THE KINGMAKER

THE KINGMAKER

How NORTHERN DANCER
FOUNDED a RACING DYNASTY

UPDATED EDITION

AVALYN HUNTER

ECLIPSE PRESS

Essex, Connecticut

ECLIPSE
PRESS

An imprint of Globe Pequot, the trade division of
The Rowman & Littlefield Publishing Group, Inc.
4501 Forbes Blvd., Ste. 200
Lanham, MD 20706
www.rowman.com

Distributed by NATIONAL BOOK NETWORK

British Library Cataloguing in Publication Information available

Library of Congress Cataloging-in-Publication Data Available

ISBN 9781493081196 (paperback)
ISBN 9781493081202 (epub)

♾™ The paper used in this publication meets the minimum requirements of American
National Standard for Information Sciences—Permanence of Paper for Printed Library
Materials, ANSI/NISO Z39.48-1992.

Contents

To Ron Turcotte, whose faith and courage
are the stuff of which champions are made

Foreword

On May 27, 1961, a small bay colt was foaled at Windfields Farm near Toronto, Canada. Although well-bred, he had several strikes against him. He was a late foal, giving away months of development to his earlier-foaled peers. He was born in Canada, a country not noted for the production of great racehorses. His sire was a chronic under-achiever despite great talent and a royal pedigree; his dam had broken down as a three-year-old. And he was small — too small, everyone said.

But dynamite comes in small packages, or so the old saw goes. And the colt named Northern Dancer was dynamite in equine form. As fiery as he was small, the little bay colt with the roguish blaze proved the best of his generation in both Canada and the United States. And, as a stallion, he set off a genetic explosion whose echoes still reverberate throughout the Thoroughbred breed.

Records can capture what Northern Dancer accomplished as a racehorse and stallion. But his personality is another question. Cold facts can convey information, but they are not enough to convey the nature of a horse whose spirit was always far bigger than the body that held it. Northern Dancer was a champion racehorse and a legendary sire, but he was more than that: He was a personality who left an indelible impact on the humans who encountered him.

This is his story.

The Breed Shapers

More than two hundred years before Northern Dancer's birth, the emerging Thoroughbred produced its first truly breed-defining sire. This was Herod (or King Herod), a son of Tartar and Cypron, by Blaze. Bred by the Duke of Cumberland in 1758, Herod was a fine racehorse whose career was marred toward its end by bleeding episodes.

Herod's true importance was not as a runner but as a sire. Standing at least part of the 1767 season (though he raced twice that year), he got his first good runner, Florizel, among his foals of 1768. Florizel, in turn, sired *Diomed, the first great Thoroughbred sire in American history. Winner of the first Derby Stakes in 1780, *Diomed enjoyed only limited success as a sire in England but, on importation to the United States at the age of twenty-one, founded a dynasty that claimed some twenty-seven American sire championships between the years 1830 and 1878. Sixteen of those championships were won by Lexington, a great-great-grandson of *Diomed whom many still regard as the greatest stallion ever foaled in the United States.

As important as Florizel was, he was only the beginning for Herod, who led the English general sire list from 1777 through 1784. Herod's other important sons include Woodpecker, whose great-great-grandson *Glencoe sired the epochal mare Pocahontas in England before becoming an eight-time leading American sire; Phoenomenon, winner of the 1783 St. Leger Stakes and a good sire; and Highflyer, unbeaten in fourteen races and England's leading sire thirteen times (1785–1796 and 1798).

The Breed Shapers

Highflyer, in turn, sired Sir Peter Teazle, whose run of ten sire championships from 1799 to 1809 was interrupted only by Trumpator in 1803. But change was in the wind. Although direct male-line descendants of Herod would win another twenty English sire championships in the years 1810–1849, the male line of Eclipse was on the rise — ironically, with a great deal of help from Herod, whose daughters, along with daughters of his sons, produced many of the best Eclipse-line horses.

By the time Stockwell (a seventh-generation descendant of Eclipse) won the first of his seven sire championships in 1860, the Herod male line was in clear decline. No Herod-line stallion has been leading sire in England since Tetratema in 1929, nor in the United States since *Ambiorix in 1961. The once-mighty Herod sire line has now dwindled to a few scattered descendants of three-time French champion sire Tourbillon, a thirteenth-generation descendant of Woodpecker.

Despite the near-extinction of his tail-male line, Herod remains one of the most profound influences on the Thoroughbred; according to some genetic studies, Herod may have contributed as much as 17 percent of the genes of the modern Thoroughbred. He may no longer stand at the head of a powerful dynasty, but he remains one of the breed's great sires.

******

Very few horses since Herod have had such a marked impact on the development of the Thoroughbred, but one that surely approaches that level of influence is St. Simon. Bred by Prince Batthyany of Hungary in 1881, St. Simon was bought by the Duke of Portland after the Prince collapsed and died of a heart attack while at Newmarket to watch his colt Galliard run for the 1883 Two Thousand Guineas (which he won). The purchase was a stroke of luck for the Duke in more ways than one, not only because the colt had come on the market at all but also because His Grace had originally gone to the Tattersalls July sale at which the Batthyany horses were being dispersed with the intention of purchasing the three-year-old Fulmen, the best juvenile of the previous season. Fulmen sold for more than the Duke was prepared to give, however, and on the advice of his trainer, Mat Dawson, the Duke purchased the next lot to come through the ring

— St. Simon. The price was a modest sixteen hundred guineas according to most modern authorities, although the Duke himself recalled the price as sixteen hundred pounds in his memoirs.

Dawson's advice no doubt was prompted by the fact that his brother, John Dawson, had been training St. Simon for Prince Batthyany. The colt was fat and out of condition at the time of the sale; furthermore, he had his hocks painted with some white substance, suggesting soreness. On examining the colt, however, Mat Dawson found nothing amiss with the horse's hocks and, between that and the horse's soft appearance, concluded that his brother was trying to discourage potential buyers, possibly with an eye to purchasing St. Simon for himself. How the Duke's purchase of St. Simon affected relations between the Dawson brothers was not recorded for posterity, but perhaps the satisfaction of training one of the great racehorses of all time helped offset any stress on fraternal affections for Mat Dawson.

No one will ever know just how good St. Simon truly was. According to the rules of racing of the day, Prince Batthyany's death voided all race nominations made for his horses, including St. Simon's engagement in the Two Thousand Guineas (he was not nominated to the Derby Stakes or the St. Leger). As nominations for major events were normally closed as much as a year in advance and supplementary nominations were then unheard of, St. Simon spent most of his two seasons of racing running for secondary events. Nonetheless, he went undefeated in nine lifetime starts. In a trial, he trounced stablemates Busybody and Harvester, who would go on to win the Oaks and the Derby (in a dead heat with St. Gatien), respectively. He also whipped the high-class stayer Tristan by six lengths in a public trial and thrashed that rival again in the 1884 Ascot Gold Cup, this time by twenty lengths.

Tristan, often used as a yardstick for comparing St. Simon to the other good horses of his day, was a rather uncertain measuring rod. Although a genuine stayer (he won the 1883 Ascot Gold Cup) and a game competitor when in the mood, he was a nasty-tempered fellow who had the reputation of sulking and refusing to extend himself at times; further, he was required to give St. Simon a twenty-three-pound concession as weight for age in both the trial and the Gold Cup. Nonetheless, the manner in which St. Simon won his races, coupled with the knowledge that he had also handily beaten his year's Two Thousand Guineas winner Scot Free and the eventual St. Leger winner The Lambkin in a trial a few days before the St. Leger, left little doubt that the son of Galopin was the champion of his generation. Although it was intended that he would race as a four-year-old, he had never quite recovered from nagging leg problems suffered when winning the Newcastle Gold Cup — his next-to-last race — over very hard ground, and he eventually retired to the breeding shed without running again, standing his first season as a five-year-old in 1886.

Like Herod, St. Simon was an immediate success. He first led the English general sire list in 1890, when his first foals were three-year-olds, and he eventually secured nine sire championships all told (1890–1896, 1900, and 1901). His sons St. Frusquin (1896 Two Thousand Guineas), Persimmon (1896 Derby and St. Leger), and Desmond (a good juvenile who later went rogue and refused to try) all became leading sires in England, while 1900 English Triple Crown winner Diamond Jubilee (a full brother to Persimmon) led the Argentine general sire list four times, as did St. Frusquin's son Saint Wolf. In France, Rabelais (1903 Goodwood Cup) led the French general sire list three times while Simonian became champion sire posthumously in 1912 and sired Nuage, leading sire in Germany in 1915–1917. Other sons of St. Simon who were influential at stud include Chaucer, Childwick, William the Third, Florizel II, Pietermaritzburg (leading sire in Argentina in 1911), and Bill of Portland.

St. Simon's daughters were also both notable as runners and able to breed on (as evidenced by St. Simon's leading the English broodmare sire list six times) though they were often high-strung after the manner of their sire. Another oddity of St. Simon's fillies — and sometimes of his sons — is that they tended to be small, many standing only a little over fifteen hands even though their sire measured a solid sixteen hands, one inch.

Since the early 1900s St. Simon's sire line has been in decline, although *Princequillo and *Ribot founded important branches in the United States during the mid-twentieth century. Nonetheless, like Herod, St. Simon remains a tremendous influence throughout the breed — in no small part, thanks to his daughters and to those of his sons and grandsons. He was also a tremendous influence on many breeders, not least Signor Federico Tesio, who spent his career trying to re-create the horse whom he considered to be one of the best, if not *the* best, of all time. In Nearco, grandsire of Northern Dancer, he perhaps succeeded.

******

"Here lies the fleetest runner the American Turf has ever known, and one of the gamest and most generous of horses." So reads the inscription on the grave of Domino. Faster horses have been seen since, but none gamer, and none that have wielded greater influence in so brief an allotted time on earth.

Unbeaten in nine starts as a two-year-old of 1893, Domino proved to be a talented sprinter at three and four but did not truly stay beyond a mile. Had his stamina matched his speed and his boundless courage, he would have been one for the ages. His greatest performance was almost certainly his match race with the 1894 Belmont Stakes winner Henry of Navarre; over a distance of nine furlongs, at least an eighth of a mile farther than he cared to go, Domino absolutely refused to be defeated and ran Henry to a dead heat.

Hampered by a foot injury and by his connections' repeated insistence that he keep trying distances beyond his tether as a four-year-old, Domino still won half his eight starts that year and retired with a record of nineteen wins from twenty-five starts. His owner, James R. Keene, thought that Domino would do best with stoutly bred mares and, to that end, had purchased a number of fine English mares specifically to breed to him.

Sadly, Domino did not have long to enjoy his splendid harem, dying suddenly at the age of six. Although the official verdict was spinal meningitis, a spinal injury suffered while playing in his paddock and colic brought on by overfeeding also have been suggested as causes of his death. He had served only two seasons in the stud and by modern standards had served a pitifully small book of mares each season.

Twenty foals constituted Domino's legacy to his breed, and the number was further reduced when one colt died while still unnamed. Of his eight surviving sons, five were geldings and another, Olympian, was presumably killed in World War I only a few years after his export to France for stud duty, having covered only a handful of mares in his native land. As if this were not enough, Domino's great son Commando, the champion of his generation, also died young, leaving only twenty-seven foals. Yet, against all odds, Domino not only founded a male line leading to 1994 American leading sire Broad Brush and 2015 Argentine champion sire Include (by Broad Brush) but also became one of the most profound influences on the American Thoroughbred.

Had Domino sired nothing but Commando, he would have done enough to etch his name deep into bloodstock annals, for Commando's handful of foals included no less than four important sires: unbeaten Colin, through whom the Domino line traces to modern times; Peter Pan, a Belmont Stakes winner who sired Colonel E.R. Bradley's foundation sire Black Toney; Celt, second only to Colin in the crop of 1905 and a first-class sire and broodmare sire; and the highly inbred Ultimus, whose dam was Domino's daughter Running Stream. Yet Domino also sired Disguise, a good sire in his own right; Pink Domino, dam of the Belmont Stakes winner and champion sire Sweep; Climax, dam of the good sire Theo. Cook; and Noonday, dam of Ultimus' son High Time, who followed in the hoofprints of his sire as a good source of speedy juveniles.

Domino's influence reached its peak through the breeding program of E.R. Bradley, who repeatedly crossed Black Toney, Black Toney's grandson Blue Larkspur, and 1926 Kentucky Derby winner Bubbling Over (whose dam carried three crosses of Domino within four generations) to his splendid matron *La Troienne. The resulting brood of daughters, bred to 1937 Triple Crown winner War Admiral (himself a maternal grandson of Sweep), produced such standouts as Busher, Buckpasser, Striking, Searching, and Mr. Busher and spread Domino's blood far and wide through the top echelons of North American breeding. And wherever Domino's blood has gone, speed and courage have followed.

******

Northern Dancer, of course, boasts a pedigree laced through and through with the blood of both Herod and St. Simon; in fact, the "Little Giant of Windfields" has twenty-one crosses to St. Simon within the first nine generations of his pedigree, an unusually high concentration for a horse foaled in the early 1960s. Through his dam, he also shares in the rich heritage of Domino. Yet breeding alone cannot explain what made Northern Dancer such a dynamo; three full brothers showed no trace of the spark that drove Northern Dancer to the heights of greatness, either as racehorses or as sires.

As the reader will see, many of the traits associated with Northern Dancer — his racing talent, his small size, and his indomitable will to win — can be traced from generation to generation through his pedigree. But Northern Dancer was more than simply the sum of his ancestors. He was himself, a unique meeting of three hundred years of selective breeding with the wild whims of chance, and the Thoroughbred has been forever changed by the little horse with the giant's heart.

Tapestry

One cannot easily pick out a beginning for the genetic tapestry that produced Northern Dancer, for its threads stretch back to the very origins of the Thoroughbred. But perhaps a good starting point is the Newmarket yearling sale of July 1894, where a small, flat-withered chestnut filly by Tristan out of the 1878 One Thousand Guineas and Two Thousand Guineas winner Pilgrimage was sold to the sixteenth Earl of Derby for 1,800 guineas.

Lord Derby was, at the time, engaged in rebuilding the family's breeding program, which had lost some prestige since the days of the twelfth Earl, the namesake of the Derby Stakes. His other acquisitions during the late 1800s and early 1900s included Lock and Key, whose daughter Keystone II would become his first homebred Classic winner by taking the 1906 Oaks, and Bridget, whose daughter Santa Brigida would win the Yorkshire Oaks and found a notable family. The seventeenth Earl, who assumed the title on his father's death in 1908, made the most of the stock inherited from his father and also made three more key acquisitions in the mares Bromus, Anchora, and Gondolette, all nowhere near top class as racers but tremendously influential as producers.

Named Canterbury Pilgrim, the Tristan filly proved anything but saintly. She was "spitefully nasty" in the words of author Richard Ulbrich, given to biting and kicking so indiscriminately that she was banished from the company of other horses while in training. Worse, she failed to stay well enough to win in five starts at two. Yet she had shown enough promise to catch at least one eye — that of veteran trainer Robert Peck, who had conditioned 1873 Oaks and St. Leger winner Marie Stuart.

"Don't be downhearted about your mare," Peck told Lord Derby's young trainer, George Lambton. "She will be a stayer and will probably win the Oaks."

Over the winter Canterbury Pilgrim formed a bond with an older gelding named Flare Up, who became her regular work companion. The relationship seemed to steady her. She added muscle during the spring of her three-year-old season and began training much more aggressively, thriving on the long gallops Lambton gave her. A hard puller, she was tough to handle on the racecourse and worse around the stable, where her manners had not improved in the least. But these faults were readily forgiven after she won the Oaks, the Liverpool Summer Cup, the Park Hill Stakes, and the Jockey Club Cup. Having won four of eleven starts, she retired at the end of her three-year-old season with the reputation of a first-class stayer.

Canterbury Pilgrim produced seven fillies from ten foals for the sixteenth and seventeenth Lords Derby, but it was her sons Swynford and Chaucer who did the most to carry her name on to future generations. The former, a son of 1904 Derby runner-up John o' Gaunt, was a big, rugged-looking brown horse who bore little resemblance to his dam. Racing for the seventeenth Earl of Derby, Swynford was rather slow to mature but won the 1910 St. Leger and the 1911 Eclipse Stakes before breaking a pastern in a routine gallop. He survived to become the leading English sire of 1923 and got a stallion even better than himself in Blandford, who led the English general sire list in 1934, 1935, and 1938.

Chaucer was a very different horse from his half brother. Standing only 15.1½ hands at maturity, he was much more like his dam in all but color, being registered as a brown. He was not exactly bred for meekness of temper, for his sire was St. Simon, who was an extremely high-strung horse and had the reputation of being quite dangerous as a stallion.

Chaucer was a nervous and stubborn sort but no more dangerous than most Thoroughbreds, and he proved a game if not stellar racehorse. He ranked among the better juveniles of 1902, winning the Gimcrack Stakes and the Boscawen Stakes, but at three and up he proved well below the best of his crop. Unplaced in all his starts at three, when he was hampered by illness, Chaucer won three plates at age four and at five won the Doncaster Spring Handicap and the Liverpool Cup. These were races far below the top grade, and Chaucer could not improve on that form at six although he scored a second victory in the Liverpool Cup.

Chaucer retired to Lord Derby's stud as a seven-year-old and proved a good stallion, his best runners including the One Thousand Guineas winners Canyon (1916) and Pillion (1926) and the 1911 Derby runner-up Stedfast, winner of twenty-two of his twenty-nine starts. Although Chaucer's stakes-winning son Prince Chimay founded a male line that reached its peak with the 1938 Derby winner Bois Roussel (sired by Prince Chimay's son Vatout) and his son Delville Wood, a five-time leading sire in Australia, Chaucer's greatest legacy was through his daughters, who made him the leading English broodmare sire of 1927 and 1933. Among them were Scapa Flow and Selene, and through them Chaucer made his primary contributions to the Thoroughbred.

Bred by Lord Derby in 1914, Scapa Flow was out of Anchora, a modest handicapper whom Lord Derby had purchased more for her soundness and toughness than for her racing talent. Scapa Flow won the Scarborough Handicap and two other races but was far from a first-rate runner. In fact, at one point during her three-year-old season, she was entered in a selling handicap at Stockton that provided the winner be sold at auction with a starting price of fifty pounds. (She ran second, and a prearranged claim by a friend of George Lambton kept her in Lord Derby's stable.)

It was in the paddocks that Scapa Flow made her name, producing Classic winners Fairway (1928 St. Leger and a four-time leading sire in England) and Fair Isle (1930 One Thousand Guineas). She also foaled Pharos, whose male line brings in a second strand of Lord Derby's breeding program.

Phalaris, the sire of Pharos (as well as of Fairway and Fair Isle), was foaled in 1913 from the mating of Lord Derby's mare Bromus with five-time leading English sire Polymelus. Bromus had won only one small race for breeder J.H. Houldsworth but was well enough bred, being by the 1890 Derby winner Sainfoin (also the sire of 1903 Triple Crown winner *Rock Sand) out of a daughter of St. Simon. Further, Bromus was closely inbred to Springfield (sire of Sainfoin and also sire of Bromus' granddam Sunrise), in his time considered one of the fastest horses ever seen in England.

As a racehorse, Phalaris proved both game and fast and was considered one of the best — if not *the* best — English sprinters of the World War I era. This was something of a left-handed compliment, however, as sprinters in that time were held of relatively little account compared to Classic winners, particularly winners of the Derby Stakes. Phalaris ran unplaced in the Two Thousand Guineas, his sole venture into Classic competition, and although he won sixteen of his twenty-four starts, he was not considered a particularly attractive stud prospect. He was, accordingly, offered for sale, but there were no takers at the stated price of five thousand pounds, and so Phalaris took up stallion duties at Lord Derby's Woodlands Stud in 1919.

Lord Derby soon had reason to be grateful that Phalaris had not been sold. Providing an injection of high-class speed into Lord Derby's generally stamina-laden breeding program, Phalaris was the leading English sire of 1925 and 1928. His five Classic winners included the already-mentioned Fairway and Fair Isle; Manna, winner of the 1925 Derby; Colorado, winner of the 1926 Two Thousand Guineas; and Chatelaine, winner of the 1933 Oaks.

Fairway, Fair Isle, and Colorado were all sired on daughters of Chaucer, as were *Sickle, *Pharamond II, and Pharos, all important sires. This apparent affinity for daughters of Chaucer is all the more impressive when one considers that only sixty-six daughters of Chaucer were registered in the General Stud Book at the time Phalaris went to stud. More were doubtless registered by the time of Chaucer's death in 1926, and Phalaris probably had better opportunities with Chaucer mares than did most other sires, given that many of Chaucer's best daughters were in Lord Derby's possession. Nonetheless, with the notable exception of Hyperion, Chaucer would have had very little impact on modern pedigrees without Phalaris, and Phalaris likewise would not have been the sire he was without Chaucer mares.

Pharos was among Phalaris' best runners, although not up to Classic standards. He ran second by a length in the 1923 Derby behind *Papyrus and eventually won fourteen of his thirty starts, including the 1924 Champion Stakes. Like his sire, he was not considered a top stallion prospect at the time of his retirement but became the leading English sire of 1931, the year his son Cameronian won the Derby. By that time Pharos had been moved to France, where he died in 1937, but he was also responsible for the 1932 St. Leger winner Firdaussi and the Irish Two Thousand

Guineas and Derby winner Phideas. In France, Pharos was highly influential, getting 1939 Prix du Jockey-Club winner and 1944 French leading sire Pharis II; the Poule d'Essai des Pouliches (French One Thousand Guineas) winners Mary Tudor II (1934) and The Nile (1935), the former the dam of 1941 Derby winner Owen Tudor; and the 1937 Prix de Diane (French Oaks) winner En Fraude among others.

Pharos' best son, however, was bred in a minor country by racing standards of pre-World War II Europe. This was Nearco, whose story introduces the great Italian breeder, Federico Tesio.

Pedigree students have been perhaps unnecessarily baffled by Tesio, a very private man when it came to his breeding program. In contrast to Lord Derby, who was greatly assisted by Lambton and by pedigree advisor Walter Alston in managing Woodlands Stud, Tesio took no one save his wife into his confidence when it came to planning matings or purchasing bloodstock.

That Tesio managed to breed four horses — Donatello II, Nearco, Tenerani, and Ribot — of international caliber in the relative backwater of Italy and on modest financial resources (by 1931, he was, in fact, sufficiently strapped that he took on the wealthy Marchese Mario Incisa della Rochetta as a partner in his Dormello Stud) speaks volumes of his genius. Nonetheless, the basics of his program were simple enough: balancing speed and stamina in his bloodlines; intelligently using line breeding, particularly to St. Simon; using mares that either were good racers themselves or came from strong bloodlines that he could "breed up" from; and selecting mates for his mares that complemented them in as many ways as possible, no matter how far he had to travel to arrange a desirable mating. And the goal of his program, as recorded in his private notebook, was simplicity itself: "… to breed and raise a racehorse who, over any distance, could carry the heaviest weight in the shortest time." In Nearco, he came as close to this goal as anyone could wish.

Although Tesio became popularly known as the "Wizard of Dormello," English horsemen may have thought him more of a madman when he reacted with delight to buying a weedy mare for seventy-five guineas at the 1915 Newmarket December sale. Although beautifully bred — by 1906 Derby winner Spearmint out of the American-bred 1899 One Thousand Guineas winner Sibola — Catnip had only one victory, in the Gosforth

Nursery Handicap at Newcastle, a race worth a mere one hundred pounds to the winner. The fact that she was selling in foal to Cock-a-Hoop, a sire whose only merit was being a full brother to the great race mare Pretty Polly, only emphasized her status as a cull.

Tesio's keen eye for breeding potential was never better demonstrated than by the purchase of Catnip. One of the great matrons of Italian history, she produced four important foals: Nesiotes (by Hurry On), a winner of fifteen races, including the Premio Omnium, and a good sire in Italy; Nomellina (by St. Amant), a winner of eight races including the Criterium Nazionale; Nera di Bicci (by Tracery), winner of the Premio Chiusura and seven other races and the dam of the Italian Classic winners Neroccia and Nannoccia; and, best of all, Nogara.

Sired by ten-time leading Italian sire Havresac II (a son of Rabelais), Nogara won fourteen of eighteen starts, including the 1930 Criterium Nazionale as a juvenile and the 1931 Premio Regina Elena (Italian One Thousand Guineas) and Premio Parioli (Italian Two Thousand Guineas) at three. She was in many ways Tesio's ideal of a Thoroughbred mare: compact, smoothly made, and muscular. If she could be faulted, it would be for being rather small (fifteen hands and one inch) and light on bone.

Tesio spent a tremendous amount of time studying pedigrees and visiting stallions to assess conformation and the quality of their care before booking a mating for one of his mares. In 1934 the results of his careful research led him to conclude that the ideal mate for Nogara would be Lord Derby's stallion Fairway, who appeared to complement the mare in pedigree, racing aptitude, and conformation. But by the time Tesio had drawn his conclusions and tried to arrange the mating, Fairway's book was already full.

Fairway's full brother, Pharos, was available, but he was not the type of stallion that normally appealed to Tesio. Although his pedigree obviously suited Nogara as well as Fairway's did, in conformation he was a coarser, blockier type. Further, his strong suit was speed over intermediate distances, and Tesio's bias was for using as sires horses with the stamina to win the Derby or the St. Leger. Nonetheless, Tesio knew the value of quality speed and had used Pharos at least once before, sending the stoutly bred Gay Gamp to him in 1933. The resulting colt, El Greco, ranked behind only Donatello II at two and three in Italy and later became a noted sire in his native land. As a foal of 1934, El Greco likely had little impact on Tesio's decision to go ahead and breed Nogara to Pharos, but Tesio would have reason to be grateful for the circumstances that had pushed him to use Pharos rather than Fairway.

Nogara produced her Pharos colt in 1935. Like his dam, the young Nearco was compact and blocky: a muscular fellow who routinely bullied the other colts at Dormello. But he took size and substance from Pharos. As he grew, he became a magnificent-looking specimen with a long, finely cut head and neck, beautifully sloped shoulders, and strong, well-rounded quarters reminiscent of his ancestor St. Simon. And he ran to his looks. No matter what the challenge, Nearco mastered it without apparent effort. The best juvenile in Italy at age two and the best Italian runner of any age at three, he crowned his career by defeating the best English and French three-year-olds of his year in the 1938 Grand Prix de Paris. An often-quoted statement from Tesio's private notebook says of him, "Beautifully balanced, of perfect size and great quality. Won all his fourteen races as soon as he was asked. Not a true stayer though he won up to 3,000 metres. He won these longer races by his superb class and brilliant speed."

Despite the excellence of Nearco's racing career, Tesio was not inclined to keep him for stud — one assumes partly because of his preference for stoutness rather than brilliance in sires and partly because of his general policy of seldom keeping a home sire for fear that he might be tempted to mate his mares based on convenience rather than on the best possible match-up. Thus, Nearco was sold for the then-record price of 60,000 pounds to British bookmaker Martin Benson and took up stud duty at Benson's Beech House Stud in 1939. There, he would lead the English general sire list twice (in 1947 and 1948) and would sire two sons whose influence on the modern Thoroughbred has been profound: *Nasrullah, sire of Bold Ruler and progenitor of the Blushing Groom (Fr) and Caro (Ire) male lines, and Nearctic, sire of Northern Dancer.

******

Selene, the second of Chaucer's important daughters, was foaled in 1919. She was produced from Serenissima, whose dam Gondolette was purchased from the Tully Stud of Colonel Hall-Walker (later Lord Wavertree) by Lord Derby in 1912 for 1,550 guineas. The purchase was in no small part motivated by the fact that Gondolette's sire Loved One was by See Saw out of Pilgrimage and, thus, a half brother to Canterbury Pilgrim. The plan was to breed Gondolette and her progeny primarily to Canterbury Pilgrim's sons Chaucer and Swynford, thus creating inbreeding to Pilgrimage.

Although Gondolette had been only a minor winner as a racer, she had already proved a fine producer by the time she came to Lord Derby's stud. Her Tully-bred progeny included stakes-winning Great Sport (by Gallinule), third in the 1913 Derby; Let Fly (by White Eagle), winner of the 1914 Dewhurst Stakes and second in the 1915 Derby; and Dolabella, whose fleet daughter Myrobella was the best English juvenile filly of 1932 and later produced the 1942 Two Thousand Guineas winner and important sire Big Game.

For Lord Derby, Gondolette produced the 1918 One Thousand Guineas winner Ferry and 1924 Derby winner Sansovino to the cover of Swynford. Her most important Derby-bred foal, however, was Serenissima, whom she was carrying at the time of her purchase. By 1909 Derby winner Minoru, Serenissima won only two minor events from fifteen starts, but her foals included 1923 One Thousand Guineas and St. Leger winner Tranquil, the 1930 Ascot Gold Cup winner Bosworth, and Selene.

Like many of Canterbury Pilgrim's descendants, including her sire Chaucer, Selene was small — so small, in fact, that George Lambton did not feel it worthwhile to nominate her for any of the English Classics. At the time, it probably would have seemed a rational enough decision to any observer; after all, Selene was only the second foal from her dam, and Serenissima's first foal, a full sister to Selene named Venetia, was not showing much promise. In hindsight, however, it was one of the few major mistakes of Lambton's career.

By the end of her racing career, Selene was widely acknowledged as the best filly of the 1919 crop. Her sixteen victories from twenty-two starts included the Rous Memorial Stakes and Cheveley Park Stakes at two and the Nassau Stakes, Park Hill Stakes, and Liverpool Autumn Cup at three. Not only did most horsemen rank her as superior to the 1922 Oaks winner, Pogrom, and the One Thousand Guineas winner, Silver Urn, but many felt she could have taken the measure of the St. Leger winner, Royal Lancer, as well. Beautifully made despite her small size (fifteen hands, two inches at maturity), Selene had a strong will to win and stayed as far as she was asked to run. If she had a fault, it was that her legs were considered slightly short in proportion to the size of her body, a trait she passed to several of her foals.

Lambton hoped to continue racing Selene at four, but he was overridden by Lord Derby, who chose to breed Selene to Phalaris in 1923. The resulting foal, *Sickle, was the first of four sons who would engrave Selene's name deep into the history of the Thoroughbred. Winner of three stakes as a juvenile and third in the 1927 Two Thousand Guineas at three, *Sickle stood one year in England before being leased to Joseph E. Widener, who imported the horse to America in 1930 (he would buy *Sickle outright two years later).

Standing at Widener's Elmendorf Farm in Kentucky, *Sickle led the American general sire list in 1936 and 1938 before his death in 1943. His forty-five stakes winners included 1938 champion three-year-old male Stagehand and 1945 champion juvenile male Star Pilot, but his most important son was the relatively moderate Unbreakable, who would become the grandsire of the great Native Dancer. Native Dancer, in turn, would become the maternal grandsire of Northern Dancer.

Selene returned to Phalaris in 1924, and the resulting colt was *Pharamond II. A blockier, smaller horse than *Sickle, *Pharamond II won the important Middle Park Plate as a juvenile in 1927 but otherwise was several notches below the best of his crop. Following his three-year-old season, he was sold to a syndicate headed by Kentucky horseman Hal Price Headley (who later bought the horse outright) for four thousand pounds and stood his first season in 1929 at Headley's Beaumont Farm. Before his death in 1953, *Pharamond II sired thirty-five stakes winners including 1937 champion two-year-old male Menow, whose son Tom Fool won Horse of the Year honors in the year of *Pharamond II's death. Tom Fool, in turn, sired 1966 Horse of the Year Buckpasser, one of the most noted broodmare sires of modern times.

Hurry On, Selene's mate in 1925, was an entirely different proposition than Phalaris. A huge (seventeen hands high) son of the 1908 Cambridgeshire Stakes winner, Marcovil, and the unraced Sainfoin mare

Tout Suite, Hurry On was purchased for five hundred guineas at the Tattersalls First July yearling sale of 1914 by trainer Fred Darling on behalf of James Buchanan (later Lord Woolavington). The big colt was not fashionably bred and was so backwards as a youngster that he did not start at two. He made up for that by going unbeaten and unextended through all six of his starts at three to be commonly acknowledged as the best English three-year-old of 1916, his victories including the September Stakes (run as a wartime substitute for the St. Leger) and the Jockey Club Cup. Many years later, as his distinguished training career drew to a close, Fred Darling said of Hurry On, "He is the best horse I have ever trained, and the best I am ever likely to train."

As a sire, Hurry On outbred his pedigree just as he had outraced it, becoming the leading English sire of 1926. A great influence for stamina, he was the opposite of the speedy Phalaris. Selene, however, showed her genetic versatility by producing Hunter's Moon, the third of her notable sire sons, to his cover. Although troubled by sore shins during much of his career, Hunter's Moon managed to win the 1929 Newmarket Stakes, defeating that year's Two Thousand Guineas winner Mr. Jinks, before being exported to Argentina. There, he became an important sire before being sent on to Brazil, where he died in the early or middle 1950s (he is recorded as having covered mares in Brazil as late as 1952). He was the leading broodmare sire in Argentina in 1954 and, like his sire, proved a notable influence for stamina.

The last and best of Selene's important sons was Hyperion, whose sire was the 1918 Triple Crown winner Gainsborough. So small as a foal that stable lads likened him to a golden retriever, Hyperion had to be specially fed from a custom-made feed bunker as a weanling because he could not compete with the larger colts. Because of his tiny size, there was some talk of gelding him or selling him off as a cull. Lambton, however, was fond of the little chestnut, and in any event was not about to make the same mistake with Hyperion that he had with Selene. He nominated the colt to the Derby and the St. Leger, and Hyperion remained ungelded and unculled.

Hyperion also remained small — he barely measured fifteen hands when he went into serious training, and stood only an inch and a half taller at maturity — but he grew into a beautifully proportioned animal. Although he had the shortish legs of his dam and was considered both ewe-necked and light on bone as a youngster, he was muscular with plenty of power for his size. Lambton's problem was that Hyperion was not at all inclined to use that power, at least not in training. The colt was that trainer's headache of a horse that is unwilling to exert himself in a workout, yet needs hard work to keep fit. Further, the curious little fellow was distracted by anything unusual that he saw and seemed particularly fascinated by skyborne objects, whether airplanes or birds.

Lambton could not have known that Hyperion was probably partially deaf, a condition only deduced after the horse's death when a thickening of the hyoid bone near the left ear opening was discovered as his skeleton was being prepared for display at the Animal Health Trust at Newmarket — possibly the result of an infection during the horse's rather sickly babyhood. Such an impairment could easily account both for Hyperion's keen interest in anything moving in his field of vision and for the difference between Hyperion as a work horse in the morning and Hyperion as a racehorse in the afternoon, for with the stimulus of a noisy crowd — something he could, perhaps, hear clearly — Hyperion became a different animal. Sent for the Zetland Maiden Plate at Doncaster for his first race, Hyperion closed strongly to be fourth of nineteen runners, and jockey Tommy Weston later admitted that he probably could have won with the colt had he anticipated Hyperion's willing response to his urging and asked him earlier.

The little golden colt went on to win three of his remaining four starts at two, including the Dewhurst Stakes at Newmarket and a dead heat for the Prince of Wales's Stakes at Goodwood. He was ranked second behind Manitoba among the juvenile colts of 1932, but both were ranked behind the brilliant filly Myrobella and her fellow females Betty and Brown Betty. At three, however, Hyperion was the best of his age regardless of sex. After winning his season opener in the Chester Vase, he turned in a brilliant performance in the Derby, galloping home ahead of King Salmon (later an Eclipse Stakes winner) and twenty-two other rivals. His official winning margin was four lengths, but many eyewitnesses made it closer to six. He finished his season by winning the Prince of Wales's Stakes at the Royal Ascot meeting and the St. Leger by three easy lengths over the next year's Ascot Gold Cup winner, Felicitation.

Hyperion remained in training as a four-year-old but had to adapt to a different trainer, Lord Derby having decided that Lambton's age and declining health warranted moving on to a successor. (Ironically, Lambton continued to be a successful trainer for other owners until his death eleven years later.) The new head trainer was Colledge Leader, a good horseman but apparently not up to the challenge of getting the lazy Hyperion to stay fit off his works.

Under the new regime Hyperion won his first two starts of the season, the March Stakes and the Burwell Stakes, but was not really impressive in either. Then he had to be pulled up from a two-mile gallop in preparation for the Ascot Gold Cup as apparently unfit to go the distance. This did not bode well for a race at two and a half miles, but Hyperion went to the post for the Gold Cup anyway despite heavy rains that had turned the course into a quagmire and placed stamina at an even greater premium. He finished a tiring third behind Felicitation and the French colt Thor II. In his final start, the Dullingham Stakes, Hyperion was beaten a short head by the three-year-old Caithness, to whom he was conceding twenty-nine pounds.

With a splendid pedigree and a race record of nine wins, one second, and two thirds from thirteen starts, Hyperion entered stud with high expectations and more than fulfilled them. He was the leading sire in England six times (1940–1942, 1945–1946, and 1955). So high was his reputation that movie mogul Louis B. Mayer offered Lord Derby a blank check for the stallion but was refused with the words, "Even though England be reduced to ashes, Hyperion shall never leave these shores." Mayer had to be content with standing Hyperion's son *Alibhai, who, despite breaking down as a yearling in training, became a first-class sire.

Hyperion, in fact, was one of the greatest sire of sires ever seen in the breed. Among the sons that earned at least one sire championship in a major racing nation are Aureole, *Heliopolis, Gulf Stream, Selim Hassan, Aristophanes, Helios, Ruthless, and Deimos, and other sons that wielded great influence include *Khaled, Owen Tudor, Red Mars, Stardust (sire of five-time Australian sire champion Star Kingdom), and the aforementioned *Alibhai.

Hyperion's daughters were no less influential, making him the leading broodmare sire in England four times (1948, 1957, and 1967–1968). Among them were *Hydroplane II, dam of the great Citation; Libra, dam of the Classic-winning full brothers Ribocco and Ribero; Aurora, dam of four stakes winners, including the 1949 Ascot Gold Cup winner and important sire Alycidon; Calash, dam of the Oaks winner Carozza and the important Argentine sire Snow Cat; and Red Ray, great-granddam of the great European racer and sire Mill Reef. But among his daughters, surely none can have wielded more influence than *Lady Angela, dam of Nearctic, whose story will be told later.

******

When the chestnut filly to be named Almahmoud first struggled to her feet in the spring of 1947, she could not have known that she represented a convergence of old American bloodlines with some of the best blood that Europe had to offer. She was bred by C.V. "Sonny" Whitney, whose own heritage in the Thoroughbred world traced back to his grandfather, William Collins Whitney. A charter member of The Jockey Club when it formed in 1894 — though he owned not a single Thoroughbred at the time! — the elder Whitney became actively involved in racing when he purchased a steeplechaser named Shillalah in 1897. Sometime during the late 1890s, Whitney also purchased the right to use the racing colors of none other than George Lambton, and so the famous colors of "Eton blue, brown cap" became enshrined in American racing history. (Lambton later repurchased the right to use the colors in England; when Whitney raced horses in England, his silks were distinguished from Lambton's by brown sleeves.)

By 1901, Whitney had not only established himself as one of the leading American owners but also had succeeded in capturing no less than the Derby Stakes with Volodyovski, a colt he had leased from Lady Meux earlier that spring. The following year he began acquiring breeding stock, and before his death in 1904, he had bred the fillies Artful, remembered for handing the great Sysonby his only defeat, and Tanya, who would win the 1905 Belmont Stakes. He died before either filly started as a juvenile, however, and both raced at two in the colors of his friend Herman B. Duryea, who leased the racing stable while the Whitney family observed the customary year of mourning. At three, Artful and Tanya raced for Harry Payne Whitney, who had purchased the two at his father's bloodstock dispersal.

The younger Whitney had already been involved in racing independently of his father since 1902, when he and Duryea campaigned the good colt Irish Lad in partnership. Following his father's death, he went into the breeding business as well. The nucleus of his breeding operation came from the dispersal of his father's horses, in which he bought the stallion Hamburg, a number of the mares, and most of the yearlings. He also bought other stock through the years. Among his purchases was the Peter Pan filly Fly By Night, whom he bought from J.N. Camden's Hartland Stud.

Under the name of Fly By Night II, the chestnut filly raced in England before returning to the United States for breeding. Among her produce was the cleverly named Flying Witch, whose sire Broomstick (by 1896 Kentucky Derby winner Ben Brush) was already famous as the sire of champion Whisk Broom II and the Kentucky Derby-winning filly Regret. One of the pillars of H.P. Whitney's breeding program, Broomstick would die in 1931, having led the American general sire list three times (1913–1915), and his 25 percent stakes winners from foals ranks him among the great stallions in the Thoroughbred breed's history.

Although Flying Witch won only one of six races for the Whitney stable, she proved her worth as a broodmare by producing two winners of the historic Futurity Stakes: Mother Goose (1924) and Whichone (1929), both by Whitney's stallion *Chicle.

A son of 1906 Derby Stakes winner Spearmint, *Chicle had enough talent to win the 1916 Brooklyn Derby (now known as the Dwyer Stakes) but was none too sound. At stud he also developed a dangerously savage disposition and was reportedly being considered for destruction when the quality of his early progeny earned him a reprieve. The decision was fortunate for American bloodstock if not for the Whitney staff, as among *Chicle's stakes-winning daughters were Chicleight, whose daughter Blue Delight founded a great family for Calumet Farm; Goose Egg, dam of 1942 Kentucky Derby and Belmont Stakes winner Shut Out; and Incandescent, second dam of 1946 Triple Crown winner Assault.

Mother Goose won only one other stakes besides the Futurity, but she placed in two other added-money events and is generally acknowledged by racing historians as the best American juvenile filly of 1924. She did not race as a three-year-old and eventually produced one foal for H.P. Whitney and four more for Sonny Whitney, who inherited the mare on his father's death in 1930.

Despite also inheriting the great Equipoise, ranked the best American runner of any age in 1932 and 1933, and Top Flight, the best American juvenile of either sex in 1931 and champion three-year-old filly of 1932, Sonny Whitney had a rather tentative commitment to racing at that time. Not only was he actively involved in running Pan Am Airways (of which he remained chairman until 1941), but he also was interested in politics, an interest not always seen as compatible with the gambling that is inextricably tied to racing; in fact, he even made an unsuccessful run for Congress.

The Whitney stable fell off in quality and earnings after 1933 (although Equipoise was once again acknowledged as the best runner in the handicap ranks in 1934), and this decline, combined with the pressures of his other interests, may have led to Whitney's decision to announce his retirement from racing in 1937. Fifteen horses were sold in a partial dispersal that November. Among them were Dauber, who would win the 1938 Preakness; The Chief, winner of the 1938 Brooklyn Handicap and Dwyer Stakes; Handcuff, the 1938 champion three-year-old filly; and Cravat, who as a four-year-old in 1939 won the Jockey Club Gold Cup and the Suburban, Brooklyn, and San Juan Capistrano handicaps.

Soon afterward, however, Whitney had a change of heart and resumed racing. He also resumed breeding horses at his father's Kentucky farm, now named C.V. Whitney Farm. One of the horses he had retained there was Mother Goose's 1937 filly Arbitrator, the Futurity winner's last foal.

A daughter of 1934 Belmont Stakes winner Peace Chance and, thus, a great-granddaughter of the great sire Fair Play, Arbitrator never raced. But she proved her worth as a broodmare, producing three stakes winners. All three were by *Mahmoud, whose importation by Sonny Whitney in 1941 brought in some of the best European strains of the 1930s as a much-needed outcross to the Domino and Ben Brush bloodlines built up by the first two generations of Whitneys.

*Mahmoud had been bred by the Aga Khan, who had purchased his sire *Blenheim II (by Blandford) from Lord Carnarvon's Highclere Stud as a yearling for 4,100 guineas. For his new owner, *Blenheim II won four good races as a juvenile and the 1930 Derby Stakes at three. He went to stud at

31

the Aga Khan's Haras Marly la Ville in France as a four-year-old and stood there for six seasons before being sold in 1936 to an American syndicate headed by A.B "Bull" Hancock at a price of 45,000 pounds (about $225,000 at the exchange rates then prevailing).

By that time, *Blenheim II had given plenty of evidence that he would be a good stallion, his European-sired progeny including the speedy juvenile Wyndham, the Italian champion Donatello II, and Mumtaz Begum, dam of *Nasrullah. Many European horsemen grumbled about such a valuable horse being sold across the Atlantic, where he would no longer be available for European breeding. The movements that would lead to World War II were already well under way, prompting some observers to conclude that the rising threat of war was behind the sale. But famed Calumet Farm trainer Jimmy Jones, who assisted his father Ben Jones in training *Blenheim II's champion son Whirlaway, had another explanation.

"He got so many crazy colts," Jones said. "Those English trainers didn't want to fool with them."

One of *Blenheim II's progeny that was *not* crazy was *Mahmoud, a beautifully refined colt who reminded many observers of his distant Arabian ancestors. He was a member of *Blenheim II's second crop and helped secure his sire's reputation by being ranked second among English juveniles at two and winning the Derby Stakes in record time (2:33 4/5) at three. The going on Derby Day in 1936 was exceptionally hard and fast; nonetheless, *Mahmoud's record for the race at its traditional Epsom setting was not bettered until 1995, when Lammtarra scorched the course in 2:32 1/5. (Several wartime runnings of the race were faster, but they were conducted at Newmarket due to the Epsom course's having been requisitioned for military use.)

*Mahmoud stood for four seasons at Newmarket without exceptional results, though he did sire the 1942 Irish One Thousand Guineas and Oaks winner Majideh and the 1941 Italian champion juvenile filly Donatella III, both later important producers. Both fillies, however, came too late to influence the decision to sell their sire, who followed *Blenheim II across the ocean in 1940. The voyage was not without some drama, for as Sonny Whitney's widow, Marylou, later related, *Mahmoud was held up at the dock due to some missing paperwork and missed the ship on which he was

to have set sail — a stroke of luck, as it turned out, for the ship was torpe-
doed and sunk before it could reach America. *Mahmoud came over on
another vessel and was safely ensconced at C.V. Whitney Farm, where he
stood until his death at the age of twenty-nine.

As with *Blenheim II, European horsemen muttered at the sale of
*Mahmoud, though probably not as loudly if their respective purchase
prices were any indication; *Mahmoud went for only 20,000 pounds, or
about $85,000 at the exchange rate then current. Undoubtedly,
*Mahmoud's price was driven down by World War II, then raging across
Europe, but regardless of the circumstances, C.V. Whitney had made an
excellent bargain. *Mahmoud would lead the American general sire list in
1946 and would also lead the American broodmare sire list in 1957.

Although *Mahmoud himself stayed well enough to capture the Derby, he
had been a speedy juvenile, and speed was the heritage transmitted by his
granddam, Mumtaz Mahal. Known as the "Flying Filly," Mumtaz Mahal
won five of six starts, all stakes events, as a juvenile of 1923 and stretched
out enough to run second in the following year's One Thousand Guineas. A
great foundation mare for the Aga Khan, who had purchased her for 9,100
guineas as a yearling — then the second-highest price ever paid for a yearling filly in England — Mumtaz Mahal produced the stakes winners
Badruddin, Furrokh Siyar, and Mirza II. She was also the maternal granddam of the great sire *Nasrullah, and her important descendants are too
many to mention.

Mumtaz Mahal was intensely bred for speed. Her sire, The Tetrarch, was
unbeaten in seven races at two (he did not race afterward due to injury) and
was considered one of the fastest horses ever seen in England up to his
time. Known as the "Spotted Wonder" and the "Rocking Horse" for his
oddly white-spotted gray coat, The Tetrarch was primarily considered an
influence for speed although he sired three winners of England's longest
Classic, the St. Leger, as well. He was the source of *Mahmoud's gray coat
(passed via Mumtaz Mahal and her daughter Mah Mahal), and *Mahmoud,
in turn, almost single-handedly made gray a popular color in American
Thoroughbreds where it had been neither common nor fashionable before.

Lady Josephine, dam of Mumtaz Mahal, was a speedy filly whose maximum distance was a mere five furlongs. She could fly within that limit,

however, which was no more than should have been expected from a union between Sundridge, the best sprinter of his day, and Americus Girl, an exceptional speedster in her own right. *Mahmoud was, thus, the result of two generations of Derby-winning sires (his broodmare sire was Gainsborough, previously mentioned as the sire of Hyperion) crossed onto a female line that carried first-class speed, and the result was a horse that in North America could transmit both speed and stamina.

The mating of *Mahmoud with Arbitrator united the cream of the Aga Khan's breeding program with a mare who combined all three of the great American strains of Domino, Ben Brush, and Fair Play in her ancestry. The result was a high-strung, moody chestnut filly whose hind legs were both cow-hocked and sickle-hocked, making her appear crooked whether viewed from the side or from behind. Although she was a full sister to 1946 Will Rogers Handicap winner Burra Sahib, the young Almahmoud apparently was not highly regarded as a yearling and was sold to Henry Knight, who, in turn, resold the filly to T.D. Taggart at the 1948 Saratoga yearling sale. Taggert died soon afterward, and Almahmoud was then acquired by William Helis.

Although Almahmoud was by an English Derby winner and out of a mare sired by a Belmont Stakes winner, she showed her best form at much shorter distances than a mile and a half, winning a division of the five and a half-furlong Colleen Stakes at two and the mile and one-sixteenth Vineland Handicap at three. She did not race past her three-year-old season and made only eleven starts all told, so whether her apparent distance limitations reflected an actual lack of stamina, her difficult temperament, or a lack of opportunity is anyone's guess.

Helis died in 1952, and Almahmoud passed back into the hands of Knight, who purchased the broodmares, yearlings, and racing stock from Helis' estate for his Coldstream Stud. Knight was, thus, the breeder of her first foal, a 1953 daughter of Cosmic Bomb who was given the name Cosmah. Racing for Eugene Mori, Cosmah won the Astarita Stakes at two and placed in four other stakes. She later produced four stakes winners including three-time champion filly Tosmah and two-time American leading sire Halo, whose descendants would later form a fruitful nick with those of Northern Dancer.

Almahmoud gave birth to stillborn twins in 1954 and was barren in 1955. In November of that year, Knight's failing health prompted him to disperse his bloodstock in a private sale at Coldstream, and Almahmoud was sold for $57,000 to Danny Van Clief, master of Nydrie Stud in Virginia. A few months after the sale, Van Clief sold an interest in Almahmoud to his aunt, Frances Augustus (the widow of Ellsworth H. Augustus and mistress of Keswick Farm in Virginia), and this partnership is on record as the breeder of Natalma, dam of Northern Dancer.

******

After producing a colt by Triple Crown winner Citation in 1956, Almahmoud was bred to Native Dancer, the "Gray Ghost of Sagamore," one of the all-time greats in racing who would become equally important as a sire.

Native Dancer was bred by Alfred Gwynne Vanderbilt, whose foundation sire Discovery had been purchased as a juvenile from Walter Salmon's Mereworth Stud. Stakes-placed that year, Discovery developed into the second best three-year-old of 1934 and the best horse of any age in 1935. Ranked only behind the three-year-old Granville in 1936, Discovery retired to Vanderbilt's Sagamore Farm in Maryland with twenty-seven wins from sixty-three starts and the reputation as one of the greatest weight carriers of all time.

A son of the "Iron Horse," Display, Discovery inherited all of his sire's toughness but none of his tempestuous disposition, and he enjoyed a long and honorable career at Sagamore before his death in 1958. Although he was never a first-rate sire, he got twenty-five stakes winners including the 1948 champion handicap mare Conniver and the hardy gelding Find, who earned $803,615 for Vanderbilt in a day when horses that earned as much as $500,000 were still a rarity.

"Breed anything to Discovery" was Vanderbilt's first formula for breeding success. He changed it to "Breed anything to a Discovery mare" after Native Dancer came along. Unbeaten in nine starts as a juvenile, the "Gray Ghost" split Horse of the Year honors with three-year-old One Count in 1952 and won the title outright off only three starts in 1954, all brilliant victories. In between, he lost one race — and with it, quite possibly Horse of the Year honors for 1953 — in ten starts. The race he lost was the Kentucky Derby, in which he, after being bumped early, failed by a head to run down Dark Star.

Retired due to nagging ankle problems after his brief four-year-old season, Native Dancer never became champion sire, but he wielded tremendous influence through a number of daughters and through two sons: the brilliant Raise a Native, sire of champion stallions Exclusive Native, Mr. Prospector, and Alydar; and Atan, who broke down after only one race but sired the important stallion Sharpen Up (GB).

Native Dancer was in his second season at stud when Almahmoud was brought to his court, so no one yet knew what kind of sire he would make. His union with Almahmoud produced a handsome bay filly whose beauty was flawed by her being slightly back at the knee. Sold to E.P. Taylor at the 1958 Saratoga yearling sale, Natalma would prove to have talent comparable to her half sister, Cosmah, on the racetrack. More important, when bred to Taylor's stallion Nearctic, she would produce Northern Dancer.

Mr. Taylor

The man who would bring Nearctic and Natalma together to produce Northern Dancer was Edward Plunkett Taylor, a man virtually synonymous with Canadian racing until his death in 1989. Known as "Eddie" to his friends and "Empty Pockets" to a few of his bolder detractors, to most of the world he was known simply as "Mr. Taylor." It seemed to fit.

Born in Ottawa on January 29, 1901, Taylor did not grow up in a "horsey" family. His interests were more those of his maternal grandfather, Charles McGee, a born entrepreneur who owned a miniature empire of small businesses. But in 1919, a chestnut colt took the Canadian sports world by storm. His name was Sir Barton, and though he was bred in Kentucky, he raced in the colors of Commander J.K.L. Ross of Montreal. A maiden going into the 1919 Kentucky Derby, he was the unquestioned champion of North American racing six months later, having taken not only the Derby but the Preakness and the Belmont as well. He was the first horse to sweep the three races that would later be known as the American Triple Crown, and his exploits sparked a fresh interest in horse racing throughout Canada.

The young E.P. Taylor was among the Canadians who caught racing fever during 1919, and he began making regular visits to the Blue Bonnets and King Edward Park racetracks near Montreal while a first-year mechanical engineering student at McGill University. His excursions (as well as much of his tuition) were financed by a new toaster design he had developed and patented, and when he began courting Winifred Duguid, he started taking her to the track as well. The future Mrs. Taylor soon came to enjoy racing as much as Taylor himself did, though she drew the line at actually getting on a horse's back and riding. She liked horses, but for the most part preferred to admire them from a distance.

Taylor's interest was more direct. Having decided that he wanted to learn to ride, he took a few lessons at an Ottawa riding school and then joined the Princess Louise Dragoon Guards, a ceremonial cavalry regiment. He did not exactly cover himself with glory during his first excursion with the Guards; too inexperienced to control his mount when it took fright at a passing streetcar, he could only hang on as his horse bolted up the steps of a nearby church. But he persevered, in due time becoming an expert rider who would continue enjoying horseback outings well into his seventies.

Horses would remain a hobby for Taylor for quite some time, though in later life he admitted to having toyed with the idea of buying a few racehorses as early as 1927. Business was his first love. He was only in his early twenties when he and a friend started bus and metered cab services in Ottawa, which had previously lacked both types of transportation. The partners sold out at a profit within a few years. Then the financial crash of 1929 came along; in typical Taylor fashion, where others found difficulties, Taylor saw opportunities.

Taylor had inherited part-ownership of a small Ontario brewery named Brading's on McGee's death in 1918, and after graduation from McGill, he was named a director of the company. It was not a propitious time to be involved in the brewing business; Canada, still in the midst of its own experiment with Prohibition, did not permit alcohol sales in bars or restaurants. Most breweries were surviving on the export trade to the United States, but in 1930 Canada passed a law prohibiting exports of alcohol across the American border, drying up that source of profit.

Change was in the wind, however, and Taylor sensed that Prohibition would not go on forever. (Most of Canada's temperance laws were, in fact, repealed not long after the Twenty-First Amendment ended Prohibition in the United States in 1933.) Taylor had also noticed that Ontario had close to forty breweries similar to Brading's, most of them struggling, and concluded that the business would be much more efficient and profitable if the industry were reorganized into one large company.

There was just one problem with his idea: he simply did not have the cash to buy out most of his rivals, and the staid Bank of Montreal considered his scheme too risky for a loan. Taylor, however, did not let a little thing like lack of ready cash stop him. After buying the Kuntz and Carling's breweries outright, he began approaching owners of other breweries, offering shares in his proposed holding company in return for a controlling interest in their businesses.

A few other owners did decide to join with him — usually at the cost of Taylor's assuming their debts — but he got an icy reception from most. By his own later admission, Taylor was using all the wits he possessed just to survive, and many observers were predicting the quick demise of his fledgling corporation.

The turning point came in 1931, when Taylor joined forces with American entrepreneur Clarke S. Jennison. Jennison, who had developed a similar consolidation plan, had the connections to the London and Glasgow financial markets to keep the partnership afloat financially; Taylor had the salesmanship and the firsthand knowledge of the Canadian brewing industry. Although Jennison died of a heart attack soon after the partnership was formed, Taylor was able to keep getting loans from the English and Scottish investors Jennison had drawn into the infant Brewing Corporation of Ontario (later renamed Canadian Breweries). By 1934 Taylor was out of financial danger and on his way to his first major success. About this same time he bought a home and some forty acres near the Toronto suburb of Willowdale, giving the estate the name of "Windfields" because of the constant wind blowing across the treeless tract.

Not only did the brewery business form the basis of Taylor's later wealth, but it also helped pave the way for Taylor's entry into the Thoroughbred industry. One of the brands of beer produced by his holding company was Cosgrave, which Taylor wished to promote.

At that time, Canadian law forbade the advertising of alcohol, but no law existed against advertising a racing stable. Thanks to that opening, Taylor saw a way to merge his business interests with what heretofore had been merely a hobby. On April 25, 1936, Taylor engaged a wily fellow named Bert Alexandra as his trainer and agent, purchased a horse named Madfest from him, and started racing in partnership with James Cosgrave, the former owner of Cosgrave Brewery, under the name of Cosgrave Stable.

Five thousand Canadian dollars, then equivalent to $4,500 in American currency, represented the sum of Taylor's initial investment in horse racing — one thousand for Madfest (plus a percentage from his first two wins in Cosgrave's colors) — and four thousand as a bankroll for Alexandra to start picking up more horses, which Alexandra did with a vengeance. Two days after Taylor had hired Alexandra and bought Madfest, he found himself the owner of five more horses, including his first winner. Between Saturday morning, when Alexandra had agreed to work for Taylor, and Monday afternoon, when Taylor received a telegram congratulating him on his winner, Alexandra had driven to Pimlico in Maryland. Once there, he bought a horse named Annimessic from an acquaintance for twelve hundred dollars (six hundred down and six hundred due when the horse won its first race for its new owner), won the second race on the card with his new purchase, and started claiming horses.

Alexandra was a master at the claiming game, and Taylor's first group of horses, cheap though they were, included a couple of real bargains. One, Jack Patches, a fifteen-hundred-dollar claim, would later that year win the Autumn Handicap at Woodbine for Cosgrave Stable; he eventually won $20,890. Another, the filly Nandi, developed into a solid allowance runner and later became the dam of Windfields, Taylor's first good homebred racehorse.

Most of the Cosgrave Stable horses continued to follow the pattern set that first season, with Alexandra making clever claims to fill the stable's ranks. Occasionally, however, Taylor took a hand. Although he did not have time to manage the stable's day-to-day operations — he left that to James Cosgrave, an avid horseman — he was actively involved in the overall running of the stable and did buy the occasional young horse to add to the Cosgrave roster. One, a twelve-hundred-dollar yearling by *Osiris II out of the King James mare Belmona, turned out to be Taylor's first real love as a racehorse — Mona Bell.

Mona Bell was not a great racehorse by any objective standard. Nonetheless, she was tough, talented, and as ready to take on colts as fillies. As a three-year-old, she became a popular idol through her rivalry with the good colt Bunty Lawless, their duels including the King's Plate (which the colt won) and the Breeders' Stakes (which Mona Bell won). Her feats gave

Taylor all the opportunity for advertising he needed. Posters of the filly — with the name Cosgrave prominently displayed on each — soon graced every bar and tavern in Ontario. Sales of Cosgrave beer rose in a most satisfactory manner, and Taylor no doubt smiled to himself as he chalked up the profits.

Mona Bell continued tilting with Bunty Lawless at four, the pair finishing one-two in the Orpen Memorial Handicap (Mona Bell the winner) and in the McIntyre and Loudon Memorial Handicap (Bunty Lawless the winner). Their rivalry was so popular that an announcement the two would be mated at the conclusion of their racing days made headlines in Canada. Sadly, it was never to be; Mona Bell slipped and broke a leg at Stamford Park in August 1939, and the injury was too severe for her to be saved.

Edward Taylor mourned his prize filly, not least for what might have been. Prior to Mona Bell, he had shown little interest in breeding racehorses for himself. He did have horses at Windfields, but they were riding horses; his racehorses stayed at the track, or else were boarded out. But Mona Bell changed all that. Taylor had tasted owning a good racehorse for the first time; now he meant to breed one for himself.

******

Taylor had already begun breeding in a small way while Mona Bell was still racing. In the spring of 1938, Taylor agreed to breed Nandi, one of his first purchases, to the top Canadian handicapper Frisius. The resulting filly, Frisinan, won twelve of 105 starts. Perhaps in hopes of getting another Mona Bell, Nandi next visited *Osiris II, but her 1940 filly Osinan never raced or produced a registered foal.

The luck turned for Taylor and Nandi after Bunty Lawless went to stud in 1941. Nandi's first Bunty Lawless foal, the 1942 filly Buntybell, won only once in thirty-eight tries, but Nandi's 1943 Bunty Lawless colt was Windfields.

As a two-year-old of 1945, Windfields won the Victoria Stakes in track-record time before being sidelined by injury. It was also the end of the road for Cosgrave Stable, which was dissolved that year; from then on, Taylor raced in his own name. The following year his turquoise-and-gold racing colors were officially registered with The Jockey Club in New York, just in time for Windfields to carry them to victory over King's Plate winner Kingarvie in the 1946 Breeders' Stakes.

Windfields raced on through 1949, finishing his career with nineteen wins from seventy-five starts before joining the American-bred Illuminable in his owner's stud. By that time, Taylor had purchased additional acreage for Windfields the farm (he eventually expanded the property to twelve hundred acres before beginning to sell off parcels in 1959) and had expanded his broodmare band to thirty-eight. He had also won his first King's Plate in 1949 with his homebred Epic, another son of Bunty Lawless.

Windfields and Epic marked another stage in the development of Taylor's racing ambitions. Windfields had been good enough to run second to American Triple Crown winner Assault in the historic Dwyer Stakes in New York as well as take the measure of a King's Plate winner; Epic had won Canada's most prestigious race. Now, having proven he could breed horses capable of racing at the highest levels in Canada, Taylor raised his sights again; he wanted to breed a horse that could win stakes on the tough New York circuit, the most prestigious in North America.

It was perhaps fitting that the horse that would provide Taylor with his breakthrough into New York racing was closely akin to Mona Bell: her full sister, Iribelle. Stakes-placed at three, Iribelle would produce only four foals for Taylor, but three would be stakes winners: Bennington, Britannia, and, best of all, Canadiana.

Canadiana was no looker; in fact, she drew the dubious distinction of being described by famed artist Richard Stone Reeves as "the ugliest horse, stallion or mare, that I have ever painted." Her defects included a hammer head, a ewe neck, and a swayback so deep that it looked as if her jockey were sitting in a hole. Nonetheless, she could run. Champion two-year-old and Horse of the Year in Canada in 1952, Canadiana won the 1953 Queen's Plate (the name of the race having been changed from the King's Plate in honor of Queen Elizabeth II's ascension to the English throne in 1952) and picked up Taylor's first victory in a major New York stakes the same year by winning the Test Stakes at Saratoga. The following year she won the Vagrancy Handicap at Aqueduct and ran second against males in the Sport Page Handicap at Jamaica. She won three Canadian stakes at five and retired with twenty wins and twenty placings from sixty-two starts.

Before Canadiana had even begun her racing career, however, Taylor's ambitions had moved up yet another step. On this occasion the catalyst was a new farm — Parkwood Farm, home of Colonel R.S. "Sam" McLaughlin. A mainstay of Ontario racing during the 1930s and 1940s, McLaughlin was seventy-nine in 1950 and no longer felt himself able to manage Parkwood as it deserved. Once it became known that he was interested in selling the property, he received several offers, but all were from developers. In desperation, the old colonel called Taylor, stating that he was willing to make substantial price concessions if the property could somehow be kept as a horse farm.

At first, Taylor was not interested in taking on a second farm. Not only did he have his hands full with Windfields, but as one of the directors of Argus Corporation, the largest holding company in Canada, he had more than enough business concerns to occupy any two ordinary men. He also was heavily involved in charitable enterprises and, in addition, had become a member of the Ontario Jockey Club in 1947; by 1952, he would be the OJC's principal shareholder, a position that would prove crucial to the future of Canadian racing.

A French friend, François Dupré, had expressed interest in having a Canadian farm in addition to his Normandy base, and Taylor contacted him about buying Parkwood. But by the time Taylor and McLaughlin could meet with Dupré to discuss the arrangements, Dupré had decided against the venture. Next, Taylor came up with the idea of forming a partnership with other wealthy Canadians to buy Parkwood and form a National Stud similar to that of England, standing quality sires to improve the breed in Canada.

It was a splendid idea but far ahead of its time in Canada, where both purses and the amount of money owners were willing to spend ran far below what their American counterparts took for granted. In reviewing the plan, Taylor rapidly came to the conclusion that it would be a major money loser for years. He called his prospective partners and, advising them of his conclusions, released them from the agreement. Then he bought Parkwood himself.

The sudden decision to buy Parkwood might well have been a surprise to

Mr. Taylor

Taylor's business associates, who were accustomed to seeing Taylor study a business proposition from all angles before making a decision. Further, Taylor already knew the farm was likely to lose substantial amounts of money for some time. Yet, in another sense, the move was quite characteristic of the man. Throughout his life, Taylor had shown the ability to take bold action when his instincts told him the time was right. And perhaps he had already foreseen that he would eventually be forced to move from the original Windfields by urban sprawl, as in fact proved the case. (Parkwood, at first renamed the National Stud Farm, inherited the Windfields name when the original Windfields ceased operations as a Thoroughbred farm and most of its remaining property was sold. The surviving Windfields Estate now consists of Taylor's house and twenty-five acres of the original property and is the home of the Canadian Film Centre.)

The acquisition of Parkwood marked a major turning point for Taylor as a racehorse owner and breeder. A 470-acre showplace, it was ideally suited for maintaining a large, quality herd of Thoroughbreds. But, by the same token, it was too large an investment for even a man of Taylor's wealth to treat as a hobby, especially by the time he had added over 1,100 additional acres through leases and purchases.

To make ends meet, not only would Taylor have to increase his racing winnings, but he also would have to breed horses good enough to attract buyers from bigger markets than Canada. And that meant consistently breeding horses that could tackle the major American races. In particular, it meant breeding a horse capable of winning one special race: the Kentucky Derby, the most sought-after prize in American racing and now the focus of Taylor's dreams and ambitions. He would spend the next thirteen-odd years chasing this goal.

Taylor being Taylor, he attacked the problem of making his Thoroughbred operations profitable from several angles at once. His first move was to put together a solid stallion roster at the National Stud under the care of general manager Gil Darlington and stallion manager Harry Green, who had been the chief stud groom at Windfields. Darlington, in turn, brought in Peter Poole, a young horseman from British Columbia, as his assistant. Taylor already had the stallion Windfields, who would eventually sire fifteen stakes winners, and with Gil Darlington came Chop Chop, who had previously stood at Darlington's own Trafalgar Farm. A stakes-winning son of the 1938 Ascot Gold Cup winner Flares (whose full brother was 1935 American Triple Crown winner Omaha), Chop Chop had already sired Canadiana for Taylor and would later sire Taylor's first Kentucky Derby starter, Victoria Park; Chop Chop would father twenty-nine stakes winners all told.

(Chop Chop's siring of Canadiana was a stroke of luck for both the stallion and Taylor. In 1949 Iribelle had actually been booked to *Boswell, the 1936 St. Leger winner and sire of her earlier stakes winner Bennington. Iribelle came into heat, but before she could be bred, *Boswell suddenly died. Unable to contact Taylor for new instructions, the Trafalgar Farm stallion manager took either initiative or license, depending on one's interpretation, and bred Iribelle to Chop Chop. The result was Canadiana — another example of "Taylor luck" in action.)

Bull Page, a colt Taylor purchased for $38,000 as a yearling, followed Chop Chop onto the National Stud roster in 1952. He was a son of Bull Lea out of a Blue Larkspur mare and, thus, bred on the same cross as the great filly Twilight Tear. Although he had soundness problems traceable to a very upright set of pasterns, Bull Page won three stakes at four and earned Canadian Horse of the Year honors in 1951 before siring the Queen's Plate-winning filly Flaming Page and Canadian Triple Crown winner New Providence for Taylor.

Taylor's other major addition to the National Stud stallion roster was *Menetrier. A son of Fairway's good son Fair Copy, *Menetrier was a high-class stakes winner in France despite a nasty temper. In Canada he would sire fifteen stakes winners and would also get several daughters that would produce champions for Taylor.

Whether Taylor knew it or not, he had laid the foundations for Northern Dancer's early stud success. The daughters and granddaughters of Windfields, Chop Chop, Bull Page, and *Menetrier helped establish the young sire's reputation with such champions as Viceregal, Nijinsky II, The Minstrel, and Fanfreluche. That was all in the future, however. In the meantime, Taylor was also tackling the problem of inadequate purses and prestige in Canadian racing.

Not unlike the Canadian brewery industry of the early 1930s, the Ontario racing scene of the first half of the twentieth century consisted of fourteen small tracks, none doing any too well. Only fourteen days of racing were allotted to each, meaning that none could generate the revenue needed to offer good purses or even maintain decent facilities. They were collectively known as the "leaky roof circuit" for good reason — dry stalls were often the occasion for fights among grooms seeking shelter for themselves and their charges. Taylor was not the only observer who feared that if the situation were left unchanged, racing would die out in Ontario, but he was the only one who held both a position to wield power over the industry and the will to use it.

Taylor applied the same consolidation strategy he had used with the Ontario breweries, buying controlling interests in the various tracks in the name of the Ontario Jockey Club. Most of the tracks were shut down and their allotted racing days transferred to the OJC, while the old Woodbine track (later renamed Greenwood in the spring of 1963 and finally closed for good in 1993) and Fort Erie both received substantial renovations. The moves were not popular with all Ontario horsemen, some of whom found Taylor's methods high-handed, but most soon acknowledged that he had probably saved racing in the province.

Under Taylor's guidance the OJC also began construction of a modern racing plant outside Toronto. The racetrack was named "New Woodbine" in honor of the old facility on the shores of Lake Ontario, but the "New" was dropped after the older track was renamed. The Queen's Plate was moved to the new track following its opening in 1956, and Woodbine is now the centerpiece of Canadian racing. New Woodbine thrived from the start, and with Ontario's 196 racing days now divided among only three tracks, Fort Erie and Old Woodbine were able to offer longer racing seasons that drew increased attendance and handle, allowing them to offer larger purses.

Taylor's need to increase the cash flow generated by his horses led to yet another innovation — the famous Windfields pre-priced yearling sales, held annually at the National Stud Farm beginning in 1954. Each year on the sale day, every yearling Taylor had was offered for inspection with a preset price listed by the yearling's identification number in the sale catalog. Potential owners and trainers were invited to look over the young horses and decide whether to buy at the stated prices. A maximum of half the youngsters would be sold; at day's end, or sooner if half of the yearlings had been sold, the sale was closed, and Taylor would keep the remaining colts and fillies to race.

Taylor's method of selling was unique, but it ensured that he could not be accused of selling only his culls; not only was every young horse he bred offered for sale, but the public got first pick. By the standards of early-1950s Canada the prices were high but so was the quality of the young horses; among the yearlings sold in the 1954 sale was Canadian Champ, who lived up to his name by becoming Canada's best juvenile in 1955 and winning the Queen's Plate on the way to Horse of the Year honors the following year. His success helped ensure the popularity of the Windfields sale in future years.

One other thing had to be tackled if Taylor was to make a success of the National Stud: he needed to upgrade his broodmare band. That meant looking for the best-bred fillies available, and in the 1950s, the finest sources of Thoroughbred bloodstock were the annual Saratoga yearling sale in New York and the Newmarket December horses of all ages sale in England. Taylor could cover New York himself but needed an agent to assist with finding the right mares in England. He contacted the British Bloodstock Agency, was assigned George Blackwell as his agent, and handed Blackwell the task of helping him buy the best mare to be had at the 1952 Newmarket December sale.

As it turned out, selecting the best mare was easy; it was buying her on Taylor's terms that was the trick. Although *Lady Angela had won only once in eleven starts, her bloodlines were among the most royal in England. Her sire was the great Hyperion; her dam was Sister Sarah, whose other produce included 1942 English champion juvenile filly Lady Sybil. And *Lady Angela was in foal to Nearco, though whether this was a plus can be debated, for *Lady Angela had already produced two Nearco foals. The first, a 1950 filly named Mary Martin, was stakes-placed twice at two but was said to be temperamental; the second, a 1951 colt named Gabriel, ended up as a gelding, suggesting that he may also have had a difficult disposition.

These results did not bode well for the Nearco foal *Lady Angela was carrying at the time of the sale, and in fact, the Nearco-Hyperion cross, so promising on paper, had proven disappointing in reality. Although Hyperion himself shared the amiable nature of his sire Gainsborough, his stock, particularly his fillies, often showed more of the high-strung, difficult temperament associated with St. Simon and Canterbury Pilgrim. When those fillies were bred to the highly dominant and willful Nearco, the result was often a horse whose disposition short-circuited its racing potential.

*Lady Angela's champion half sister Lady Sybil was, however, a daughter of Nearco, suggesting that her family might have an affinity for the great son of Pharos. Further, the filly Noory, by Nearco out of the Hyperion mare Sunny Day, had won the Prix d'Aumale in France earlier in 1952 to rank among the season's better French juveniles. (She would go on to win the Irish Oaks the following year.) Perhaps these facts were playing in Taylor's mind when he made up his mind not only to purchase *Lady Angela but to have her remain in England to foal and be bred back to Nearco before being shipped to Canada.

Arranging for *Lady Angela to be booked back to Nearco took some intensive pre-sale negotiation. As it happened, the mare was owned by Martin Benson, also the majority shareholder in Nearco following the horse's syndication in 1942. Through Blackwell, Taylor conveyed his interest in purchasing *Lady Angela at any price but only on the condition that she be sold with a return breeding to Nearco.

Benson was at first reluctant to the point of obstinacy, doubtless not wanting to use one of his own nominations to the stallion on a mare no longer his own. Taylor, however, was equally obstinate, making it clear (via the luckless Blackwell, who could not afford to antagonize either Benson or Taylor and must have found his position between the two stubborn men a most uncomfortable one) that he would not buy *Lady Angela without the return booking to Nearco.

To Blackwell's undoubted relief, Benson eventually yielded on condition that the stud fee be paid in American dollars. The reason for this seemingly odd stipulation was the English currency restrictions of the time, which limited the amount of money that Benson could take out of the country with him on his annual vacation to Palm Beach, Florida. Taylor's agreement to the deal ensured that the free-spending Benson would have plenty of American money for his vacation, and *Lady Angela was duly purchased for a sale-topping 10,500 guineas — about $35,000 in American money at the exchange rates then prevailing. Another $3,000 of Taylor's money went to Nearco's stud fee, and he wrapped up his English shopping spree by buying *Nephthis, another Hyperion daughter, for 4,200 guineas. (Even Taylor could not be lucky all the time; he might as well have saved his money on *Nephthis, who produced only one foal of no merit whatsoever.)

Thus, *Lady Angela remained in England until the spring of 1953, when she gave birth to her Nearco colt. Her return date with Nearco resulted in pregnancy, and *Lady Angela, her suckling colt, and her unborn foal sailed for Canada in late July.

Taylor's success in securing the mating with Nearco notwithstanding, the drama surrounding *Lady Angela's importation was not yet over. She arrived in Montreal after an uneventful voyage, but the trip nearly ended in tragedy when the ship's crew, inexperienced with horses, tried to lead *Lady Angela into the unloading crate without her foal. The mare, frantic to avoid separation from her baby, fought them desperately. The situation appeared ripe for injury to the mare or her handlers — or for a possible stress-induced miscarriage of the foal *Lady Angela was carrying — when Harry Green took charge.

It was no small stroke of luck that the Windfields staff had sent Harry Green to collect the new Taylor horses at the dock, for Green was no stranger to dealing with volatile animals. As the stallion manager at Windfields and later the National Stud, his charges had included *Menetrier, a horse of such ugly disposition that a man with a rifle was stationed near the paddock gate every time the stallion was led in or out in case he should try to savage his handler. *Lady Angela, fortunately, was not nearly so dangerous by nature; she was simply in a panic, and Green knew how to deal with that. He waved the crewmen back and got the mare quieted, then maneuvered the foal into the crate so he could disembark first. The crate had only enough room for one horse at a time; fearing that the little fellow would be overly frightened by riding in the crate without his mother, Green swallowed his own trepidation and climbed aboard as well, petting and reassuring the squealing youngster as the crate lifted from the deck, then swung to the dock.

With the foal safely landed, Green went back for *Lady Angela. Now anxious to rejoin her foal, the mare loaded willingly, and Green steadied her through his second trip in the swaying, shuddering crate until the mare — and the precious cargo *she* carried — reached the dock safely. The foal she had fought so hard to protect, *Empire Day, would grow up to win only three of thirty-six starts with one stakes placing and would sire only one stakes winner, 1964 Canadian champion older male E. Day. But the foal she carried was Nearctic, a much superior racehorse and the sire of Northern Dancer.

Nearctic and Natalma

N earctic was foaled at Windfields on February 11, 1954. A striking near-black colt with the powerful lines of his sire, he was a much sturdier type than his older brother *Empire Day. Like Nearco, he was also unusually independent even at an early age, ranging far from his mother's side and fighting his handlers determinedly at every new procedure. Tesio, perhaps, would not have been surprised; in later years, John Aiscan of *The British Racehorse* stated, "Of all Nearco's sons with racing class, Nearctic bears the closest resemblance to his sire."

Like all the Windfields crop of 1954, Nearctic was offered for sale at the pre-priced yearling sale of 1955. There is reason to believe that Taylor had no real intention of selling him, however. The handsome colt carried a price tag of $35,000, a price that would have been fairly high even in America. In Canada, where the average yearling at the 1955 Canadian Thoroughbred Horse Society sale brought only $2,392, it was astronomical, especially as *Empire Day had only a maiden victory to his credit at that point. At day's end, Nearctic remained unsold, leaving Taylor in possession of the best horse he had bred to that point.

As a racehorse, however, Nearctic proved enigmatic. He was blessed with abundant talent but cursed with the volatile temperament typical of the Nearco-Hyperion cross. Aggressive, willful, and highly strung, he was a colt that few riders were capable of handling. Further, he battled physical problems throughout his career.

Nearctic's early training was handled by Gordon "Pete" McCann, who had become Windfields' head trainer on the recommendation of Gil Darlington after Bert Alexandra's retirement in 1950. "If I had my choice of all the trainers on the Canadian circuit, this fellow is the one who would have my horses," Darlington told Taylor.

Darlington was not the only one who held such a high opinion of McCann. Reminiscing many years later, champion jockey Ron Turcotte said, "He was one of the greatest trainers of all time. I rode for many great trainers during my career — trainers like Jimmy Jones, Hirsch Jacobs, Eddie Neloy, and Frank Whiteley — but I never rode for one who was a better horseman ... He never shied away from any work, whether it was making up his horses' feed or mucking out stalls. Just about everyone who knew him loved him."

Sadly, too few people outside Canada know much about McCann. Yet by any objective standard, his career was remarkable. He trained six Queen's Plate winners, including Canadian Triple Crown winners New Providence (1959) and Canebora (1963). The first really good horse he trained was none other than Bunty Lawless, whom he took over from Jack Anderson as a four-year-old. For Windfields, he trained six horses that gained Horse of the Year honors in Canada, beginning with Bull Page in 1951 and ending with Viceregal in 1968. (By way of comparison, the famous father-and-son training team of Ben and Jimmy Jones trained five American Horses of the Year for Calumet Farm, all in the 1940s.)

A former jockey, McCann did much of the training of his best horses from the saddle. He had an uncanny instinct for picking out those young horses that had real potential; he also rode the toughest horses in the barn, the problem children he did not want to entrust to anyone else.

Nearctic was one of the horses McCann chose to ride.

******

A young racehorse has to learn a tremendous amount in a short time. Within the space of six to nine months, it must learn how to carry a rider, how to break from the starting gate, and how to obey a rider's signals regardless of whether it is walking quietly or stretched out at a full gallop. It must learn to accept many strange sights and sounds and, most importantly, it must learn to trust the humans who work with it.

Little concrete information exists regarding Nearctic's early training, but the evidence from his racing days strongly suggests that he was a colt who could easily have been spoiled for racing by a trainer less skilled and patient than Pete McCann. He was not an easy ride by any means, even for McCann, but over time a deep trust grew between colt and trainer, never better demonstrated than when McCann broke an ankle. As McCann's long-time assistant, Bill Reeves, later told author Muriel Lennox, Reeves took over exercising the colt for three days; then McCann was right back in Nearctic's saddle, wrapping an extra-long stirrup leather around his cast and hooking that to the saddle to serve as a substitute for a stirrup. Nearctic must have wondered at the change in his friend's equipment but behaved as well as he ever did, and McCann healed up without incident while daily galloping his favorite.

Except for the times when Nearctic was in another trainer's barn and the three days taken off for the broken ankle, McCann exercised Nearctic personally for the four years the horse raced. Many other trainers have been equally conscientious in the care and feeding of their charges; like McCann, they have devised individual feeding plans for each animal's needs, checked each horse personally on a daily basis, and have been alert to small changes in behavior that might signal problems. Some even have had McCann's almost instinctive ability to communicate with horses and discern their needs and quirks. But McCann's riding of Nearctic added another dimension to his awareness of the colt's behavior and personality and may well have been the difference between Nearctic's becoming the racehorse he was and Nearctic's not making a racehorse at all. What might have been had Nearctic remained consistently in McCann's care throughout his career will never be known.

******

Nearctic made his debut on May 10, 1956, in a four and a half-furlong maiden race at Old Woodbine. He won gate to wire in brilliant fashion, earning himself the headline "Nearctic Easy Winner in First Start" in the next day's *Daily Racing Form*. Eleven days later he won another four and a half-furlong race, this one an allowance for non-winners of two, in the same front-running style.

Two weeks after the opening of New Woodbine, Nearctic went to the post there for the Swansea Plate, a five-furlong allowance event for two-year-olds. Although the Swansea represented a step up in class from the competition Nearctic had previously faced, it made no difference; Nearctic leaped out of the gate first as usual and sped home ten lengths in front under a hand ride. Then, on July 2, Nearctic demolished another overmatched field in the Clarendon Stakes, again over five furlongs. The colt concluded the first phase of his racing career by handily winning the five and a half-furlong Victoria Stakes on July 14 from Mister Jive, who would go on to win the Summer Stakes in Canada and the Cowdin Stakes in New York before the season's end.

At that point Nearctic had won five straight races by a combined margin of some twenty-eight lengths and had never been fully extended. Had he been retired for the season then and there, he could possibly have been Canada's Horse of the Year. As it was, he was to lose more races than he won over the remainder of the year. But no one knew that when the colt loaded aboard a van bound for Saratoga.

The oldest and most prestigious of New York's race meetings, Saratoga annually draws the cream of the Eastern stables and is especially known for its juvenile racing. To have a colt or filly break its maiden at Saratoga is considered a mark of quality; to win a stakes there, doubly so.

Taylor was quite familiar with the traditions of Saratoga racing. Every year he and Winifred would pack up and travel down to the stately old track, where the Taylors would rub elbows with the elite of the American owners. Friendships were made there as well as friendly rivalries, and the proudly nationalistic Taylor was undoubtedly keen to show his American counterparts that Canada could produce more than just snow and ice.

McCann did not share his eagerness. An extremely shy, self-effacing man, McCann hated publicity and generally did not care to travel farther from his home base at Woodbine than Fort Erie, some ninety minutes away. In any event, he was responsible for some fifty Windfields horses other than Nearctic; even had he been enthusiastic about the venture, it is questionable whether he could have been spared from his other duties. And so

Nearctic was sent to veteran American trainer Charley Shaw, who would handle the colt throughout the Saratoga meeting.

******

Horses are creatures of habit, some more so than others. For the high-strung Nearctic, who had never been more than two hours' drive from his birthplace, the day-long van ride to Saratoga and a new barn were strange enough. But more changes awaited him. New tastes of hay and grain and water, all subtly different from what he was used to. New smells and sights. A new exercise routine and a new exercise rider. And, to top off everything else, a new jockey.

Nearctic had already had three jockeys. His first, Vic Bovine, had been summarily dismissed by McCann after using a whip on the colt while well out in front; McCann was never one to tolerate what he considered abuse of a horse. Nearctic's second jockey, George Walker, had been more satisfactory but nothing spectacular. But his third had proven a near-perfect fit for him and had ridden him in his last three Canadian starts. This was future Hall of Famer Avelino Gomez, a Cuban exile who wound up winning more than four thousand races, mostly in Canada, before his death in a three-horse spill at Woodbine in 1980. Energetic, cocky, and charismatic, Gomez seemed to understand Nearctic and let the free-running colt roll, concentrating on keeping his mount balanced and focused on his task.

Gomez, however, was persona non grata in the United States. He had been riding in Chicago in 1951 and, as required for a legal alien residing in the United States, had registered for the draft. The Korean War was raging, however, and when it looked as though Gomez might be coming up for the draft, he returned to Cuba. Thus, he was listed as a draft dodger in the United States and, although he had resumed his riding career in Canada in 1955, he could not cross the American border to ride at Saratoga. Eric Guerin was engaged to ride the colt instead; he had gained fame a few years earlier as the regular pilot for the great Native Dancer.

Nearctic was entered in the Flash Stakes on Saratoga's opening day, and the usual crowd was swelled by Canadians who had crossed the border to see their hero tackle America's best. McCann was also there as a spectator rather than trainer, having been driven down from Fort Erie by Windfields racing manager Joe Thomas the night before.

******

The pairing of McCann and Thomas was ironic in view of their future clashes in the handling of Nearctic. Both genuinely loved the horse; in his obituary in the *Daily Racing Form* of June 10, 1984, Thomas was quoted as having repeatedly said, "I think my favorite horse was Nearctic ... He had tremendous speed and an air of electricity about him." Yet the personalities of the two men would bring them into what was perhaps an inevitable conflict over the colt's management, a conflict that often did not work to Nearctic's advantage.

Thomas first began working for Windfields as the result of Taylor's visit to the 1955 Keeneland July yearling sale. While at a dinner, Taylor mentioned his need for a man who could handle both the financial side of the Windfields operation and the publicity for the farm, including the development of the catalog for the annual yearling sale. His hostess, Mrs. Roy Carruthers, and Warner Jones, then the president of Churchill Downs, both recommended the same man: Joe Thomas, a UCLA graduate and former groom who at that time was working in the Lexington bureau of *Daily Racing Form*. The developer of the Stallion Directory and Farm Register sections of the *Form*, Thomas was a regular columnist for the *Lexington Herald* and had also done publicity work for Keeneland; on top of that, he had an extensive knowledge of pedigrees. After some phone calling among Taylor, Jones, and Thomas, Taylor became convinced that Thomas was the man he needed and hired him on February 1, 1956.

The problems began not too long after Thomas assumed the title of Windfields racing manager. Pete McCann was a hands-on horseman and had neither the inclination nor the verbal expressiveness to spend time making a case for how he felt the racing stable should be managed; he apparently felt that his care of the horses and their success in racing should speak for themselves. Thomas, on the other hand, was articulate and outgoing, and much more comfortable in dealing directly with Taylor than was McCann; further, hindsight suggests that he was more in tune with Taylor's long-range ambitions for his stable than was McCann. The net result was that McCann, while remaining responsible for the care and training of the horses, found himself increasingly pushed to one side when it came to making major decisions about his charges' racing campaigns, such as what targets they would be pointed toward and which specific races they would enter. According to author Muriel Lennox, Thomas even began taking over such traditional prerogatives of the trainer as hiring jockeys and giving riding instructions for specific races.

Thomas shared Taylor's dream of making Windfields a world-class racing and breeding operation, and he had a keen sense of how to manage the strategic aspects of developing a horse business. A measure of his success in helping Taylor achieve his ambitions is that he was named Windfields' vice-president for Thoroughbred operations on the death of Gil Darlington in 1968; later, his contributions to the Canadian Thoroughbred industry were recognized in 1983 when he was named "Man of the Year" at the annual Sovereign Awards dinner and in 1985 when he was inducted into the Canadian Horse Racing Hall of Fame in the "Builders" category. But Thomas' one great weakness when it came to Nearctic was the area of McCann's strength: Thomas lacked an intimate, hands-on knowledge of Nearctic's physical and mental condition and, in fact, had no experience at all with training horses. And, thus, Nearctic sometimes was treated — however unintentionally — as a pawn in the overall Windfields strategy, rather than as an individual horse with needs and vulnerabilities of his own.

******

McCann may not officially have been in charge of Nearctic while the colt was at Saratoga, but he could not have liked what he saw in the Flash Stakes, which was run on a muddy track. Apparently either unaware of Nearctic's front-running style or afraid that the colt would use himself up too early, Eric Guerin tried to restrain Nearctic off the lead. The effort was futile. Nearctic fought both his jockey and a rival named Willing Worker to get the lead, tired, bore out, and finished eighth behind Missile, a good son of War Relic who won four stakes that season. McCann went back to Fort Erie that night.

Nearctic and Natalma

Nearctic should have been Canada-bound as well, at least according to statements made by Charley Shaw prior to the Flash. Shaw had told reporters that if Nearctic did not prove himself in the Flash, he would be promptly returned to Toronto with no excuses. Further, the *Daily Racing Form* reported that Nearctic had come out of the Flash with bucked shins (the equine equivalent of a human runner's "shin splints"), probably the reason he had tried to bear out. The condition is not generally considered serious, but it is painful and is usually treated by rest, applications of cold water, and anti-inflammatory medications. Yet Nearctic stayed at Saratoga and — according to one unnamed source, at the insistence of E.P. Taylor himself — remained in training.

One week later Nearctic went to the post for the Saratoga Special. This time he was ridden by George Walker, who had been aboard the colt in his second race in Canada. Although the track was again muddy, Walker did not repeat Guerin's error and let the colt roll. He made one of his own, though — one that probably would have gotten him sacked immediately if McCann had been in charge. Nearctic scorched the first half-mile in :46 2/5 — the fastest half-mile split to that point in the meet despite the off track — but bore out badly on the turn, and Walker struck him several times about the head with the whip to get him back on a straight course. One of those blows struck the colt in the eye. Nearctic just hung on to win by three-quarters of a length over Clem, a namesake of sportscaster Clem McCarthy. Clem would go on to be one of the better members of the crop at ages three and four.

Nearctic's victory was sweet to Taylor, especially after the debacle in the Flash, but it had come at a price. The colt's eye was not seriously injured, but the reason he had tried to bear out became painfully apparent when he came back sore after the race. His bucked shins were badly inflamed, and the *Daily Racing Form* report indicated that the colt would be forced to miss the meeting's marquee event for juveniles, the Hopeful Stakes.

Yet, when the Hopeful Stakes rolled around nineteen days later, Nearctic was in the post parade. Although he led for the first half-mile, he was unable to withstand the challenge of King Hairan, one of the season's best juveniles, and according to the *Daily Racing Form* chart, "gave way suddenly when challenged" to finish fourth. Eyewitness accounts indicate that he was bearing out again toward the end of the race, suggesting that his shins had not fully recovered and perhaps had been reaggravated during the running.

The Saratoga meet having ended, Nearctic went back home to Canada and Pete McCann. Back in familiar environs at Old Woodbine, the colt recovered well enough to score an easy win in the inaugural Carleton Stakes, a race restricted to Canadian-breds, on September 22, three weeks after the Hopeful. With his old partner, Avelino Gomez, in the saddle, he seemed back to his best form. But after the race, McCann detected the beginnings of a quarter crack in the colt's left front hoof. This injury, a vertical split in the hoof beginning just below the coronet (the equine equivalent of a human's nail bed), is often treated in the modern era with a patch of silicone or some other material that can contract and expand in the same way that the horse's hoof wall normally does, enabling the horse to continue racing and training without pain.

In Nearctic's time, however, the only cure for a quarter crack was to permit the hoof to grow out until the quarter crack could be cut away, then let the hoof finish growing out to its normal form — a procedure that required long months of rest, yet better than continuing to train and race the horse. An untreated quarter crack is a painful injury in and of itself, but it also can cause stress in other areas of the horse's anatomy as the animal attempts to accommodate its painful foot, increasing the risk of additional injuries. What could happen with an untreated quarter crack is illustrated by the tragic history of Black Gold, the 1924 Kentucky Derby winner; troubled by a quarter crack for much of the first phase of his racing career, Black Gold developed leg problems when returned to the races at age six after two years at stud and, perhaps compromised by fatigue from a too-heavy work schedule as well, suffered a fatal breakdown in his first start at age seven.

In hindsight, the logical and humane thing to do would have been to send Nearctic back to Windfields, where the quarter crack could have grown out while the colt enjoyed a well-earned winter's rest. But instead, Nearctic was sent back to New York and Charley Shaw, with the venerable Futurity Stakes at Belmont Park as his target. Perhaps his connections reasoned that with the quarter crack still in an early stage and Nearctic apparently in top form otherwise, the colt might still have a shot in the big race.

Nearctic might as well have stayed in Canada. In both his prep race for the Futurity and the Futurity itself, he flew from the gate, only to end up unplaced after beginning to tire at about the half-mile pole. Pain from his left forefoot may well have been a factor in his inability to sustain his run, but a mental problem was developing as well. Already a confirmed front runner, he was becoming "speed-crazed," running all out from the gate regardless of whether he was being challenged or not and using up his energy much too early in a race. On returning to Canada, Nearctic followed the same pattern in the Coronation Futurity: uncontrollable early speed followed by an unplaced finish.

McCann had not wanted to run the horse in the Coronation Futurity to begin with, and after the race, he had seen enough. He took Nearctic back to Windfields with the intention of resting him. But he was overruled by Joe Thomas, who insisted that the colt enter the Cup and Saucer Stakes. (Whether Thomas' insistence was at Taylor's behest is not clear from available records.) This was the last major event for juveniles on the Canadian calendar and the desire to win it was understandable, but Nearctic was simply not physically capable of delivering what was wanted of him. For once in his life, he was slow leaving the gate, and though he got up to third at the head of the stretch, he faded thereafter.

Back to Windfields he went, but once again he did not get the prolonged rest he needed. This time the intervening factor was trainer Horatio Luro, who had been acquainted with Taylor since the late 1940s and had been instrumental in arranging the lease that initially brought Taylor's good stallion Chop Chop to Canada. Luro was heading to California for winter training and racing, but prior to his departure, he ran into Taylor in New York. Naturally, they began talking about horses; before too long the conversation had veered around to Nearctic. Whether on his own initiative or at Taylor's prompting, Luro offered to take Nearctic with him to be prepared as a Kentucky Derby prospect.

A few days later Nearctic was on his way to California.

******

Horatio Luro, then and now, was a man who tended to stir either deep admiration or, less commonly, an equally deep antipathy. Gifted with a

Latin verve for life, he loved speed in any form: fast airplanes, fast cars, and fast horses. He liked the good life of fine restaurants and the polo set, and the company of beautiful women. With the gracious manners of a Spanish aristocrat and the dark good looks and stylish dress of a Hollywood star, there was no question that "El Gran Señor," like him or not, was one of the most striking figures ever seen around an American racetrack.

The love of the Thoroughbred ran deep in Luro's blood. His grandfather, Pedro, emigrated from Spain to Argentina at age seventeen and became one of the country's foremost cattle ranchers. Having escaped ambushes by local Indians several times through the aid of his horse El Moro, Pedro Luro had an appreciation for a fast horse, a trait passed to his son Adolphe, a founder and president of the Argentine Jockey Club and the owner of one of the country's premier breeding farms in Haras El Moro.

One of six sons of Adolphe, Horatio Luro was born in 1901 in Buenos Aires. He was required to work with the family's horses in between educational requirements (he spent three years at the University Veterinary Schools in Buenos Aires) and romantic pursuits, which on at least one occasion led him as far as Paris, France.

Paternal authority and control of the younger Luro's allowance enabled Adolphe to get his son back from France and steadied down somewhat, but it was only a matter of time before Horatio broke out on his own. In the 1930s he began exporting Argentine horses to the United States, both taking horses there to sell and acting as agent for Americans who came to Buenos Aires to buy.

Luro came to the United States permanently in the spring of 1937, his father having died a few months earlier, and formed a partnership with the young trainer Charlie Whittingham, then working as a jockeys' agent. As Luro did not yet have an American trainer's license while Whittingham did, the partners shared the work along logical lines: Luro wooed clients (along with assorted Hollywood starlets and leading ladies); Whittingham did most of the hands-on horse work; and the two managed to hustle out a living until Pearl Harbor rocked the headlines and Whittingham enlisted in the Marines.

Luro had lost his partner, but he still had his wit, his charm, and his eye for a good horse. He quickly got his own trainer's license and began training horses for a number of owners, among them Princess Audrey Djordjaze, the American-born wife of an exiled Georgian prince. Luro talked the Princess into partnering with him in claiming a colt named *Princequillo for $2,500 in 1942; the following year, *Princequillo developed into the best stayer in the country, winning the Saratoga Cup and the Jockey Club Gold Cup.

*Princequillo made Luro's reputation, and by the time Whittingham got back from the Marines to re-enlist as Luro's assistant in 1946, Luro was training horses for the likes of Arnold Hanger, Josephine Ryce, and Mary Elizabeth "Liz" Whitney. The last-named lady not only helped solidify Luro's reputation as a trainer with the fine horses she supplied him but furthered his reputation as a ladies' man by carrying on a torrid affair with him. (According to horse dealer and raconteur John "Trader" Clark, the affair ended abruptly when Luro allowed one of Whitney's horses to get claimed by running it below its true value so he could deduct money Whitney owed him: "Money business comes before monkey business," he reportedly told her afterward.)

Luro's womanizing days were behind him when he entered Nearctic's life (he had married Frances Weinman in 1951, his second marriage and one that would endure until Frances' death in 1989), but other habits remained. Shirley Post, writing for the *Los Angeles Times–Washington Post* news service, said of him, "The dapper figure of señor Luro can be seen all over the major tracks in the barn area in the morning, in the posh clubhouses and turf club areas during the day's races." The problem was that one place Luro was seen perhaps less often than he needed to be was in the barn itself, doing the hands-on work. That was usually left to his assistants, particularly during the summer, when Luro customarily vacationed for several weeks in Europe to avoid the American hay fever season.

This is not to imply that Luro was incompetent as a trainer. Known for his patient and careful approach to horses and a meticulous eye for detail, he was well respected by his peers. Yet to a great extent, his success depended on the competence of his assistants. Whittingham, who went out on his own in 1948 with Luro's active encouragement, beat his old partner to the National Museum of Racing's Hall of Fame by six years, getting inducted in 1974. David Englander, who assisted Luro while Whittingham was in the

Marines, actually trained *Princequillo to several of his more important victories because Luro had become ill from the stressful racetrack life. (Luro eventually had to check into the famed Mayo Clinic and take six months' vacation before he was fit to resume his career.) In later years Reggie Cornell (who trained 1959 Preakness Stakes winner Royal Orbit in his own right), Norman Bowles, and Thomas "Peaches" Fleming all played important roles in Luro's stable.

Luro's dependence on his assistants for much of the day-to-day, hands-on contact with his charges may well have been to his detriment in coping with Nearctic. Luro had no trouble in observing that Nearctic was rank and headstrong but apparently missed the quarter crack at first, perhaps because it was still in an early stage. He concluded that the colt's problem was the sharp, fast works that he had been given while in Charley Shaw's barn in New York. Luro tended to model his training program after the more relaxed, patient style typical of the best English and French trainers, and he believed that the speed drills had made Nearctic overly anxious; long, slow gallops would settle the colt's nerves and make him more amenable to a rider's restraint.

It was a good idea as far as it went, but the problem of Nearctic was compounded by the fact that none of Luro's people had the strength and skill to ride him. Luro, however, had previously made the acquaintance of Australian-born jockey Rae Johnstone, one of the best riders in Europe in the 1950s. Johnstone had sometimes ridden for Luro when the trainer had horses running in France, and it was natural enough that the two would renew their acquaintance while the jockey was wintering at Santa Anita, far from the dank cold of a European winter.

Johnstone sometimes worked horses during his winter vacation to keep himself fit, and he agreed to work Nearctic for Luro, sometimes on the track and sometimes in the wooded area surrounding Santa Anita. The long, slow works did seem to have some benefit. By the end of the winter, Nearctic was more relaxed and no longer as anxious.

He still had the quarter crack, however — Luro had discovered its presence during the winter — and it apparently hampered efforts to get him prepared for a race. The one benefit to Nearctic of being in Luro's care rather than McCann's at this time may have been that Luro, a self-assured man with a gift for charming clients and the advantage of not being Taylor's full-time employee, was well equipped to withstand any pressures that Taylor or Thomas might have brought to bear to run the colt before he was ready.

Nearctic shipped to Belmont Park with the rest of Luro's stable, but by the time Luro considered him fit to run, both the Kentucky Derby and the Queen's Plate were out of the question. The colt did not appear on the race-course until July 1, 1957, and finished a well-beaten second to an unre-markable horse named Dancing Feet in a six-furlong allowance. Twenty-five days later he faced his old rival King Hairan in another Belmont allowance and ran wide through the stretch to finish fourth without ever having shown any of his usual speed.

That lackluster effort got Nearctic sent back to Canada, where he was reunited with Pete McCann and Avelino Gomez. The results were little short of astonishing. Within the period from August 9 to August 24, Nearctic won two allowance sprints over Fort Erie's main track, then won by six lengths in the mile and one-sixteenth Canadian International Handicap on the Fort Erie turf course. But no sooner had Nearctic apparently come back to his best form than he was shipped back to Luro at Belmont.

By this time, Nearctic's record strongly suggested that the high-strung colt simply did not cope well away from the friendly confines of his home base in Canada. He also may have been past his best form, for his entry in the one-mile Atlantic Beach Purse on September 2 marked his sixth start in just over two months and followed that peak effort in the Canadian International. In any event, he bore out badly in the stretch after leading early and ended up sixth behind Promised Land, a good colt whose six 1957 stakes victories included the Pimlico Special against older horses. Just over three weeks later Nearctic ran a tremendous race in the six-furlong Mitchel Field Classified Handicap, an overnight event, but was beaten a half-length by the speedy *Mahmoud colt Cohoes after dueling with that rival through most of the race.

Nearctic's next race was not quite up to that standard, though the colt ran a respectable fourth in another six-furlong allowance race, beaten less than a length and a half. But his next start was incredibly ambitious given the form he had displayed to that point. He was entered in the Vosburgh

Stakes, where he would face the mighty Bold Ruler in the midst of the latter's Horse of the Year season. Perhaps the Windfields team was encouraged by the fact that Nearctic had been assigned the field's lightest weight at 109 pounds compared to 130 on Bold Ruler, but few others took the colt's chances all that seriously; Nearctic went off at odds of 16-1.

Nearctic did his best, catching Bold Ruler after the latter had gotten the best of the break and actually wresting the lead from him briefly. But after three-eighths of a mile, Nearctic was done. He staggered home dead last, while Bold Ruler won by nine lengths and broke Roseben's fifty-one-year-old track record for seven furlongs at Belmont.

Physically exhausted, Nearctic was shipped back to Pete McCann but not for a rest. Ten days after the Vosburgh, he was out for the nine-furlong Bunty Lawless Stakes at Old Woodbine — reportedly on orders from Joe Thomas and over McCann's protests. Up to that time Nearctic had never won at so long a distance; to expect that he would do so after a disastrous finish in his last start seems wildly optimistic in hindsight. For some inscrutable reason Thomas also decided to retain Conn McCreary to ride the colt. McCreary, it is true, had ridden Nearctic several times, most recently in the Vosburgh Stakes, but he had not been successful with the colt and was, in fact, best known for his skill in bringing horses from off the pace, not in managing front runners. Nearctic finished a well-beaten fourth behind the solid stakes horse Dorenes Lad after getting into a speed duel with four-year-old Canadian Champ, the previous year's Queen's Plate winner.

Why Nearctic was shipped back to Luro for yet another crack at New York racing is something of a mystery, for he had already raced ten times in four months and had not shown anything close to his best form in his last three starts. Yet on November 6, Nearctic was in the starting gate at New York's old Jamaica racetrack for the Rockville Centre Classified Handicap, an overnight race at five and a half furlongs. He ran third. Twelve days later the colt bore out badly and finished fifth in the six-furlong East Marion Purse, beaten just under five lengths as the odds-on favorite.

One week later Nearctic was entered in the Middleville Purse, another six-furlong allowance. On paper this seemed a questionable move, given that severe bearing out such as Nearctic had shown in his last start usually reflects a physical or mental problem. But Luro's judgment was borne out by the race, for Nearctic took the lead early and never looked back, winning by a length. The colt apparently went back to Canada afterward, for there is no record of him on the work tabs in Southern California, where Luro's stable wintered.

******

Wherever Nearctic spent the winter, he at last got the long rest he needed to heal completely from his physical ailments. When he reappeared in April 1958, it was under the care of Pete McCann, who engaged Benny Sorensen to ride Nearctic in the stead of Avelino Gomez. (Gomez had once again returned to his native Cuba, where he had bought an apartment complex and opened a bar called the Toronto Club; he eventually returned to riding in Canada after Fidel Castro's takeover.)

As at the beginning of his juvenile season, Nearctic was fresh, happy, and fit, and it showed in the way he raced. Beginning with the April 19 Bold Venture Handicap at Fort Erie (in which he set a new Canadian record for five furlongs), Nearctic reeled off five straight wins, his skein including the Vigil Handicap, the Swynford Stakes, the Jacques Cartier Stakes (setting a Canadian record for six furlongs), and the Canadian Maturity Stakes. In the last-named race, however, Nearctic was visibly tired at the finish and won by only a nose, just outlasting Our Sirdar for the mile and one-sixteenth. His next effort, the July 1 Dominion Day Handicap, was actually a fairly good one as he was beaten less than a length and a half in the nine-furlong race, but four days later he stopped badly in the one and one-sixteenth-mile Connaught Cup Handicap to finish sixth.

That performance did not inspire confidence in the betting public two weeks later when Nearctic shipped to Detroit for the Michigan Mile; the colt went off at odds of 21-1 as part of the mutuel field. The favorite was Swoon's Son, an excellent racehorse who won twenty-two stakes during his career. The 1958 Michigan Mile would not be one of them, however. Swoon's Son took himself out of contention early by stumbling into the speedy Red God, creating a traffic jam. Nearctic was not affected as he had broken in front, and in front was where he stayed throughout the race. He won by two and a quarter lengths over *Shoerullah in track-record time.

The Michigan Mile is generally considered the biggest win of Nearctic's career, and it was certainly the most lucrative; the $40,746.55 Nearctic picked up as the winner's share was the largest purse ever won by a Canadian horse up to that time. It was also the only time that Pete McCann voluntarily went to the United States with Nearctic, and as soon as Nearctic had safely cooled down from his victorious effort, McCann put him on a horse van and headed right back for Canada.

******

Nearctic's win in the Michigan Mile had two important spinoffs. First, it gave him a win over good American competition, his first since the Saratoga Special as a juvenile, helping to enhance his potential value as a stallion. Second, it put some extra money in Taylor's pocket, which he used to go shopping at the 1957 Saratoga yearling sale.

Taylor was not after racehorses at that time; the stalls allotted to Windfields at New Woodbine and Fort Erie were well filled. But he was in the market for fillies that could make fine broodmares; if they could race well prior to retirement, so much the better. With the money provided by Nearctic, he was determined to buy something special — the kind of filly who could become a foundation mare for Windfields.

One of the consignors at that sale was Danny Van Clief, whose string of sale horses included the bay filly by Native Dancer out of Almahmoud that he had bred in partnership with his aunt, Mrs. Ellsworth H. Augustus. The filly, later named Natalma, was a half sister to stakes winner Cosmah and had the kind of bloodlines Taylor was looking for to help upgrade his brood-mare band.

As related by Edward Bowen in *Matriarchs: Great Mares of the 20th Century*, some superb tomato preserves might also have played a role in Natalma's purchase. Danny Van Clief's cook, Rosa Page, had made the preserves and baked up a batch of fresh bread for buyers looking over Van Clief's string, and when Taylor and Luro came by to look at Natalma, they both had a generous helping of Rosa's preserves and bread. Whether it was the filly herself or the memory of those preserves (as Van Clief himself claimed) that brought Taylor back for a second look at Natalma, the fact remained that Taylor ended up paying $35,000 for the daughter of Almahmoud. It would prove money well spent.

******

Nearctic had barely gotten back to the familiar confines of Fort Erie when Pete McCann got orders — whether from Joe Thomas or from Taylor himself is not clear — to turn around and take Nearctic back to Detroit, where the colt could win a bonus if he could add the Detroit Sweepstakes to his Michigan Mile win. McCann protested; he knew that the chances of Nearctic's getting away with an easy lead again were slim to none. Given that the Michigan Mile had been Nearctic's eighth start in three months, perhaps he also felt the horse needed rest, but his protest went for nothing. Back to Detroit Nearctic went, only to run seventh in the Sweepstakes. Then, in an even odder development, Nearctic was sent on from Detroit to Saratoga, where he joined Horatio Luro's barn once more.

Perhaps Nearctic's connections felt that with a familiar jockey in the saddle, one that had worked well with the colt before, he would handle the transition in trainers this time. Benny Sorensen, who had ridden Nearctic throughout the year, was retained to ride him at Saratoga, and the horse was entered in the seven-furlong American Legion Handicap on August 8. But something may well have been physically wrong with Nearctic by this time, for once again he bore out during the race, finishing unplaced, and once again he was sent back to McCann — apparently to be patched up, for it was nearly a month before he appeared under silks again.

Nearctic returned in the seven-furlong Sandown Stakes at Old Woodbine on September 1 and won easily, a performance he repeated in the one-mile Greenwood Handicap twelve days later under a hefty 130 pounds. Sent to the post for the ten-furlong Autumn Handicap on September 27, he tired under top weight of 126 pounds and finished second by three-quarters of a length to the filly Kitty Girl, who carried 117 pounds. The distance was probably beyond his scope, but a week later Nearctic showed that the effort had not harmed him by setting a track record for six furlongs in the Seaway Handicap.

Continuing to race at Old Woodbine, Nearctic was assigned 126 pounds for the nine-furlong Kingarvie Stakes on October 13. He ran well but was unable to stave off the closing run of Our Sirdar, a good stakes horse who carried 116 pounds. Five days later Nearctic had another hard race, this against the speedy English import *Arcandy in the Challenge Handicap at six and a half furlongs. Top-weighted under 130 pounds against 122 on *Arcandy, Nearctic dueled with *Arcandy throughout most of the race before losing by a length.

Nearctic had run sixteen times in six months, winning nine stakes events and finishing second in three more. Coming off two hard races back to back, he would seem to have earned a trip back to the farm for some rest. Instead, he returned to New York and Horatio Luro. The Windfields people should have saved the money for the van ride, for Nearctic showed none of his usual spark in the November 4 Sport Page Handicap at Jamaica, breaking slowly and finishing a dismal twelfth. He ran better thirteen days later in the Port Jefferson Handicap, an overnight race, getting third money. But he was clearly not at his best, and Luro sent him back home to recuperate. Nearctic did not reappear for the rest of the year.

******

Nearctic opened his five-year-old campaign on April 27, 1959, in a five and a half-furlong race at Fort Erie, finishing third after barely being able to make the lead. Although he had run with marked determination, his effort suggested lingering physical problems, for at four he had run very sharply off an extended layoff. But five days later Nearctic looked as good as ever, winning the six-furlong Vigil Handicap in time equaling the Fort Erie track record. That made his performance a week later in the seven-furlong Ultimus Handicap at Old Woodbine all the more shocking: unable to make the early lead, Nearctic battled to be with the pacemakers and then stopped badly, finishing sixth of seven.

Nearctic, as it turned out, had developed what horsemen call a "blind splint" — a bony enlargement between the cannon bones that, because of its location, can be difficult for even an experienced horseman to detect. Although Joe Thomas insisted that Nearctic would continue racing, the horse did not appear for a scheduled start in the June 1 Jacques Cartier

Handicap. The following day Nearctic was officially retired. He had won twenty-one of his forty-seven starts and a total of $152,384.

Canada's Horse of the Year in 1958, Nearctic retired with the reputation of being the best Canadian runner of his day — a left-handed compliment, given that Canadian racing in the 1950s did not enjoy anywhere near the prestige that racing at Woodbine would later have. A measure of how he rated against the best American older horses is provided by the *Daily Racing Form*'s Free Handicap for older males of 1958, which assigned him 110 pounds versus 132 on co-highweights Bold Ruler and *Gallant Man and 131 on American Horse of the Year Round Table. Yet there were tantalizing hints that Nearctic might have achieved far more.

Under McCann's handling Nearctic won nineteen of thirty starts, compared to a record of two-for-seventeen when trained by Shaw and Luro, and the discrepancy cannot all be put down to weaker competition in Canada; in fact, McCann's record with Nearctic would probably have been even better had he not been pushed to run the colt against his better judgment on several occasions. That Taylor could not consistently use McCann for the colt's American forays is understandable given the trainer's personality and the need not to disrupt the training of the other Windfields horses, but why Taylor continued to send Nearctic to Luro after it became clear the horse did not race well for him is a secret Taylor took to the grave. Under a more compatible trainer, better results might have been achieved. As for Charley Shaw, he was handicapped not only by a training style probably ill-suited to Nearctic's disposition but also by the fact that the colt was plagued with injuries while in his care.

Distance was another area that, in retrospect, could have been better handled. Although on pedigree Nearctic had the bloodlines to stay almost any distance in American racing, in real life he was clearly best at sprint distances. He was only two for ten at distances longer than a mile and repeatedly lost in routes to horses that he was much superior to in shorter races. Given the bias in breeding circles against pure sprinters, the desire to have the horse prove himself over longer routes is understandable, but why the persistence once Nearctic had clearly proved that he could not stay?

A still more haunting question is why, time and again, Nearctic was asked to race with injuries that should have demanded a rest. Taylor was not ignorant of horses. Joe Thomas, his racing manager, had never trained horses, but in his time on the backstretch, he had surely seen lameness before. Luro had learned horsemanship from the ground up on his family's farm in Argentina and rode well enough to be considered a good polo player. Yet, from the bucked shins Nearctic suffered as a juvenile to the quarter crack that plagued him through much of his career to the splint that finally forced his retirement, he was repeatedly expected to run, regardless of his physical condition.

Part of the answer may have lain in the fact that, too often, decisions about where and when Nearctic would run were made by people who did not have day-to-day contact with him. But the ultimate answer may perhaps have lain in Nearctic himself. Courageous and determined to run whatever the cost, the horse may simply have convinced his connections that he could run and win in spite of the injuries — or even that the injuries were not as serious and painful as they likely were — and then found his body unable to answer the demands of his fiery spirit. If that indeed were the case, then Nearctic may have been his own worst enemy, and his own biggest obstacle to lasting greatness. Perhaps Abram Hewitt, in *The Great Breeders and Their Methods*, put it best: "Nearctic was in all probability inherently a high-class racehorse who never realized his full potential on the track."

******

Natalma, the filly Nearctic's earnings had helped to purchase in 1958, might also have fit Hewitt's description. She showed so much promise in her early training that she was sent to begin her career in the United States rather than Canada and joined Horatio Luro's barn in early 1959.

The daughter of Native Dancer proved to have talent at least comparable to her half sister Cosmah. After winning her first two outings at Belmont, Natalma was entered in the important Spinaway Stakes at Saratoga. She finished first but did not get to keep her victory, for she was disqualified to third for interfering with Warlike as the Windfields runner ducked away from jockey Bobby Ussery's whip. The chief beneficiary of the disqualification, Irish Jay, was a first-class filly who also won the Demoiselle, Fashion, and Schuylerville stakes that year, so on her Spinaway form, Natalma was right up with the first flight of the fillies of her year.

The whip crack from Ussery may have cost Natalma more than her Spinaway trophy, for the filly absolutely refused to go to the track the next morning, and the next, and the next. With that one sharp blow during the Spinaway, Natalma had associated going to the racetrack with feeling pain, and she wanted none of it. Peaches Fleming, left in charge of the stable in Luro's absence, was unable to persuade the filly otherwise, and Luro, who had gone to France following the conclusion of the Saratoga meet, returned several weeks later to find Natalma at Belmont Park with the rest of the stable but no less adamant that she was *not* going to the track.

If Natalma's loss of several weeks' training and racing time betrayed Luro's chief vulnerability as a trainer, her return to the track highlighted his strengths. With the aid of a minor tranquilizer and his stable pony, "El Gran Señor" gradually overcame Natalma's fear. Every day he would have the filly given her medicine; then, mounted on his pony, he would escort Natalma and her exercise rider on a tour of the Belmont grounds, often stopping and visiting other barns. As Natalma began to relax under a rider, the tours began ending at the track, where the filly was encouraged but not forced to walk out, look around, and satisfy herself that she had nothing to fear. The whole procedure was an example of what a psychologist would call "systematic desensitization," or eliminating fear by gradual exposure to the thing or situation that triggers it. It worked; Natalma eventually consented to begin training again.

By the time Natalma was ready to go back to work, however, the important races for two-year-old fillies were all but past. Any remaining chance of her winning a stakes before the end of her juvenile season ended when a bone chip was found in her right knee. The chip was removed at the University of Pennsylvania veterinary school, and Natalma went back to Windfields to recuperate.

Despite her setbacks Natalma had shown enough promise that the decision was made to train her for the 1960 Kentucky Oaks while her stablemate Victoria Park would contest the Kentucky Derby. (The first Derby starter for Taylor, Victoria Park would finish third; he later finished second in the Preakness and won the Queen's Plate.) The following spring, the filly was working brilliantly for her chance at stardom but pulled up lame six days before the Oaks. Examination showed that she had developed a calcium deposit in the same knee that had been operated on earlier, ending her Oaks hopes.

A decision then had to be made. Natalma had shown considerable ability, and it was conceivable that surgery could enable her to return to racing. Further, it was getting late in the season for breeding; even if she conceived on her first cover, the resulting foal would not be born before late May at the earliest. That meant it would be giving away months of development to its peers since the official birthday of all Thoroughbreds in the Northern Hemisphere is January 1 regardless of whether a foal is born in January or June.

On the other hand, Natalma was a valuable broodmare prospect, purchased primarily to help upgrade Taylor's broodmare band, and there was no guarantee that she would ever return to her earlier form following surgery. At the very least, she would be sidelined until the fall, missing many valuable races. Further, there was a risk that she might suffer a fatal breakdown if she returned to racing. And she seemed to match up well with Nearctic, who was having trouble getting enough mares to fill his first year's book.

In the end, the mare herself was allowed to make the decision. She was bred to Nearctic — according to Joe Thomas, she was the last mare the young stallion covered that season — with the understanding that if she did not conceive on her first cover, she would not be bred again that season; she could either be rested to begin her broodmare career the following spring, or she could still possibly undergo surgery and try for a racing comeback.

She conceived.

Just Another Colt

Everyone who has ever owned a broodmare knows that mares seldom time foaling for the convenience of their human owners. Humans prefer to be up and about during the day, but mares prefer the relative safety of the middle of the night, when their major predators in the wild are less active.

Natalma was no exception to the rule. Going into labor shortly before midnight, she delivered her firstborn foal without incident at 12:15 a.m., May 27, 1961 — "a tight but normal foaling," according to assistant farm manager Peter Poole. The bay colt was small — not uncommon for a first foal — but healthy and vigorous. A roguish-looking fellow, he sported three white socks (only the right forefoot was dark) and a large star above and between his eyes connecting to a crooked blaze that trickled down to his left nostril.

Although it is not certain who gave Northern Dancer his name, the most likely candidate is Winifred Taylor, who usually took time each fall to select names for the new Windfields foals. The colt's foal pictures, submitted with his registration application, show a normal youngster: long-legged, bright-eyed, and inquisitive about the camera. Yet there is something else there, too: a dominance, even an arrogance normally seen mostly in mature stallions, and not always even then. Perhaps the beginnings of the "look of eagles" are more easily seen in hindsight than at the time, however, for the Windfields staff did not remember Northern Dancer as a particularly outstanding youngster.

Just Another Colt

"I guess you could say he stood out a bit," said Poole when asked about the young Northern Dancer several years later. "But, really, we have a lot of fine-looking weanlings." Joe Thomas was less complimentary, describing the year-old Northern Dancer as "so short and so damned chunky that he was a real disappointment." Apparently, no one remembered that the combination of shortish legs with a normal-sized body had not kept either Selene or Hyperion, this colt's ancestors, from being runners of the highest class.

Disappointment or not, Northern Dancer enjoyed the normal life of a young Thoroughbred, his hours taken up with feeding, playing with his peers, and napping in the sun when his energies ran out. By fall he had graduated to a pasture with the other weanling colts, now no longer dependent on their mothers.

January 1, 1962, rolled around, making Natalma's son officially a yearling even though he was actually only a few days past seven months. A few months later he and his pasture mates were separated into individual paddocks to prevent their putting too many cuts and scrapes on each other before the farm's annual yearling sale in September — probably none too soon in the case of Northern Dancer, whom Windfields yearling manager André Blaettler recalled as "a real devil." If left to themselves, yearling colts spend a good bit of their time sparring with one another in instinctive preparation for the day when, in the wild, they would challenge a herd stallion for control of a band of mares. Most of the time, the play inflicts no more than minor injuries, but there is always the possibility of a colt getting seriously hurt; the possibility is multiplied when an unusually dominant youngster such as Northern Dancer is involved. And even minor blemishes can hurt a colt's sale value.

The downside of individual paddocks for sales preparation is the young horses do not get the same conditioning they would naturally give themselves if left in a group. The great early twentieth-century breeder John E. Madden, who routinely left his colts in group pastures as much as possible, noted that while his youngsters were usually smaller and thinner than colts individually prepared for the sales, they were dead fit and generally caught up or even surpassed the others quickly once put into serious training. Madden, however, trained and raced many of the youngsters he raised, often selling a horse after it had won a race or two, and so could afford to ignore the fact that his yearlings did not look as attractive as the more pampered youngsters when offered for sale; more commercially oriented breeders generally cannot afford to follow his methods. Although ponying and hand-walking the young horses help, both require too much time and manpower for enough to be done to equal the amount of exercise a group of colts at pasture would normally get.

Northern Dancer was agile enough to stretch his legs even in a small paddock, though, and he came up to the sale well-muscled and gleaming with health. Years later Ron Turcotte recalled seeing him at the sale:

"He was short, not even fifteen hands, but you couldn't really call him small; he was so broad and muscular. He must have weighed as much as some of the bigger colts. You could tell looking at him that weight wouldn't bother him any; he was that strong."

Despite his lack of stature, Northern Dancer was one of the three highest-priced yearlings in the sale with an asking price of $25,000. Given that the Windfields staff did not seem to have seen anything outstanding about him as a potential racehorse, why the high price, which discouraged all but a few potential buyers from even considering him?

Perhaps Northern Dancer's price reflected Edward Taylor's faith in Nearctic. Northern Dancer was one of only seventeen foals in his sire's first crop, but sixteen would become winners; the group would include stakes winners Arctic Hills, Belarctic, Langcrest, and Pierlou, as well as, of course, Northern Dancer. Yet at his yearling sale, Taylor parted with several other sons and daughters of Nearctic for lesser prices than what he was asking for Northern Dancer.

Norman Bowles, who was an assistant trainer to Horatio Luro during Northern Dancer's racing career, thought the price might have had something to do with Natalma. "There just weren't that many daughters of Native Dancer around, and she was a good one," he recalled many years later. "She wasn't real big, maybe sixteen hands tops and not a big frame, but she had a nice disposition."

Any conjecture is pure speculation now, but it is just possible that the reason for Northern Dancer's high price tag may have been Winifred Taylor, who had taken a liking to the little bay while he was still a foal. The feeling was apparently mutual; years later the stallion would nicker a greeting any time Mrs. Taylor came to visit, though whether he remembered her or the bag of sugar cubes she invariably brought for him was a moot point.

At any rate, only a few people seriously considered buying Northern Dancer, and none followed through. The brothers Phil and Jim Boylen went so far as to have the colt pulled from his stall three times for a closer look but were eventually steered away from him by their trainer, Art Warner, who thought the horse was too small. Another would-be owner, Larkin Maloney, was also discouraged by his trainer from buying Northern Dancer, going instead to a tall *Menetrier colt also priced at $25,000. Morris Fleming, a client of Horatio Luro's who actually had the trainer's encouragement to buy Northern Dancer, decided he wanted an animal with some residual value if racing didn't pan out and chose a Nearctic filly.

Both Maloney and Fleming got some value for their money. The *Menetrier colt, named Brockton Boy, became a stakes winner and earned $67,548 while the Nearctic filly, named Muskoka, became the dam of stakes winners Muskoka Weekend and Miss Hyperion. But neither Maloney nor Fleming got Northern Dancer.

The sale day over, thirty-three of the original forty-eight Windfields yearlings moved on to the Windfields training division where they began their education as racehorses by being introduced to saddles, bridles, and carrying a rider. Being ridden was not high on Northern Dancer's agenda, however, especially if it meant submitting his will to that of a human.

Northern Dancer came by his highly dominant nature honestly; it ran in the blood of his sire and his maternal grandsire. Nearctic had required all the skill of Pete McCann, a superb horseman, to restrain the horse's desire to run headlong as he willed. Native Dancer was more calculating; if he caught an exercise rider napping, he would swing his massive head around, clamp his teeth on one of the rider's boots, and heave the hapless human right out of the saddle.

Northern Dancer lacked the sheer impetuosity of Nearctic and the raw strength of Native Dancer, but he had plenty of tricks of his own. Often described as more like a Quarter Horse than a Thoroughbred in conformation, he had a Thoroughbred's explosive energy coupled with the quick action and agility of a seasoned cow horse; without warning he could change direction, stop cold, duck, or spin, often right out from under a luckless exercise boy. No one wanted to draw Northern Dancer as his morning ride; too often, the ride ended with a jarring thud and the sight of Northern Dancer's muscular quarters rapidly receding into the distance.

Although he succeeded in dumping his rider and running loose with some regularity, Northern Dancer managed to get through the initial breaking period without seriously injuring himself or a human. Nonetheless, he was still no more than half broken when he went to the Canadian division of Horatio Luro's stable to begin serious training with Luro's assistant, Peaches Fleming. Worse, the colt had begun using his teeth to express his displeasure with human meddling. By most accounts, he was not at all vicious, but he was determined to have his own way. Humans who chose to interfere with his doing as he wished faced the same rough discipline as would any subordinate horse that dared challenge the herd stallion.

Taylor was by this time aware of Northern Dancer's behavior, for Luro's people had contacted him with a recommendation that Northern Dancer be gelded to bring him under control. The recommendation would be repeated several times, but each time Taylor said, "No." The loss to the breed would have been incalculable had Taylor said, "Yes," but at the time, he had no grandiose notions that he was preserving the colt's future as a great sire. He was simply following his belief that gelding would have been a waste of time and money; as he later said, "My experience has been that, once a colt starts acting ugly, his manners aren't improved by castration."

Taylor's experience may have been based in part on a *Ribot colt named *Roman Flare, whom he had purchased as a yearling the same year Northern Dancer was foaled. *Roman Flare was a half brother to Nantallah, whose son Ridan was the top juvenile colt of 1961, and Taylor thought that his colt would make a good stallion prospect. Unfortunately, *Roman Flare had inherited much of *Ribot's difficult disposition, and Luro finally persuaded Taylor to have the colt gelded on the grounds that he would never make a good racehorse otherwise. *Roman Flare may not have made a good runner as an entire horse, but he did not make a good racehorse as a gelding either and ended up as a low-level claimer.

Taylor may also have guessed that Northern Dancer's rambunctiousness was in part due to having more energy than the youngster knew what to do with. A racehorse in training may spend twenty-two to twenty-three hours per day pent up in his stall, his only opportunity for serious exercise coming in his morning workout. If he is fortunate, he may be taken out and hand-walked or allowed to graze for a little while, poor substitutes for the slow but constant moving about that horses display when left at pasture.

Northern Dancer's situation was complicated by his developing cracked heels, a form of psoriasis at the back of the pastern. The affected skin becomes red, scaly, and blistered, cracking easily as the horse moves about. The cracked skin is quite vulnerable to infection and further irritation, and a trainer may be reluctant to work the horse for fear of worsening the condition. Luro, who kept in touch with the progress of his Canadian-based horses via regular visits from Southern California, was never one to rush a horse in any event; combined with the colt's late birthday, the cracked heels gave the trainer ample reason to take his time.

It was June before Northern Dancer was able to start more serious workouts — probably high time, from the colt's viewpoint. The little firebrand made his first official breeze on June 8, going three-eighths of a mile in :39 4/5 according to *Daily Racing Form*. Nearly a month later the colt blasted the distance in :37 flat during his first test at breaking from the starting gate.

Virtually any Thoroughbred can turn in one furlong in twelve seconds, a pace known in racing vernacular as a "twelve-clip." Most can run two twelve-second furlongs back to back without any trouble. From there on out, the pace usually starts dropping off. A twelve-clip for a mile (eight furlongs) gives a time of 1:36, good enough to win many stakes races even today; a twelve-clip for a mile and a quarter (ten furlongs) gives a time of 2:00, good enough to have won all but two runnings of the Kentucky Derby; and a twelve-clip over a mile and a half (twelve furlongs), gives a time of 2:24 — the time of Secretariat's record-breaking Belmont victory. For a green two-year-old only a month into serious training to throw in a thirty-seven-second work over three-eighths of a mile at Woodbine wasn't exceptional, but it was quite respectable and indicated to Northern Dancer's connections that the colt might have some real ability.

The workout also indicated a potential problem with sensitivity to the whip. Luro, who had been in town for the work, felt Northern Dancer had become a trifle lazy. To ensure the colt got off alertly in his first try from the starting gate, Luro had ordered exercise rider Ramon Hernandez to tap the colt on the shoulder with his whip as the gate opened. If "lazy" had ever been an accurate description of Northern Dancer, it was no longer true a split-second after the starting bell rang and Hernandez' whip came down; the colt had sprung from the starting gate like a startled jackrabbit and nearly run off with Hernandez. One wonders if Luro, witnessing the scene, remembered Natalma, who had been traumatized for weeks by a single crack of the whip.

A few weeks later the Windfields horses moved over to Fort Erie to prepare for that track's summer meet. Northern Dancer was clearly progressing quickly, for on July 13 he worked a half-mile in :48 4/5, only one second off the track record. The work was fast but also dangerous; when the starting bell rang, Northern Dancer bolted, apparently associating the starting bell with the sting of the whip he had felt a month earlier. Had he thrown his rider in that first wild burst of speed, or had the track been more crowded as the colt went careering down the straightaway, the results could have been lethal.

As it was, the workout had results of a different kind. Taylor knew about it, of course — he kept tabs on his horses' works through the track work sheets and *Daily Racing Form* — and he started asking when the colt would make his first start. So did Joe Thomas, whose decisions to override Pete McCann's judgment had worked to Nearctic's detriment more than once.

In truth, Fleming was not eager to get Northern Dancer into a race. Luro was headed for the Saratoga meeting via Europe and had left orders that Northern Dancer was not to run until he returned; he felt that the colt needed more conditioning to make up for the time he had lost with his cracked heels in the spring. Fleming fully agreed; further, having seen Northern Dancer's last work, he felt the colt was still too green and headstrong to race with any degree of safety — even the frail illusion of safety involved when eight or ten charged-up, skittish juveniles are on the track for the first real race of their lives.

Thomas, though, was looking at the overall Windfields stable, and he didn't like what he was seeing. Although Northern Dancer wasn't the only two-year-old in the barn, by late July, the Windfields juvenile division was looking very thin. The other colts and fillies that had begun training with

Northern Dancer were either injured, lacking in talent, or showing that they would need much more time to develop. If Windfields was to have a major two-year-old in 1963, it was pretty much up to the Dancer.

Thomas kept pressing; Fleming, backed up by communications with Luro, kept stalling. Finally, Thomas became frustrated and demanded some action.

"Oh, hell, go ahead and run him," Thomas later remembered having told Fleming.

(John "Trader" Clark had another version of how Northern Dancer's first start came about; according to him, after learning of the Dancer's fast work, Taylor told Fleming, "I'm paying the bills, so start him in the next maiden two-year-old race that comes up.")

So, on August 2, 1963, Northern Dancer pranced from the backstretch to the saddling enclosure, eyes bright and ears flicking as, for the first time, he met the charged atmosphere of a race-day crowd. Neither he nor the crowd knew it, but Canada was about to witness the birth of a legend.

The Making of a Racehorse

Thoroughbreds are bred to run and to compete. The instinct shows early as foals venture from their dams' sides to chase about with other youngsters. Later, as weanlings and yearlings, the young horses start pushing themselves more seriously, their gallops becoming less playful and more competitive in nature.

But no amount of pasture play can prepare a young horse for what it will face as a racehorse. In the wild a horse uses its speed in relatively short bursts, either in play or to evade a predator. A horse that straggles or that speeds too far out in front is alone and vulnerable, so the instinct to stay with the herd is strong. And the home range of a band of wild horses — or even a farm pasture — is a relatively quiet and familiar place for its residents.

Compare this to what a young horse faces on its first venture into competition. It has already learned to accept saddle and bridle, to put up with the unnatural weight of a human on its back, to submit to basic guidance from that human, and to break from a starting gate without becoming unhinged at the clanking of the machinery and the ringing of the starting bell. Now, in addition to what it has already learned, it must tolerate the sights, sounds, and smells of a noisy and excited crowd — a far different environment than the relative quiet of the same track during morning workouts. When asked, the young horse must run at high speed for farther than it would probably ever do in any natural or semi-natural setting. And to win, it must be willing to leave the safety of the herd for at least a few fractions of a second if the race is not to come down to a head bob.

The Making of a Racehorse

Fort Erie was Northern Dancer's introduction to the hustle and bustle of the racetrack. It is not a major track, and so the crowd gathered about the paddock for Northern Dancer's first race — a five and a half-furlong event for maiden two-year-olds bred in Canada — was not a big one. Nonetheless, it was more people than Northern Dancer had ever seen close-up in his life. Some young horses are unable to handle the excitement and spend their energy on fretting or worse: They may rear, buck, or skitter about, with stable personnel trying desperately to keep them from hitting spectators or other horses. But Northern Dancer passed this first test, letting Peaches Fleming tighten his girth and toss jockey Ron Turcotte up into the saddle without trouble. Perhaps the colt was so interested in the activities around him that he forgot about acting up himself, or perhaps he was a bit intimidated by the unusual sights and sounds; in any event, he was quiet enough that Turcotte later actually described his behavior as "docile." It was probably the last time that anyone would apply that particular adjective to Northern Dancer.

******

Ron Turcotte had not grown up dreaming of racing stardom. Born in New Brunswick in 1941, he had followed his father, Alfred, into the logging trade at age fourteen. His primary job was handling the logging horses: big, patient animals a world away from racehorses.

Alfred Turcotte was quite particular about the care of his horses, and his attitude rubbed off on his son. "My father taught me how to be patient with horses," the younger Turcotte said later. "He taught me how to give them confidence and not abuse them. And he gave me a lot of confidence about how I could handle horses."

Still, lumberjacking was hard work and not that lucrative, so Turcotte decided in 1960 to look for work in Toronto — in construction, not in racing. He hadn't thought about horse work as a career, even though he had been good at it. But the job market was slow, and those builders that were hiring weren't interested in taking on a man only five feet, one inch tall, no matter how tough. According to journalist Eddie Donnally, it was Turcotte's landlord who, while watching the 1960 Queen's Plate on television with

Turcotte, suggested that the young man should think about becoming a jockey.

Turcotte hitched a ride out to New Woodbine the next day and landed a job as a hotwalker for the Windfields horses. A week later Pete McCann took Turcotte off walking hots and gave him two Thoroughbreds and a couple of ponies to look after; the ponies were quickly replaced by two more Thoroughbreds. In August, McCann sent Turcotte to Windfields to begin learning how to ride; by September, Turcotte was breaking yearlings and working some of the Windfields racers that were recuperating from injuries. He kept that job until he signed his first riding contract the following spring — not with Windfields, but with trainer Gordon Huntley.

"I liked working for Windfields," Turcotte recalled. "Pete McCann was the boss, but he was one of the boys, too. We'd play hockey in the winter and he'd be right in there. He put me on some tough horses, but not the really bad ones; he rode those himself. He'd tell me generally what he wanted and let me figure it out from there. And he never rode you about a mistake; he'd point things out in a way where you realized your own mistakes. He built a lot of confidence in me.

"Actually, I could have signed a contract with Windfields, but it wouldn't have paid very much and I didn't see much opportunity for me. Avelino Gomez was riding for Windfields then, and they weren't going to sit him down to ride me. And there were several lighter boys in the stable to ride the horses Gomez didn't get. So I signed a contract with Mr. Huntley."

On June 21, 1961, the young jockey got his first leg up in a race, this on a six-year-old gelding named Whispering Wind at New Woodbine. The horse finished sixth, and Turcotte finished out the year winless after getting only fourteen mounts in 1961. He did not get his first winner until April 9, 1962, when he came home first at Fort Erie aboard a three-year-old colt named Pheasant Lane. But after that, the winners kept coming. Turcotte scored his first stakes win on October 6, piloting eventual Canadian Horse of the Year Crafty Lace to win the Breeders' Stakes.

By the end of 1962, the twenty-year-old apprentice was Canada's leading rider with 180 wins under his belt. The following year Turcotte would repeat as Canada's leading jockey by number of wins, bringing his horse home first 215 times. Three of those wins would be with Northern Dancer.

The Making of a Racehorse

******

Decades later, Turcotte vividly remembered Northern Dancer's first race. "He was lazy at first and just kind of galloped along. He went to the leader all right when I asked him, but he wouldn't go on.

"I waited until the sixteenth pole, and he was just running along happily with this other horse; he wasn't giving me everything he had. But I had been told not to use the whip on him. So I switched the whip over to my left hand where it couldn't be seen from the stands and just gave him one little tap on the shoulder. My God, what an explosion! If I had done that at the quarter pole, he would have won by fifteen or twenty lengths!"

Instead, Northern Dancer won by "only" six and three-quarters lengths over Nacuba. Despite racing greenly (not keeping a straight course in the stretch — often a problem with inexperienced runners, which may tend to shy away from the noise of the crowd in the grandstand), he had run the five and a half furlongs in 1:06 1/5, just a tick off a "twelve-clip" for the distance and quite respectable for a first-time starter. But for Turcotte, what he had felt beneath him in that wild run to the finish line was far more than just "respectable."

"I went over to Mr. Fleming after the race and told him, 'This is the best two-year-old in Canada, for sure,' " Turcotte recalled.

Fifteen days later Northern Dancer went to the post for the Vandal Stakes. The six and a half-furlong race was run under allowance conditions, so Northern Dancer carried a mere 109 pounds against 122 on the favorite, Ramblin Road, who had won the Victoria Stakes on July 13. Because Ramblin Road was trained by Gordon Huntley, Turcotte was aboard as Huntley's contract jockey, leaving Northern Dancer to be ridden by Paul Bohenko. Northern Dancer was also wearing blinkers for the first time, perhaps because of the green behavior he had displayed during his first race; he would race in blinkers for the remainder of his career.

Northern Dancer broke sharply, but his eagerness worked against him as he got into a speed duel with the filly Shackalot, who took the field through an initial quarter in :23 1/5 with Northern Dancer in close attendance. The Dancer had disposed of Shackalot by the half, which went in :46 4/5, but had Ramblin Road at his throat by then and had nothing left with which to stave off the favorite. Northern Dancer finished second, beaten by four lengths, with Brockton Boy another two and a half lengths back in third. It was a good effort for the inexperienced Dancer; behind him at the finish were three current or future stakes winners in third-place Brockton Boy, sixth-place Slithering Sam, and last-place Shackalot.

"I think Mr. Luro was a little irritated with me over that one," Turcotte said later. "He had wanted me to ride Northern Dancer, but I had to ride Ramblin Road instead because of my contract with Mr. Huntley and wound up beating the Dancer."

Only a week later Northern Dancer and Bohenko were back in action for the Summer Stakes, a mile event on turf and the most valuable juvenile race of the Fort Erie summer meet. The course was very soft and deep from recent rains, allowing the horses' hooves to sink in deeply. Northern Dancer floundered in the boglike conditions but managed to thrash his way to the lead and stayed there to defeat Slithering Sam by a length and a quarter in a slow 1:43 2/5. The effort was an exhausting one, and when Luro arrived from Saratoga a few days later, the first thing he did was order a rest for his new star.

Northern Dancer did not return to racing until the Woodbine fall meet, but when he did, it was for a big prize: the Cup and Saucer Stakes, a mile and one-sixteenth race on turf for Canadian-bred two-year-olds and traditionally a major factor in determining the country's champion two-year-old. Because of his Summer Stakes win, the Dancer had the top-weight of 124 pounds, conceding up to eleven pounds to his rivals. This time Ron Turcotte was back aboard.

"He had really changed after that first time I rode him," Turcotte recalled. "The first time, he was real easy to take to the gate and content to just run along with the other horses until I gave him that little tap. This time he was a real handful to get to the gate, and he had his mind on running. He was all horse, all right."

Breaking sharply, Northern Dancer made all the pace while pressured throughout but at the end could not stave off longshot Grand Garçon, who beat him three-quarters of a length under 113 pounds. Ironically, Grand Garçon had been sold for $10,000 at the same Windfields sale at which Northern Dancer had gone unsold. It was not the only time a Taylor color-bearer had been beaten by a horse Taylor himself had bred, but it was sure- ly one of the more painful — and costly — occasions.

Northern Dancer appeared to have tired at the end of the race, raising speculation as to whether he could stay more than a mile. Something else may have been at play, however. Although the Cup and Saucer Stakes had been run on September 28, almost five weeks after the Summer Stakes, it is possible that Northern Dancer had incurred some injury during his tremendous effort in the earlier race and had not yet fully recovered.

Turcotte had not been aboard for the Summer Stakes, but he knew some- thing was not right when he rode Northern Dancer in the Cup and Saucer. "He kept wanting to bear left, and I couldn't get him on his right lead at all," the jockey recalled. "He was really favoring his left fore. He probably wasn't as tight as he should have been, either. He was supposed to have had a work a few days before the race, but Mr. Luro canceled it. I don't remember now if he ever said why."

Nine days after the Cup and Saucer, Northern Dancer was sent to the post for the Bloordale Purse, an allowance race over a mile and seventy yards on Woodbine's main track. Under the race's conditions Northern Dancer was required to concede five pounds to the next-weighted horse, another son of Nearctic by the name of Northern Flight, and seven to ten pounds to the other five horses in the field.

As it turned out, Northern Flight was the only one of the Dancer's five rivals that mattered. Although Northern Dancer broke sharply, Turcotte steadied him and let Northern Flight sail into an uncontested lead. At the half-mile, Northern Dancer, running in third, trailed Northern Flight by about five and a half lengths. Then Turcotte relaxed his hold on the Dancer and let him run. Under intermittent urging, Northern Dancer caught Northern Flight to beat him a length, with the next horse more than twen- ty-five lengths farther back. The final time of 1:42 flat was just one second off the track record set by the good stakes mare Kitty Girl as a five-year-old in 1959.

The Bloordale marked another stage in Northern Dancer's development as a racehorse. In the Cup and Saucer he had been too anxious and had used too much energy in the earlier stages of the race; in the Bloordale he had relaxed nicely for Turcotte, allowing the jockey to take him back and conserve his speed for when it counted. But he was still favoring the left fore, and no one except Turcotte seemed to be paying attention, perhaps because Northern Dancer himself gave no sign of trouble except at full racing speed.

Whatever the problem was, Northern Dancer appeared sharp and ready for the Coronation Futurity, traditionally the season-ending event for Canada's top juveniles. Although it was only five days after the Bloordale, the crowd made Northern Dancer the favorite in a field of fifteen colts and fillies. The bettors were not mistaken in their choice. Northern Dancer rated nicely in fourth until the field straightened out in the backstretch; then he moved and, that quickly, it was over. Although Turcotte tried to throttle his mount down during the stretch run, Northern Dancer winged home by six and a quarter lengths over Jammed Lively, leaving no doubt in anyone's mind as to the identity of the best colt in Canada. Grand Garçon, his former conqueror, finished a well-beaten fifth.

******

Northern Dancer was clearly Canada's champion juvenile, but to the surprise of many observers, the Coronation Futurity marked the end of Turcotte's partnership with the colt.

"Mr. Luro gave me orders to keep him in midpack until about the three-eighths mark," Turcotte recalled. "But my saddle slipped rounding the first turn and that was it. You can't keep tight control over a horse when you're just trying to hang on, and a slipped saddle tends to ride up and down with the horse's motion and encourage him to run faster. I told Mr. Luro about it after the race, and he said, 'Your saddle won't slip no more.' I thought that meant he would add something to the equipment to keep the saddle from slipping again, but instead he took me off the horse. I guess he thought I was just making excuses for not following orders. And you had to ride a horse exactly to orders for Mr. Luro; otherwise, you didn't ride for him."

Orders or no orders, Luro may have had another motivation for dropping Turcotte. The Windfields team was planning a New York foray for Northern Dancer. Turcotte may have been the hottest jockey in Canada, but Canada was still considered provincial compared to the major American circuits.

Luro may well have felt that Turcotte was not experienced enough for the colt's venture into the big time.

Turcotte himself later recalled, "Mr. Luro said, 'I need a New York rider for the U.S. races.' I made up my mind then that I would be a New York rider and show them I was good enough." Less than ten years later Turcotte and Secretariat would rewrite the Belmont Stakes record book and, together, enter immortality.

******

By November most of the season's good two-year-olds have gone to winter quarters; those that remain on the track are for the most part either lesser lights or late developers that have raced only lightly earlier during the year. Northern Dancer was neither, his Coronation Futurity win marking his sixth start in a mere ten weeks since opening his racing career. But on November 6, twenty-five days after the Coronation Futurity, the colt was back in action and not in New York, where the prestige and the purses attached to the races might have justified the decision. Instead, the race chosen for him was the Carleton Stakes, a minor event at Greenwood, formerly known as the old Woodbine track.

The decision to run in the Carleton was questionable for two reasons. First, Northern Dancer had come out of the Coronation Futurity still favoring his left forefoot, and he was beginning to show signs of stress. The second reason was the track itself. At the best of times, Greenwood had chronic problems with water. The track was perilously close to the water table (the infield lake was actually at the same level as Lake Ontario, to which it had an outlet) and was easily waterlogged by any kind of rain. To complicate the situation, a dense grove of alder trees grew near the three-quarters pole, shading the track and making it almost impossible to get the final turn thoroughly dried out. The only time the shaded area was completely dry was those days the wind was blowing in from the West; then, the wind would dry the track so badly that track officials couldn't get the water trucks out often enough to keep billows of dust from being raised.

No suitable race with the right timing was available in New York, however, and Joe Thomas thought the Carleton might be a good prep race for the

New York trip even though Northern Dancer had not really been prepared to run in it. With good track conditions and a completely healthy colt, Thomas might have been right. But the weather turned up raw and blustery, Greenwood was a sea of mud, and Northern Dancer did not want to run. Under a steady whip from Jim Fitzsimmons from the top of the stretch to the wire, the colt defeated his five overmatched rivals but clearly did not have his heart in the fray. The reason was discovered as the colt was being bathed after the race. A groom spotted blood trickling from the coronet band of the colt's left forefoot and sent for Luro. The trainer diagnosed a quarter crack — the same type of injury that had plagued Nearctic.

Common sense would have suggested that following the discovery of the quarter crack, Luro would send Northern Dancer home to Windfields for rest and recuperation, especially in light of his sire's history. Instead, the colt was on the road to Aqueduct two days later. The goal chosen for him was the historic Remsen Stakes, a race first run in 1904.

Whether due to the unimpressive showing in the Carleton or to wanting the colt to have a race over the track, Northern Dancer's connections felt he needed another prep race before the Remsen, quarter crack or no quarter crack. Thus, on November 18, the colt went to the post for the one-mile Sir Gaylord Purse, an allowance race. In the saddle was twenty-two-year-old Manuel Ycaza, who had ridden Victoria Park to a third-place finish in the Kentucky Derby for Windfields three years earlier. Although only a year older than Turcotte, Ycaza had been riding since the age of fourteen and had ridden champions Sword Dancer, Bald Eagle, Ridan, Never Bend, and Lamb Chop since coming to the United States in 1956.

The race could not have been easier; Northern Dancer sailed home eight lengths ahead of Bupers, winner of the Futurity Stakes earlier that year. But the colt's post-race examination proved ominous: the quarter crack had worsened. Consultation among Luro, Joe Thomas, and the blacksmith followed: Could Northern Dancer run in the Remsen? The consensus was yes, but as a precaution, Northern Dancer's regular racing plate was pulled and a bar shoe applied to the damaged hoof to stabilize it. (A bar shoe, which has a solid bar running from heel to heel of the shoe — hence the name — limits the normal expansion and contraction of the hoof, protecting a cracked or damaged area but reducing the ability of the hoof to

91

absorb concussion, which is then passed on further up the leg.)

On November 27, Northern Dancer and Ycaza answered the call to the post for the Remsen Stakes. Over forty years later Ycaza still remembered the race well.

"He was very calm when I took him to the post and broke very smoothly," he recalled. "I just hardly asked him to go, and he just went so easily. He won with tremendous authority.

"I remember him as an ideal horse for any kind of situation. He would do anything you asked; he had the speed to go right from the wire, or he could lay back and wait. He was built just like a little bulldog, but he was a very smooth-traveling horse. He wore one-cup blinkers, but I don't know why for he never tried to get out on me or duck in.

"He was a great horse."

The official margin was an easy two lengths over Lord Date, who would go on to be a stakes winner for the next three years. The victory was impressive enough to earn the little Canadian a weighting of 123 pounds on the Experimental Free Handicap, sixth overall among colts raced in the United States and only three pounds less than top-weighted Raise a Native.

Under ordinary circumstances, the Windfields team would have been delighted with the outcome. Here at last was the colt who could fulfill Edward Taylor's Derby dream: he had all the speed and courage of his headstrong sire combined with the mental flexibility to handle shipping from track to track, the ability to rate off the pace, and the stamina to go as far as any horse of his age had been asked to run. But the quarter crack was still there, and one look after the race told Luro all he needed to know. Despite the bar shoe, the crack had worsened. To train the colt further was to risk breakdown; the only intelligent choice was to send him back to Windfields and let the hoof grow out. The Derby seemed out of the question; the hope now was that the colt could recover in time to make the Queen's Plate two months later.

Luro had the colt brought to Belmont with the rest of his stable and kept him on stall rest while waiting for the van that would take the horse back to Windfields. Then Lady Luck stepped in. Luro was an avid reader of all things related to horse racing, and only a few days before Northern Dancer was supposed to go back to Canada, his reading brought him across a magazine article on Adios Jr., a top Standardbred pacer. Adios Jr. had, it seemed, been sidelined by a quarter crack himself but had been treated with a new technology — a vulcanized rubber patch that filled the crack and allowed the hoof wall to flex normally without pain for the horse. Not only had he returned to training, but he also had won several important events in California while racing on the patched hoof.

Luro's old friend Laz Barrera, himself a first-class trainer, was in California at the time, and Luro called him to see if he knew anything about the new method of treating quarter cracks. Barrera had no first-hand experience with the patch, but he was able to track down the name of the blacksmith who had developed the patch, Bill Bane, and gave Bane's phone number to Luro.

Bane listened when Luro called and explained the problem. He could, he said, try to treat Northern Dancer's hoof, but only if the crack was in a certain part of the hoof wall. After Luro sent detailed photos of the colt's left forefoot, the blacksmith rendered a verdict: Yes, the crack was in a treatable location, but he could not promise that it would work, and he would require a fee of a thousand dollars plus traveling expenses to and from California to make the trip.

After consultation with Taylor — who, one presumes, was easily persuaded to grasp at anything that might let Northern Dancer train safely for the Derby, especially when Luro offered to pay for the treatment himself — Luro agreed, and Bane flew to New York. The chief worry at that point was that Northern Dancer might not tolerate the patch, but the fears proved groundless. The colt stood calmly while the patch was applied, showing no signs of pain or stress.

With his new patch firmly in place, Northern Dancer walked onto a horse van but not one going to Windfields. He was headed for Luro's own farm in Cartersville, Georgia, where he was turned out into a small paddock. There, he could wander about and get used to the way his mended hoof felt without having the room to get up a full head of steam and possibly hurt himself.

Nine days passed; everything was going well, and the Dancer seemed to be enjoying his brief vacation. On the tenth day he was back on the road. His destination was Hialeah Park in Miami, where he would begin preparing for the Kentucky Derby.

Derby Bound

Hialeah is now a casino; no Thoroughbred racing has been held there since 2001. Yet there was a time when Hialeah was the undisputed queen of winter racing in America. Originally part of an entertainment complex that included a greyhound track, a jai-alai court, a dance hall, and a roller coaster, the track was exclusively devoted to horse racing after the Great Miami Hurricane of 1926 destroyed the other facilities.

Following its purchase by Joseph E. Widener in 1931, the track underwent major renovations that included a compete replacement of the clubhouse and grandstand and the construction of an infield lake, which was populated with flamingos imported from nearby Cuba. The result was hailed as one of the most beautiful racing facilities anywhere in the world. Placed on the National Register of Historic Places on March 2, 1979, Hialeah was famed for its lovely Mediterranean-style architecture, its landscaping, and its trademark flock of flamingos.

Under Widener's guidance Hialeah became *the* place to be for the Northeastern elite following its grand reopening in 1932. As a winter counterpart to the Saratoga meeting, it drew many of the country's best horses; the stands reverberated to cheers for the likes of War Admiral, Nashua, and Bold Ruler. A statue of Citation, placed in memory of the great horse's victory in the 1948 Flamingo Stakes, stood watch near the saddling paddock.

Northern Dancer settled in comfortably at Hialeah following his arrival in late December 1963. Now that his foot no longer hurt, he was putting on weight and muscle, and Luro prescribed a series of long, slow gallops for him. He knew the colt possessed plenty of natural speed; his concern was that Northern Dancer would develop the same speed-craziness that had plagued his sire and would not relax when asked to go a distance.

Still, some sharpening would be necessary before Northern Dancer went for the Flamingo Stakes, his first major target of the season — the more so since the colt was forced to miss several works due to poor weather. Accordingly, Luro entered the Dancer in a six-furlong allowance race as a tightener.

In line with his belief that Northern Dancer needed to be taught to relax if he was to carry his speed over a mile and a quarter, Luro had been trying to secure the services of Bill Shoemaker as his jockey. More than any other jockey of his time, "The Shoe" was known for his ability to establish a rapport with his mounts. Horses ran for him willingly; he seldom needed to use the whip more than sparingly, and he was known for his ability to get horses to rate either in front or off the pace.

Shoemaker was not available for the February 10 race Luro had chosen, however, so Luro called on Bobby Ussery. Perhaps remembering Ussery's ride on Natalma in the 1959 Spinaway Stakes, Luro reminded Ussery that this race was merely a tightener and explicitly told him not to use the whip.

Minutes later Luro was livid. Having been slammed hard coming out of the gate, Northern Dancer was forced to work his way from the back of the pack and became blocked behind the good colt Chieftain and a longshot named Mom's Request. Northern Dancer had no hope of getting through in time (he finished third, two lengths back), but whether out of competitive instincts or frustration, Ussery laid into the Dancer with the whip. Under similar circumstances, Pete McCann, a former flyweight boxing champion, had been known to deck an offending jockey; Luro contented himself with publicly raking Ussery over the coals for his ride.

Luro had even better reason than he knew to be upset. The next day, everything seemed fine with Northern Dancer — until he was taken to the track for a little light exercise. At that point he reared, bucked, and lashed out; no amount of persuasion could get him to go forward, and there was no coercing him. Like his mother had years before, he seemed to associate the sting of the whip with the track, and he had no intention of going where he had met the pain before. Why he had not shown a similar reaction after being driven under the whip by Fitzsimmons in the Carleton Stakes is unclear; perhaps Ussery had struck him in a particularly sensitive spot, or perhaps the Dancer was smart enough to resent being punished when he had no chance to win.

Luro knew better than to force the issue. He had the Dancer ridden away from the track and walked in the company of a stable pony up and down the avenue of pines that borders the Hialeah barn area until the colt was calm again. Then, for the next five days he applied the same strategy that had worked with Natalma: a light tranquilizer with a gradual approach back to the track. He was successful; Northern Dancer finally consented to resume training. The Windfields camp no doubt heaved a collective sigh of relief.

For the colt's next race Luro managed to get him into a seven-furlong exhibition race on February 24 in which there were only two other starters: Chieftain, who had defeated the Dancer in the earlier allowance, and the lightly raced but well-regarded Trader. From Luro's viewpoint it could not have been a better setup. Northern Dancer was not likely to encounter any of the bouncing around he had gotten in his first race of the season, and this time Shoemaker would be in the saddle. A good experience for the colt would surely overwrite any lingering memories of the treatment he had received from Ussery.

Northern Dancer romped by seven lengths in 1:23 2/5, a brisk time for Hialeah and three-fifths of a second under a twelve-clip for the distance. A week later the colt and Shoemaker teamed up again for the Flamingo Stakes. After prompting the pace in the early going, Northern Dancer took command at the top of the stretch from Mr. Brick, another Kentucky Derby hopeful, and strode home by two lengths, despite lugging in intermittently throughout the stretch drive; Quadrangle, winner of the previous year's Pimlico Futurity, was eight lengths behind Mr. Brick in third. The time was 1:47 4/5, only four-fifths of a second off Bold Ruler's track record. The win made Northern Dancer the first Canadian-bred to take down a race worth $100,000 or more.

Winifred Taylor happily accepted the Flamingo trophy in the stead of her husband, whose flight from Toronto had been delayed by fog. Despite the victory, however, Shoemaker would not commit himself to ride Northern

Dancer in the Kentucky Derby, not after feeling him trying to lug in down the Hialeah stretch.

As with bearing out, lugging in is often seen when a horse has a physical or mental problem. It can also be the result of fatigue, and Shoemaker believed that Northern Dancer had tired in the final sixteenth of a mile, an assessment shared by the *Daily Racing Form*'s Joe Hirsch in his post-race write-up. In addition, Shoemaker may well have heard the rumor that the colt had shown signs of splint trouble after the Flamingo. The Shoe was being courted by the connections of two other Derby candidates, Hill Rise and The Scoundrel; he could afford to wait to make a decision on which colt he would ride for the roses.

Twenty-five days after the Flamingo, Northern Dancer was back in action, this time for a seven-furlong allowance race at Gulfstream Park. Shoemaker had a prior commitment, so Manny Ycaza filled in for a race that turned out to be little more than a paid workout for the Dancer. The colt won easily by four lengths over The Scoundrel and equaled the track record of 1:22 2/5 for the distance; at Luro's orders Northern Dancer galloped out another furlong for a mile in 1:36 3/5.

Luro was said to have been displeased by the quick time, considering it to be unnecessary use of the colt. Nonetheless, even the most hardened doubters were beginning to concede that E.P. Taylor just might have something in this undersized chunk of a colt from Canada. Three good wins over well-regarded colts, one in track-record time, were credentials too solid to write off. And there was something electric about the colt that was hard to ignore; as one veteran writer in the Hialeah press box put it, "He has character and a strangely disturbing personality ... He exudes explosive excitement."

But doubt needs only the slightest excuse to flare up again. In the April 4 Florida Derby, Northern Dancer's doubters got that excuse.

It wasn't that Northern Dancer did anything wrong; in fact, he won the Florida Derby over The Scoundrel without being fully extended. The contrast between the first two finishers is beautifully caught by the *Daily Racing Form* photo of the finish; it shows Shoemaker hand-riding Northern Dancer, with The Scoundrel clearly stretched to the limit a length back. But the time was a relatively slow 1:50 4/5, and Northern Dancer had once again lugged in during the stretch run. Many observers took this to indicate that Northern Dancer had tired at the end. Tongues began to wag: "He won't stay a mile and a quarter."

Railbirds and fans were not the only ones to express doubts. Joe Hirsch, writing for the *Daily Racing Form*, said, "… it did not appear Shoemaker had a lot of horse left at the wire" and noted that the time had been the slowest for the Florida Derby since 1955. Many others in the American media echoed similar doubts regarding the Dancer's stamina.

Human memory is notoriously fickle, but surely at least some of the doubters recalled that the Dancer had run the very same distance three full seconds faster at Hialeah. And what most of the doubters either didn't know or ignored is that Northern Dancer had every reason to be tired at the end of the Florida Derby, for it was his second big effort in two days. With an unfamiliar exercise rider aboard (his regular rider, Ramon Hernandez, was back in Toronto honoring another commitment), Northern Dancer had managed to get the bit in his teeth and had turned a scheduled four-furlong breeze the day before the race into a totally unplanned five-furlong blowout, going the distance in :58 3/5.

Shoemaker knew about the work. But he also knew that he had been offered the mount on Hill Rise for the Kentucky Derby. And he knew that when Hill Rise had won the Santa Anita Derby on February 29, the son of Hillary had left The Scoundrel over seven lengths behind in fifth place while winning easily. Further, Hill Rise's time was a brisk 1:47 2/5, and he had had a month's freshening since then.

To most observers, the Shoe among them, Hill Rise appeared to be a colt ready to make fast progress at the right time; Northern Dancer, perhaps, had hit a plateau or even regressed. And there was the troublesome fact that Northern Dancer was continuing to lug in. That he was racing on a patched hoof was common knowledge; while the patch did not appear to be giving him any problems in training, there was always the possibility that the foot was still hurting him at racing speed. Further, Luro had by now openly acknowledged the presence of the splint that had been suspected after the Flamingo, though he told Joe Hirsch, "… that splint on the inside of his left front has been there throughout his career without appearing to bother him at any time." (Norman Bowles, then Luro's assistant trainer, differed slightly when interviewed in 2005; while acknowledging that Northern Dancer did not appear to be in any discomfort during his spring campaign, he noted that the Dancer "would probably run through anything — he was a tough little man — and you never can tell when one of those things may start stinging.")

But perhaps the biggest point in Hill Rise's favor was that he simply looked the part of a Derby horse more than little Northern Dancer. A tall, elegant dark bay who appeared nearly black in some lighting, Hill Rise was "of the universally accepted classic stamp" according to *Daily Racing Form*. By contrast, *The Blood-Horse* described Northern Dancer as "… built low to the ground and wide, appearing of the sprinter type …" No matter what Northern Dancer did on the track, most people simply could not get over how small he was.

Whether it was race times, soundness concerns, looks, or the old racing adage that "a good big horse will beat a good little horse" that swayed him, Shoemaker made his choice. (Years later, Shoemaker indicated that pressure from his old friends Rex Ellsworth and Meshach Tenney, respectively the owner and trainer of The Scoundrel, had been the deciding factor; apparently, if they couldn't get him for The Scoundrel, they preferred seeing him on Hill Rise to Northern Dancer.) At the victory dinner following the Florida Derby, Shoemaker announced that, while he had appreciated the opportunities to ride Northern Dancer, he would be riding Hill Rise in the Kentucky Derby. Luro did his best to change the jockey's mind, but to no avail. The following day, Luro received a phone call from Shoemaker's agent, Harry Silbert, letting him know that Shoemaker was officially committed to Hill Rise.

Ironically, Hill Rise could have been a stablemate of Northern Dancer's. Luro had already trained several horses for prominent California owner-breeder George Pope in the late 1950s and early 1960s, not least the 1962 Kentucky Derby winner Decidedly, so when he was offered the chance to train one of Pope's 1963 two-year-olds for racing in New York, he agreed, provided he was allowed to select the candidate. Pope consented, and Luro went to Pope's California ranch to choose the newest addition to his barn.

As Joe Hirsch related the story in *The Grand Señor: The Fabulous Career of Horatio Luro*, Pope liked to see action from his horses. Luro, keeping this in mind, selected a colt that had shown precocious speed in workouts at the ranch — one that would be ready to race by early summer at the latest. But a few days later when the van transporting Pope's colt pulled up at Santa Anita, the colt that the handler led off the van was not the one Luro had selected. Luro tossed an exercise boy up on the newcomer and watched the colt gallop, then called Pope's farm manager.

It was no mistake, the man assured Luro. He explained that Luro's original choice had gone lame, and Pope had sent the new colt as a substitute. Luro politely turned the young Hill Rise back, stating he would not mature quickly enough to be ready for the summer two-year-old racing in New York. According to Hirsch, Luro even predicted that the big colt would not break his maiden before November. If that part of the story is true, Luro was dead right; Hill Rise, by then in the barn of William Finnegan, broke his maiden on November 22, 1963.

Since then, Hill Rise had done nothing wrong. Before the year was out, he had won the California Breeders' Champion Stakes and the Golden Gate Freshman Handicap to rank among California's best juveniles. With the San Felipe Handicap and Santa Anita Derby under his belt at three, he was considered the "hot horse" by almost all of the American sportswriters, who felt Shoemaker's decision to switch to him from Northern Dancer vindicated their judgment. (It was only in hindsight that some writers would question George Pope's decision to replace Hill Rise's regular jockey Don Pierce with Shoemaker; Pierce had been on the colt in both the San Felipe and the Santa Anita Derby and had never lost with him.)

Shoemaker's defection left Luro casting around for another jockey. Ron Turcotte had hopes that he might get the call; following Ussery's ride on the colt, Turcotte had received a letter from E.P. Taylor himself.

"Mr. Taylor said he'd love to have me ride Northern Dancer," Turcotte recalled. "I thought I had a chance to get back on him when Shoemaker took off."

Manny Ycaza also might have entertained thoughts of securing the Dancer for a Derby mount; after all, he was three for three on the colt and had won with him both on the lead and from off the pace. The problem was that, as the contract rider for Cain Hoy Stable, he could not guarantee his availability.

"I would have liked to ride Northern Dancer in the Derby," he said later. "But Cain Hoy might have had a colt with some promise; I don't really remember now. Anyway, with my contract I could not commit myself to ride until the last minute because Cain Hoy had first call, and Luro understood that. Luro needed someone he knew would be there, so he called Bill Hartack."

At first glance, Hartack might seem an odd match with the aristocratic and sometimes autocratic Luro. The son of a Pennsylvania coal miner, Hartack had cut his teeth on racing at the Charles Town racetrack in West Virginia. This was one of the "bull ring" tracks where a jockey needed to make good decisions fast to cope with tight turns, short stretches, and racing conditions that could range from fast to frozen.

Under the tutelage of trainer Norman "Junie" Corbin, Hartack rode his first race on October 11, 1952, and had his first winner three days later on a horse named Nickleby. From there, he took off in meteoric fashion. Having finished second to Shoemaker by number of winners in 1953 and 1954, he won his first national riding title in 1955. By the time he hooked up with Luro and Decidedly to win the 1962 Derby, Hartack was already in the Racing Hall of Fame (he was inducted in 1959) with four national riding titles by number of winners, two titles by money earned, and two Kentucky Derby winners in Iron Liege (1957) and Venetian Way (1960). Had he not broken a leg a week before the 1958 Derby, he might well have earned another bouquet of roses, for his scheduled mount was Tim Tam, who won under Ismael Valenzuela.

Hartack had unquestioned riding skills and smarts, nor could he be faulted for his desire to win. Rohit Brijnath, writing for *Sportstar* magazine in 2001, recounted an incident in which Hartack was riding a race after having torn a muscle in his back two days earlier. Another jockey congratulated him on coming in second despite his injury; Hartack reportedly snarled back, "I don't care if I have one leg. I wanted to win!"

But Hartack's intense drive was coupled with an equally intense personal style that many felt bordered on pure arrogance. He did not suffer fools gladly, and in his book, a lot of the media fell into that category. (He once remarked, "I admire the Turf writers because it must be tough to write about something you know nothing about.") Nor was he inclined to apologize when a trainer or owner took offense either at some remark of his that did make it into a newspaper or at the candid opinions Hartack provided of their horses.

Luro, though, respected proven ability, and he was less interested in getting into an ego contest with Hartack than he was in winning races. As blunt-spoken as Hartack was, he had a reputation for both absolute integrity and keen insight into his mounts' qualities, and Luro would listen to him where he might not have another jockey. Hartack, in turn, appreciated Luro's gracious approach to him.

Decidedly's Derby win may just possibly have been the payoff for Luro's listening to one of Hartack's suggestions. After riding Decidedly in the Forerunner Purse and the Blue Grass Stakes, Hartack suggested putting blinkers on the colt; he felt that Decidedly didn't have his mind one hundred percent on business. Luro did not ordinarily care for making a major equipment change right before a big race but agreed after due consideration. Whether it was the blinkers or not, Decidedly turned in the race of his life in the Kentucky Derby, winning by two and a quarter lengths and setting a track record of 2:00 2/5.

Hartack agreed to ride Northern Dancer in the Blue Grass Stakes, the colt's next prep and his final start prior to the Derby; the jockey would make his final decision on the Derby itself after that race. It was a measure of both Luro's confidence in Northern Dancer and his respect for Hartack's ability that he agreed to these terms instead of finding another jockey who would commit through the Derby.

Northern Dancer shipped to Keeneland without incident and settled in. Even when not planning to run in the Blue Grass, many Derby-bound horsemen like to have their colts train at Keeneland because of the relaxed atmosphere; some will wait until only a few days before the Derby itself to transfer to Churchill Downs, avoiding as much of the Derby media circus as possible. The Keeneland track, located just outside Lexington, is surrounded by lovely, park-like grounds rather than being crowded into an urban landscape, and the April weather is usually mild. For horses coming in from the heat of Florida and Southern California, the change can be quite invigorating.

Northern Dancer had not done badly in Florida, but he thrived at Keeneland. He muscled out, his coat beginning to take on the dappled sheen of peak condition. As horsemen put it, he was a "big little horse"; short he might be, but he girthed seventy-three inches (the average sixteen-hand Thoroughbred has a girth of about seventy-two inches) and was as broad across the back and rump as most of the bigger colts, causing *Daily Racing Form*'s Charles Hatton to liken him to "a vest-pocket Hercules."

Hill Rise was at Keeneland, too, but the two colts were not slated to meet prior to the Derby; Hill Rise was going in the Forerunner Purse, a seven-furlong allowance, six days before the Blue Grass. If they happened to cross paths on the way to or from the track to train, it meant nothing to them beyond one horse meeting another; they were blissfully unaware that they had been cast in the roles of uncrowned champion and upstart challenger, or the Good Big Horse and the Good Little Horse.

On April 23, Northern Dancer met four challengers in the Blue Grass Stakes. For many of the racegoers in attendance, it was their first chance to get a look at the Canadian runner, and they crowded around the walking ring where the colt was being saddled. They might not have thought he was a match for Hill Rise, but they were happy to make him a 1-5 favorite against a weak field.

Following the race, many American sportswriters were more convinced than ever that if there was a colt in Kentucky capable of taking Hill Rise's measure, Northern Dancer wasn't it. Oh, he had won, all right, but his margin was only a half-length over lightly raced Allen Adair. His time was 1:49 4/5, nothing spectacular, and it had taken him another :13 1/5 to gallop out another furlong, giving him a time for one and a quarter miles — the Derby distance — of 2:03.

To Luro and Hartack, though, the race had told a very different story. First, Northern Dancer had rated for Hartack — grudgingly, perhaps, but enough that he had gone the first three-quarters of a mile in a slow 1:14 1/5. Second, he had run the last three-eighths of a mile of the race itself in :35 3/5 — the final eighth in a sparkling :11 2/5 — and he had not been all out to do it; as *Daily Racing Form* put it, he had "won with complete authority."

Hartack had his Derby mount. Northern Dancer had his rider. And Luro knew he had a colt with as much of a chance as any man could ask.

Snow and Roses

T wo days after the Blue Grass, Northern Dancer took the short van ride over to Churchill Downs. He might as well have ridden into another world. Crowded amid Louisville's urban sprawl, Churchill Downs has nothing of Keeneland's serene elegance. Almost every inch of space at the 140-acre plant is used for something; the only significant amount of open space is in the track infield, and on Kentucky Derby Day even that is lost to view beneath a raucous crowd that can go well into five figures, forming a large proportion of the track's usual six-figure Derby Day attendance. Like an old patchwork quilt, Churchill Downs' unique character arises from a hodgepodge of seemingly disparate elements accumulated through the years; even following the track's renovation in 2003–2005, elements of the "old" Churchill still exist, not least the track's trademark twin spires, which now rise between two massive glass-and-steel structures containing luxury suites, a simulcast theater, two private club rooms, and extensive balconies for viewing the action below.

What Churchill Downs does have is excitement and plenty of it. During the week prior to the Derby, the place swarms with journalists, many with no acquaintance with horse racing other than during Derby week. For the trainer of a favorite or of a horse with an unusual story behind it, the experience can be nerve-wracking; trying to keep an excitable young Thoroughbred quiet and relaxed while fending off a flood of reporters and photographers is no small challenge.

As the trainer of a volatile colt with several unusual angles to his story and status as second favorite for the big race, Luro had his hands full dealing with the press, the more so because many knew he had also, however briefly, trained Hill Rise. But the wily Señor was up to the challenge. Pressed to bring Northern Dancer out for photos, he substituted a stable pony. Most of the photographers only knew that Northern Dancer was supposed to be small; the fact that the pony was chestnut and Northern Dancer was bay made not the slightest difference as flashes popped and shutters clicked. As for the reporters, Luro handled them deftly, giving them good copy while steering them away from his colt.

It helped somewhat that Hill Rise was still the Derby favorite. Although he had not really impressed in the Forerunner Purse (he won by three-quarters of a length), he made up for that by taking the Derby Trial four days before the Kentucky Derby itself in a smart 1:35 1/5. That victory made him the winner of eight straight races coming into the Derby. He had Shoemaker, generally regarded as the country's best jockey, in the saddle. And he was eye-catching. Like Northern Dancer, Hill Rise had that self-assurance that good horses have; he couldn't read his own press clippings, but he *knew* he was good, and the people who watched him knew he knew it. He strode the track like a king, and most of the American media seemed more than happy to dance attendance at his court.

It also helped that Northern Dancer was in familiar hands. His groom, Bill Brevard, had been with Luro for more than twenty years and had taken care of Northern Dancer throughout his campaign. A naturally placid man, he was instrumental in keeping Northern Dancer in a contented mood.

Fortunately, the Dancer was blissfully unaware of a controversy within his own camp. Whether the dissent originated with Taylor or with Joe Thomas himself, it was Thomas who picked a newspaper interview a few days before the Derby to express his opinion that Hartack was not the best possible jockey for Northern Dancer. Luro erupted — "I am running the stable!" — and stuck by his guns; Hartack remained the colt's rider.

Nothing could keep all the excitement away from Northern Dancer, of course; it could have been as quiet as a graveyard and the colt would have created plenty of excitement for himself, given half a chance. He was on the muscle and eager to run in his morning workouts. Luro kept him to slow gallops until April 30, when the colt had his final pre-race breeze. With exercise rider Raymond Cerda straining to keep the colt from repeating his blowout from the day before the Florida Derby, Northern Dancer clicked off five furlongs in 1:00 2/5 and galloped out six furlongs in 1:14.

He was ready.

On May 1, Derby Eve morning, Luro met with the other trainers in the racing secretary's office, along with some of the owners and members of the press. Each entrant's name was printed on a card and placed in a box; Luro, as the most recent trainer of a Derby winner present, was given the honor of drawing the cards out, one by one, to be lined up in the order in which they were chosen. Then, at 10 a.m., the Churchill Downs racing secretary shook twelve ivory balls, each incised with a number from one through twelve, out of a leather bottle; their order, matched with the order of the cards, would determine the post positions.

Northern Dancer was assigned post seven, to Luro's apparent pleasure. Hill Rise would make his run for glory from four places outside him. The stage was set.

******

May 2, 1964, dawned overcast and strangely quiet; the horde of reporters and photographers that had swarmed the track all week were mostly elsewhere, waiting for the race. There were no works to follow this morning, and anyway, no one would care; the pre-race stories had all been written. It was now just a matter of waiting for the main event.

Like the other Derby colts, Northern Dancer got his first cue that this was a race day at breakfast. A voracious eater, the colt normally got oats plus a net full of hay that he could nibble at will. (Given the chance, Northern Dancer not only would polish off the hay but also would snack on the straw used for bedding as well, so Luro had long since switched him over to peat moss for bedding material.) But a horse usually will not run well if it is in the process of digesting a stomach full of bulky food; digestion takes blood that is needed to fuel muscles. So Northern Dancer got only oats for his breakfast; more easily broken down than hay, they would supply energy for his afternoon's exertions. He would get another light meal of oats about midday, his last until after the race.

The hours dragged. The sun banished the early clouds; the day grew hot and humid. Trainers and grooms occupied themselves quietly and tried to stay calm; some grooms walked their charges up and down the shed row for a little light exercise. Coats already abloom with health were brushed to a high gleam. The farrier made rounds, checking the Derby horses' shoes and making any needed adjustments. As post time approached, some colts — Northern Dancer among them — had their manes braided, a touch that would keep their jockeys from being whipped in the face by a mass of waving horsehair as they crouched low over their mounts' necks.

After the sixth race, it was time. One by one the Derby contenders were led from their stalls, around the backstretch, and over to the saddling paddock and their assigned stalls. A huge crowd gathered outside the paddock; as much as possible, Bill Brevard kept himself between the crowd and Northern Dancer. The colt was on edge; Brevard talked to him and patted him, trying to keep him as quiet as possible while Luro got the saddle in place.

The call to the post sounded. All around the enclosure, trainers were getting in last-minute instructions, then tossing the jockeys onto their mounts. Luro gave Hartack a leg up. In the infield the band struck up "The Star-Spangled Banner" as the horses began the short walk from the paddock to the track.

Mr. Brick, first in the post parade, emerged from the gap in the stands out onto the track; almost simultaneously the band swung into "My Old Kentucky Home." One hundred thousand voices, give or take a few, joined in with the familiar lyrics. Meeting the incredible storm of noise, Northern Dancer bounced like a rubber ball, hind legs lashing; Hartack, used to the antics of excitable Thoroughbreds, stayed glued to the saddle. The colt settled down after one buck, but his ears were flicking and his eyes were bright and alert.

Winifred Taylor held her husband's hand and watched from the owners' box. There on the track, Windfields' turquoise and gold colors were being carried by her special colt, the one no one had wanted to buy; the one Luro had wanted gelded; the one Shoemaker had rejected. Against all odds he had won his way here. Now he was going to the post as the second choice for the Kentucky Derby. Perhaps for a brief second her eyes flicked to Hill Rise; black and gleaming with sweat, the favorite strode easily, looking every inch the champion.

The horses reached the starting gate. As though he had gotten something out of his system with that one fierce buck at stepping onto the track, Northern Dancer had been well behaved through the post parade and his warm-up. But the instant an assistant starter took his bridle, something in the colt snapped; Northern Dancer backpedaled, dragging the man with him. The Taylors watched tensely; one thousand-odd Canadians who had come down to Louisville for the big race froze in place. And as suddenly as he had balked, Northern Dancer changed his mind and walked into the gate.

The final horses were loading; last of all, Roman Brother went in. Northern Dancer stood quietly. For a fraction of a second, everything at Churchill Downs was absolutely still.

"They're off!" The announcer's shout was drowned by the roar of the crowd as twelve horses leaped from the gate. Northern Dancer, away alertly, responded to Hartack's guidance, dropping in toward the rail and saving ground as the field thundered into the first turn. He was under restraint but running easily.

The horses around the little colt closed and shifted; he was boxed in as the field began the run up the backstretch. Hartack held the colt off the heels of the ones ahead of him and bided his time. The box was okay with him for the moment. Hill Rise was the one he was worried about; he didn't want the Dancer chasing the speed up front. Mr. Brick, the leader, had zipped the first half in :46 flat; he wasn't going to last.

As quickly as the box had shut, it opened, but it wasn't going to stay that way. Hill Rise was moving up smoothly on the outside and Hartack knew without ever looking that if Shoe got the chance, he'd close the box and shut Northern Dancer in like a mouse in a trap.

Realization and action were nearly simultaneous; Hartack sent the Dancer for the closing hole. As Mr. Brick hit the three-quarters mark in 1:10 3/5, Northern Dancer burst free practically under Hill Rise's nose and was gone before the bigger colt could react. While Shoemaker was still trying to get his mount in gear, Northern Dancer rushed to the leaders.

In the stands at Churchill Downs, a thousand Canadians cheered wildly amidst the noise of the greater crowd as Northern Dancer charged forward. Across Canada millions more watched on TV: cheering, shouting, knuckles tightening on chair arms, mouths going dry as their little hero took command. The mile had gone in 1:36 flat; two furlongs remained between the Dancer and victory.

Six horses hit the quarter-pole with only three lengths between the first and the sixth. Hartack wasn't concerned about four of them; they were falling away. His worry was the big colt he knew would be coming fast: Hill Rise.

Luro had warned Hartack about the whip: "When he is hit, it can turn him sour," he said. But Hartack needed everything that the Dancer could give him to stave off the onrushing shadow on the far outside. The whip came down; not hard, just a light tap. With the same catlike burst of coiled energy that had gotten him out of the box, Northern Dancer exploded forward. He was on top by two lengths with three hundred yards to go.

Hill Rise was in full flight. A roar went up from the crowd as he took dead aim on the little bay leader, whose feet were flickering so fast it seemed as if Northern Dancer had eight legs instead of four. Under Shoemaker's urging, the favorite came on in huge strides, each jump looking like two of the Dancer's.

But there was no quit in Northern Dancer. Hartack was scrubbing on him with everything he had, using a light but steady left-handed whip, and the Dancer was giving everything, his short neck stretched to the limit and his feet churning for dear life. Hill Rise was lapped on the Dancer; the black nose inched past the little colt's flank, past his girth. All the crowd could see of Northern Dancer in the final furious yards was his head and neck sticking out in front of his larger rival, and that head and neck were still in front when the two colts hit the wire.

A new roar went up from the crowd as the time was posted: two minutes flat, a track and stakes record. And throughout Canada people yelled crazily in their living rooms and slapped total strangers on the back in the streets; car horns honked wildly from drivers listening to radio broadcasts. Those Canadians lucky enough to be in the stands at Churchill Downs were in sheer ecstasy, some of them breaking into a spontaneous chorus of "O Canada" — perhaps to the bemusement of the natives, who were much more used to hearing "Bred in Old Kentucky" as the post-race music.

"This is a great day for Canada!" Edward Taylor shouted joyously as he greeted his colt in the winner's circle. And so it was.

Canada's Hero

The champagne was flowing in the Windfields camp after the Derby, and no wonder. Not only had Northern Dancer won the greatest victory ever taken by a Canadian-bred and set a track record, but he also had set another mark as well; he was now the youngest Kentucky Derby winner on record, for he had won the great race while still twenty-five days short of his actual third birthday. It was a remarkable feat indeed for the little bay son of Nearctic and Natalma, and there was every reason to think that still further improvement might come with continuing physical maturation.

Yet the media didn't see it that way. Already, the wise guys were buzzing that the Derby had taken more out of Northern Dancer than out of Hill Rise. The Canadian upstart had gotten the benefit of a clever ride while Hill Rise had been forced wide on the last turn, they said; Northern Dancer would not be so lucky a second time.

Oblivious to his disparagers, Northern Dancer settled into his stall at Pimlico in Maryland without incident. The fourteen-hour van ride had been a little wearying, coming only two days after the Derby, but the colt was in good condition. Rather than putting him in the Derby winner's traditional stall in the barn set aside for the Preakness horses, Luro had specifically requested a stall in a barn near the six-furlong pole of the track, well away from the others. Most of the media clustered around the Preakness barn containing Hill Rise and the others, leaving Northern Dancer in relative peace. Plus, Luro's chosen barn had a good grazing area for the colt.

As the days progressed toward the Preakness, Luro kept Northern Dancer's training quiet, for the most part continuing the same slow gallops that the colt had had before the Derby. Things were not nearly so quiet elsewhere. Northern Dancer didn't know it, but his presence in the Preakness had innocently spawned an amusing diplomatic incident.

"I was the publicity director at Pimlico at the time," recalled Joe Hickey Jr. during a 2005 interview, "and I knew they had this cavalry unit up in Ontario, the Governor-General's Horse Guards, that took part in the ceremonies surrounding the Queen's Plate every year. I think it was Joe Hirsch who suggested that I see if I could get them to come down for the Preakness.

"Well, in a few days I could have killed him. The Guards were happy to send a contingent, Pimlico was delighted, and everything was fine until somebody pointed out that the Guards were an armed military unit and could not cross the United States border according to a treaty dating back to the War of 1812. (Along with the large silver axe carried by the farrier-sergeant, the Horse Guards were equipped with swords and lances — long since outdated as weapons of war but still "arms" by the terms of the treaty.)

"Before I got everything straightened out for them to come into the country, the State Department, the Pentagon, and the Canadian embassy had gotten involved. Then I ran into another problem; with the Pimlico meet going and the Preakness coming up, there wasn't a stall to be had anywhere near the track for the Guards' horses. The Baltimore Police Department finally agreed to move some of their horses out to the country and let me have enough stalls to accommodate the Guards."

The day before the Preakness, Luro gave Northern Dancer a three-furlong "pipe opener" to hone his speed for the race. The colt spun the distance in :35 4/5 and galloped out another furlong for a half-mile in :48 3/5 — not outstandingly fast but a good indication that he was sharp and ready. By contrast, Hill Rise had gone three furlongs in :40 flat in his speed drill the day before. Yet conventional wisdom still held that Hill Rise had emerged from the Derby in better shape than the Dancer. Certainly, the California colt looked magnificent. On Preakness Day the track handicapper pegged Hill Rise at 7-5 and Northern Dancer at 2-1 in the morning line; Hill Rise's odds would drop to 4-5 by post time.

Those believing that Northern Dancer was a tired colt following the Derby might well have rethought their position after watching his antics prior to the race. He left the barn on his hind legs and continued rearing and snorting all the way to the saddling area on the Pimlico turf course, only settling down to business when the tack started going on.

Hill Rise certainly made a more impressive appearance in the Preakness post parade, gleaming and prancing; Northern Dancer, in a mercurial about-face to his behavior while coming from the barn, ambled to the post almost casually. But when the starting bell rang, Northern Dancer charged out as though he meant to run the others into the ground from the start. Hartack took the colt back off the moderate opening pace set by longshot Big Pete for the first half; then the action heated up as the Dancer, Hill Rise, and Quadrangle hit the three-quarters mark nearly abreast, with Quadrangle the leader by a half-length. At the stretch call it was Hill Rise and Quadrangle who were faltering, unable to keep up; the Dancer was in front by three and wound up a comfortable winner by two and a quarter lengths. The Scoundrel came on to head Hill Rise for second; Quadrangle finished fourth.

With all the trouble he had gone to, Joe Hickey perhaps took a bit of extra satisfaction in watching the Governor-General's Horse Guards canter down the track to greet E.P. Taylor as he walked across the main and turf tracks to the winner's circle in the infield. After receiving the Woodlawn Vase, Taylor raised the trophy high, to the cheers of the crowd. Once again the Canadians had conquered.

******

Northern Dancer had barely settled to his own supper when he became the subject of a new controversy, the author of which was none other than Horatio Luro. Along with the Taylors and a group of enthusiastic friends, Luro was part of the post-race party at the Members Club near the Pimlico clubhouse turn. Taylor was happily receiving the congratulations of the other partygoers and the champagne was flowing freely when Luro dropped his bombshell.

"I do not plan to run Northern Dancer in the Belmont," he said.

Stunned silence ensued, followed by a buzz from the newsmen present. "Why?" asked Taylor, clearly taken aback.

"I think this colt has distance limitations," Luro replied. He went on to explain that as a short-striding horse, Northern Dancer was not well suited to a race of one and a half miles. Further, he felt that Northern Dancer had earned a short rest; if a break was not forthcoming, then the Jersey Derby, he proposed, might be a better fit both in terms of distance and in terms of the competition that Northern Dancer would probably face.

Whether Luro had discussed the issue with Bill Hartack or not prior to the party, the trainer may well have been aware that Hartack, too, had reservations about the colt's ability to get twelve furlongs. Taylor, however, was probably not privy to any such information. After the initial shock had passed, he told Luro that the two of them would discuss plans for Northern Dancer the next morning. In the meantime, of course, the news of Luro's announcement was spreading far and wide — which, presumably, was Luro's intention, given that he had taken his stand in so public a setting.

Luro reiterated his objections when he met with Taylor the next day, but Taylor was not ready to let the dream of a Triple Crown go. He had never been a man to rest on past laurels; now that he had reached the culmination of his Derby dream, his ambitions naturally expanded. Perhaps, too, he still felt the sting of past media gibing at Northern Dancer's expense; let his colt win the Triple Crown and no one would ever laugh at the "Canadian runt" or Canadian breeding again. And he had already announced his intention of going on to the Belmont during the Preakness post-race interview before Luro's announcement, making it hard for him to back down.

No final decision was reached, but a compromise of sorts was made. Luro, honoring Taylor's wishes, would take Northern Dancer with him for training at Belmont. He would size up both Northern Dancer's condition and the Belmont field as it took shape; if both appeared favorable, Northern Dancer would try to become the ninth Triple Crown winner.

Luro had originally planned to ship Northern Dancer with two other horses, but that plan had to be thrown out when Northern Dancer became upset. "We got him in the van," recalled assistant trainer Norman Bowles, "and then we started putting those others in and he just went to roaring and stomping; he wasn't going to have it. He just didn't like to be that close to other horses. I had to go back to Mr. Luro and tell him to take the other two horses out of there. Once they were gone, he settled right down and made the drive without any trouble."

Continuing the regimen of slow gallops that had worked so well before the Derby and the Preakness, Northern Dancer trained well at Belmont, giving Luro cause to hope that maybe, just maybe, the little colt would stay better than he thought — on class, perhaps, if not on pure stamina. Adding to his growing confidence, the emerging Belmont field contained only three real challengers, all of them horses that the Dancer had already whipped twice: Hill Rise, Quadrangle, and Roman Brother.

Hartack was apparently less sanguine, though he was determined to do his best to help Northern Dancer get the trip. Whether he was still concerned about Hill Rise is open to question, but he may well have remembered a prediction that he had made regarding Quadrangle prior to the Kentucky Derby. Quadrangle had been the third choice in the Derby betting; Hartack, looking forward to the big race, had said that he respected the colt's ability but thought he was still a few weeks away from his best form. As usual — at least when it came to assessing a horse — he was right.

Belmont Park was undergoing a complete replacement of its old, run-down grandstand, so the 1964 Belmont was run at nearby Aqueduct. On June 6, eight horses went postward for the Belmont under an overcast sky, among them Northern Dancer. For the first time in the Triple Crown series, he was the favorite, going off at odds of 4-5.

But the Triple Crown was not to be. Hartack took the Dancer back early behind a sluggish early pace; after a half in a pedestrian :49, Northern Dancer was fifth behind the early pacesetter, Orientalist, and pulling hard. Quadrangle was only a length ahead in fourth but was able to slip through on the inside on the first turn, saving ground all the way, and grabbed the lead just after the mile. "I won the race right there, when I was able to cut inside," said winning jockey Manuel Ycaza later.

Northern Dancer went inside the tiring Orientalist at the mile and set sail for the leader, who was only a length ahead. To the roars of the crowd, he got to within a half-length of Quadrangle with an eighth of a mile to go … but he could do no more, and the cheering waned as it became apparent to all that the Dancer was beaten. In the last eighth of a mile, Quadrangle drew away easily to win the Belmont by two lengths. Roman Brother came on to take second, four lengths ahead of a leg-weary Northern Dancer. An even wearier Hill Rise was fourth, having faded after prompting the early pace.

Following the race, Hartack became the focus of a firestorm of criticism. Disappointed Northern Dancer supporters, Taylor among them, felt the Dancer had used himself up fighting his jockey and should have been turned loose earlier. Luro, too, came in for his share of the Sunday-morning strategists' ire; had he not publicly expressed his belief that Northern Dancer could not stay? Some writers expressed the opinion that if Luro had held more confidence in the colt and had not given Hartack instructions to rate him so tightly, Northern Dancer might have come out the winner.

Others, however, felt that Northern Dancer had simply failed to stay the distance, among them the *Daily Racing Form*'s Joe Hirsch and Charles Hatton. And there may have been another explanation. Neither Luro nor Hartack ever replied publicly to the charges of poor judgment laid against them, but Hartack later confided to his good friend Ron Turcotte, "Instructions didn't beat Northern Dancer. Soundness did."

Precisely when Northern Dancer suffered the tendon injury that eventually forced his retirement has been a matter of some debate. Both Joe Hirsch and racing historian Edward Bowen wrote that the injury occurred during a workout while the colt was preparing for the American Derby. But Hartack's statement would suggest that the injury had much earlier origins — most likely during the Belmont itself, when fatigue would have made the Dancer vulnerable to a misstep. This would agree with the position taken by Muriel Lennox in her biography of Northern Dancer, though it seems safe to presume that Hartack would not have agreed with Ms. Lennox that his rating of the colt was the cause of the injury.

Whether Northern Dancer could have won the Belmont even if everything had set up perfectly for him is debatable, for Quadrangle was coming into his own as a top stayer. Clearly relishing the Belmont distance, Quadrangle would go on to win the Travers Stakes at ten furlongs and the Lawrence Realization at thirteen furlongs, beating Roman Brother by a neck in the latter. Roman Brother, who got the worst of the running during the Realization, won the American Derby at ten furlongs and ran second to Kelso, the defending Horse of the Year, in the two-mile Jockey Club Gold

Cup; behind him in the Gold Cup were such proven stayers as Quadrangle, the San Juan Capistrano Handicap winner Cedar Key, and the Epsom Oaks winner *Monade. At four Roman Brother would win the Jockey Club Gold Cup en route to a Horse of the Year title.

Could a completely healthy Northern Dancer have defeated either Quadrangle or Roman Brother at a mile and a half on class? Perhaps; the question was never to be answered. But it seems very unlikely that he could have beaten either on superior stamina, particularly during the second half of the season when both were reaching their best form.

******

Eight days after the Belmont, Northern Dancer arrived at Woodbine to an enthusiastic welcome by track personnel, trainers, grooms, and reporters who had come to pay homage to Canada's hero. The disappointing loss in the Belmont had not dampened Canadians' adoration for their little champion. Toronto's mayor, Alan Lamport, asked to have the honor of holding a ticker-tape parade for Northern Dancer through the heart of the city; when Taylor explained that the parade, while well meant, would doubtless be too much for the nerves of a high-strung Thoroughbred, the mayor altered plans slightly and feted Taylor at a reception at City Hall, during which Lamport presented Taylor with a key to the city for Northern Dancer. Carved from a single carrot, the key was enthusiastically gobbled by Northern Dancer later in the evening.

Northern Dancer's target was now the Queen's Plate, Canada's premier race for three-year-olds. Whatever criticism Luro may or may not have deserved following the Belmont, the fact remains that Northern Dancer's presence at the Queen's Plate was a remarkable tribute to Luro's skill as a trainer as well as to the colt's constitution. Following the rigors of a Triple Crown campaign, most horses of the post-World War II era have needed a month or more to recover; yet only two weeks separated the Belmont and the Queen's Plate, and here was Northern Dancer prancing his way to the post as if he had not been racing hard since February.

Never before had the Queen's Plate boasted a Kentucky Derby winner among its entrants, nor had it ever hosted such a huge crowd. Thousands, many of whom had never before attended a horse race, poured into Woodbine. Seven colts and one filly had been entered in the Plate, but only one mattered: Northern Dancer, who went off at odds of 1-7.

Many fans' hearts must have been in their throats in the early going when the crowd saw Northern Dancer boxed in and running next to last, then last as Hartack tried to find racing room. As Hartack later explained, the Dancer was faster than his rivals even under a stranglehold, and he couldn't get the colt to take back enough to escape the box. But then a small hole opened and Northern Dancer did the rest. Given his head, he bulled through the narrow opening and then accelerated past the field in one huge burst that had him in front before the horses reached the final turn. In the stretch it was all Northern Dancer, his ears flicking to the wild cheers of the crowd as he drew off to win by seven and a half widening lengths.

It was a great day for Windfields; not only had Northern Dancer absolutely demolished his field, but the runner-up, Langcrest, was also by Windfields stallion Nearctic. In addition, Windfields had bred and sold third-place Grand Garçon. But for the Taylors, Windfields' accomplishments in the Queen's Plate paled beside what Northern Dancer had just done in front of their fellow Canadians.

Together, Edward and Winifred Taylor led their gallant little champion into the winner's circle. To roars of approbation from the crowd, they received the traditional fifty guineas' purse and the trophy from the Governor-General of Canada, representing Her Majesty, Queen Elizabeth II. Northern Dancer snorted and pranced as though eager to go around the track again.

No one knew that the race would be his last.

******

Northern Dancer enjoyed a few weeks' respite from serious training while the Windfields team considered its options. The Travers Stakes at Saratoga — historically known as the "Midsummer Derby" — was a logical target; it would be run on August 22. But the American Derby, slated for August 29 at Arlington Park, was also a tempting target and carried a larger purse than did the Travers ($100,000-added against $75,000-added). Both races were at one and a quarter miles, and Northern Dancer would be required to carry 126 pounds in either event.

Whatever injury or unsoundness Hartack had sensed in Northern Dancer during the Belmont apparently did not receive any consideration. The problem, whatever it was, seemed to reveal itself only at racing speed, when the pressures on the colt's legs were greatest. Once again Hartack had felt something was not quite right with Northern Dancer, this time in the Queen's Plate. Despite the colt's easy win, Hartack felt his performance was "dull" and owed much of its apparent brilliance to the weakness of the competition. Yet, courageous to a fault, Northern Dancer had showed no distress following the race.

Taylor may well have been unaware of the possible lameness problem, and if Luro knew, he may have felt it was minor enough that he could continue with the colt. This was not an uncommon decision or necessarily inhumane; many racehorses have soundness issues that can be managed with care, and part of the skill of an expert trainer is in distinguishing between the problems that can be worked around and the ones that will force him to stop on the horse. Further, Luro's European style of training, with its emphasis on long gallops rather than speed drills, tended to be easier on a horse's legs than the traditional American style.

The Windfields team eventually chose the American Derby as Northern Dancer's next conquest; according to Joe Hirsch, Luro had made arrangements with Burley Parke, trainer of Roman Brother, to share a plane to Chicago and split the cost between them. But before shipping, Luro wanted Northern Dancer to get in at least one serious work. He had planned to work the colt Sunday before shipping out Monday afternoon, but rain delayed the work to Monday morning, and even then conditions were still rainy and wet. Nonetheless, Luro, now pressed for time, decided to work the Dancer anyway.

The work went beautifully; Northern Dancer breezed nine furlongs in controlled fashion while scarcely breaking a sweat. But on the way back to the barn, Luro thought he saw a slight misstep. Examination revealed heat in the main tendon of the left foreleg, and Luro immediately phoned Parke: the Dancer would not fly out with Roman Brother. If the injury proved minor enough, the colt would ship to Chicago later in the week.

Treatment was begun immediately; Northern Dancer was given an anti-inflammatory medication to bring down the swelling in the tendon and a diathermy machine (a therapeutic device for supplying radiant heat to an injured area) was brought into use. Luro thought the colt might recover fairly soon because the tendon sheath had not ruptured — the tendon was strained rather than truly bowed — but the days passed with little sign of improvement. The American Derby came and went, won by Roman Brother in the absence of the Dancer, and nothing changed.

Luro probably knew the truth within the first few weeks, but Taylor was not ready to let go and admit that Northern Dancer's racing career was over. He had received an invitation for the colt to the November 11 Washington, D.C., International at Laurel Park in Maryland. In retrospect, Northern Dancer probably had no chance of winning this race even if healthy. Although he was a proven commodity on turf, he would have had to tackle the mighty Kelso at his best form over a mile and a half, a distance far more favorable to the four-time Horse of the Year. But Taylor was still unconvinced that Northern Dancer could not truly stay twelve furlongs, and the chance to see his little colt prove himself against the best horses in the world was tempting.

Nonetheless, no amount of wishful thinking could heal Northern Dancer's leg, and Taylor's dream at last gave way to the inevitable. On November 6, 1964, Northern Dancer was officially retired. Five days later Kelso won the International, setting a course and American record of 2:23 4/5 and locking down American Horse of the Year honors for the fifth consecutive year.

Stud

A little over a week before Northern Dancer's retirement became official, the champion's adoring fans were given an opportunity to say goodbye. Arrangements were made for an exhibition gallop at Woodbine on October 24, 1964, as part of Canadian Championship Day. At Edward Taylor's request, Ron Turcotte was aboard for the ride, which was staged just before the feature race.

"It was a real pleasure for me," Turcotte recalled. "He was much more mature than when I first rode him, so much easier to handle. He was kind of disappointed that I only just galloped. And then I went out in the next race and won the Canadian Championship Stakes with Will I Rule. It was a great day."

Disappointed or not, Northern Dancer was not going to get the chance to damage his strained left foreleg further; he was far too valuable as a stallion prospect. His value was further emphasized by the awards that came flooding his way.

On November 14, the Toronto edition of the *Daily Racing Form* announced Canada's year-end champions. No one was surprised that Northern Dancer was unanimously voted both champion three-year-old male and Horse of the Year except those who realized that the voting rules had been rewritten on the Dancer's behalf. Prior to 1964, *Daily Racing Form*'s rules governing its awarding of Canadian championships required that a prospective champion be bred in Canada and do its best racing there. Northern Dancer met the Canadian-bred requirement and had certainly been devastating in the Queen's Plate, but his lone 1964 start in Canada hardly constituted his "best racing"; hence, that requirement was quietly dropped. One doubts if anyone protested the change, given Northern Dancer's clear superiority over anything else running in Canada. Given 132 pounds in the Canadian Experimental Handicap, he was rated five pounds better than champion grass horse Will I Rule, six pounds better than champion older male E. Day, and twelve pounds better than three-year-old runner-up Langcrest.

(Ironically, Northern Dancer would not have been eligible for the modern-day Sovereign Awards either. Although the Sovereign Awards do not require a horse to be bred in Canada to be eligible, they do require at least three starts in Canada for an animal to be considered in the championship voting.)

December 3 rolled around, and with it another award: Edward and Winifred Taylor jointly accepted the award for Northern Dancer as the American champion three-year-old male at the Thoroughbred Racing Associations' annual awards banquet. One of three organizations then choosing divisional champions in the United States, the Thoroughbred Racing Associations was not alone in assessing Northern Dancer as the best of his generation anywhere in North America. *Daily Racing Form* also named Northern Dancer champion and assigned him 128 pounds on its Free Handicap for three-year-olds, a pound more than Quadrangle and Roman Brother, who shared the second spot; in the overall standings, Northern Dancer ranked behind only three older males — Kelso (136 pounds), the formidable Gun Bow (136 pounds), and the top-class grass specialist Mongo (133 pounds). *The Blood-Horse* likewise rated Northern Dancer as the best three-year-old in North America, so all of the major American organizations were united in proclaiming what Canadians had known since May: Northern Dancer was the king of his generation.

The colt even conquered the best competition *Homo sapiens* could throw at him, for at the end of December he received a totally unprecedented honor for a racehorse. Besting several Olympic medalists, a slew of hockey players, and his old friend Ron Turcotte, Northern Dancer was named Canada's Athlete of the Year by a vote of Canada's sports editors and journalists. While the decision outraged a few hockey supporters, it was popular with most Canadians. Northern Dancer's admirers drove to the National Stud Farm to see him in such numbers that visiting hours eventually had to be curtailed to keep the chaos in check.

That Northern Dancer was still in Canada at all was a tribute to E.P. Taylor's dedication to Canadian racing and breeding. Once the colt's retirement had been announced, Taylor received numerous offers either to syndicate the colt or to stand Northern Dancer on his behalf; under either arrangement Northern Dancer would have been moved to Kentucky. But Taylor refused all offers. Northern Dancer was a Canadian hero, he said, and he would remain in Canada.

In truth, even before the last offer came in, Northern Dancer's initial book of thirty-five mares was already full. Taylor was providing the young stallion with ten of his best mares; the other twenty-five were coming from breeders in Canada, Kentucky, Maryland, and Pennsylvania. This was strong support for Northern Dancer, particularly in view of his $10,000 stud fee — the same that his sire Nearctic then commanded.

The very first mare Northern Dancer was assigned to cover was his owner's Flaming Page. A daughter of Bull Page, she had been sold at the 1960 Windfields yearling sale but had been turned back by purchaser Frank Sherman because of an ankle problem discovered shortly after the sale. One can only imagine Sherman's feelings two years later on seeing Flaming Page run second in the Kentucky Oaks behind the American champion Cicada, then return home to romp in the Canadian Oaks against her own sex and in the Queen's Plate against males.

On paper Flaming Page looked like a perfect mate for Northern Dancer. A high-class racer, she was a big, strong, rather masculine-looking mare who offered plenty of size to offset Northern Dancer's lack of inches, which was exactly the problem when the two were brought together in the breeding shed. Try as he might, Northern Dancer simply wasn't tall enough to mount Flaming Page successfully. The mare finally ended the unintended comedy by getting fed up and letting fly with both heels, catching Northern Dancer squarely in the ribs.

That ended the attempted breeding; fortunately, Northern Dancer was not seriously injured in either body or libido. (Some stallions, on getting kicked by an early mate, become so mentally traumatized that they either refuse to breed at all or become reluctant breeders — or they may develop quirks such as refusing to breed a mare of the color of the one that kicked them.) Still, there was the problem of getting Flaming Page bred before she passed out of heat, necessitating a three-week wait before she would come into season again. The solution was simple; a shallow pit was dug in the dirt floor of the breeding arena. Concrete and asphalt were poured in to provide a stable surface, and the depression was then lined with non-slip matting on top of the asphalt. When the time came for the return tryst, Flaming Page was led to stand in the depression; Northern Dancer, standing on the higher ground of the main floor, was able to make a successful cover. (A different strategy was used following the Dancer's move to Windfields Maryland, as the breeding shed there had a solid floor that could not be dug into. Instead, a low ramp was used to give Northern Dancer the extra inches he needed to cover his mates — an arrangement never entirely popular with the Windfields staff, who feared that the stallion might slip or fall off the ramp when dismounting his mares. But as Joe Hickey Jr. said, "He scared us a few times, but nothing ever really happened.")

Northern Dancer had always shown a strong interest in fillies and mares; now that he had actually mated with one, his sex drive intensified. He had every intention of breeding every mare on the farm and every mare brought to it, and he would become enraged if he realized another stallion was being taken to the breeding shed in his stead.

"It was really rather funny," recalled Hickey, who became quite familiar with Northern Dancer's behavior while general manager at Windfields Maryland. "I don't know how he did it, but he could tell whether a van coming onto the farm had mares aboard or not. If it was carrying hay or other stuff, he'd not pay it any attention, but if there was a mare on board — well, he had this half door with a screen on the front of his stall, and he'd have his front hooves up on the wooden edge of that lower half like a big dog and be whinnying and hollering for all he was worth. Even if the mare never called or made a sound, he'd do that. I don't know how he knew, but he knew."

With eight other stallions to share stud duties at the National Stud Farm, Northern Dancer wasn't going to get to breed every mare there, but there was no telling him that. The Windfields staff rapidly learned that he could not be left in a paddock while another stallion was breeding; he would gallop himself into a lather. Leaving him loose in his stall was nearly as bad, for he would stomp, kick, and maul his water buckets and feed tubs while screaming his displeasure. The one remaining solution was to tie him up with a chain (he could snap any rope made) in his stall, and even that had its pitfalls; left with too much length on one occasion, he tried to climb the partition separating him from freedom and nearly hanged himself instead.

Northern Dancer's behavior was that of a highly dominant stallion, and it continued as such even when mares were not around. Left in a paddock, most horses will quickly settle to grazing or even lie down, but not Northern Dancer. In a manner reminiscent of wild herd stallions guarding their territories, he would patrol his paddock periodically, head up and alert for potential dangers. Perhaps because of his constant activity, he continued to present a hard-muscled appearance well past an age at which most stallions have long since become comfortably fleshed out. The mere humans he dealt with quickly learned that one did not go into Northern Dancer's paddock, even to take him to his supper; one waited until it pleased the horse to come over to the gate and signal his readiness to leave his territory.

Dancing, prancing, and hollering, Northern Dancer serviced the thirty-five mares he had been assigned over the course of the breeding season and gave every indication that he would have tried to cover thrice that many given the chance. Twenty-six pregnancies resulted from his first season's efforts. Flaming Page, alas, gave birth to stillborn twins; four other mares failed to produce live foals for various reasons. But twenty-one sons and daughters of Northern Dancer made it through birth to frisk in pastures from Canada to Kentucky during the spring of 1966. They were the beginning of Northern Dancer's legacy.

Rising Star

A nytime a Thoroughbred goes to stud, breeders are looking at a gap of three years between the time the horse services his first mares and the time his first crop comes to the races. Until then, how good a sire a horse will prove to be is a matter of speculation, no matter how good a racer he was or how stellar his bloodlines. The wait can be even longer if the horse is of the type whose foals cannot reasonably be expected to do their best running until at least three years of age.

Neither Taylor nor his chief advisors, Gil Darlington (who died in 1968) and Joe Thomas, seem to have been enamored with any particular bloodline when selecting Northern Dancer's mates, though Taylor certainly was not shy about his own good mares. Aside from Flaming Page, Northern Dancer's first group of mates included Taylor's good stakes winners Windy Answer (Windfields—Reply) and Victoria Regina (*Menetrier—Victoriana); Victoriana (Windfields—Iribelle), who had already produced four stakes winners for Taylor by the time of her tryst with Northern Dancer; *Queen's Statute (Le Lavandou—Statute), another proven matron with Windfields-bred stakes winners by Epic, Chop Chop, and *Menetrier; and Taylor's 1963 Canadian Oaks winner Menedict (*Menetrier—*Queen's Statute). Inbreeding to Hyperion appears to have been frequently tried, as was inbreeding to Phalaris and the great broodmares Selene and Scapa Flow, but at least as important as pedigree in choosing mares for Northern Dancer was general conformation; mares with some size and substance to offset the Dancer's lack of inches were considered ideal.

In accordance with his established custom, Taylor offered all of his Northern Dancer yearlings at the Windfields pre-priced yearling sale of 1967. The sale itself was to be conducted among somewhat different lines, however. To accommodate the anticipated demand for these first sons and daughters of the Dancer, as well as the demand for yearlings by Nearctic and his other proven stallions, Taylor decided to hold a pre-sale ten days before the main event. Preferred buyers — those who had bought Windfields yearlings at previous sales — would get the first opportunity to buy horses from the 1966 foal crop; then, at the main sale, the remaining yearlings would be offered to the general public. If two or more buyers wanted the same youngster, the colt or filly would be auctioned with the preset price as the starting bid. Of the sixty-two yearlings offered on auction day (eight of which were Northern Dancer's), eighteen sold for $303,300 (Canadian). The top price of $75,000 was paid for a Northern Dancer colt out of *Queen's Statute.

Northern Dancer's other seven yearlings did not sell, but his yearlings were among the most expensive offerings, including the handsomest colt in the sale — a blaze-faced golden chestnut out of Victoria Regina, by *Menetrier. Aside from his exquisite good looks, he was a "nephew" of Victoria Park (a half brother to Victoria Regina), and his dam was a stakes winner at both two and three. His pedigree and conformation should have excited keen interest, but he was flawed by a puffy ankle, the result of a paddock injury suffered several weeks before the sale. At $50,000, no one wanted to take a chance on him, and so Taylor retained ownership of the colt eventually named Viceregal.

Viceregal's ankle remained a constant source of concern, but under the care of Pete McCann, he was brought along slowly. In the meantime, others of Northern Dancer's first crop matured enough to get to the races. The first to reach the track was Jitterbug, a filly bred by Greentree Stud out of the Sailor mare Port of Call. Racing at Hialeah on January 26, 1968, she won a three-furlong baby race to become her sire's first official winner.

Jitterbug, alas, would never make it to the track again, nor would she achieve any note as a broodmare. But a better fate awaited Northern Dancer's second starter, a youngster out of Bold Ruler's half sister Hill Rose. Named True North, he broke Santa Anita's twenty-two-year-old track record for four and a half furlongs in March and later ran second in the Futurity Stakes. The chestnut gelding was slow to reach his best form but won the Churchill Downs Handicap at four and the historic Widener Handicap at age five for Sonny Whitney. The wins kept coming; all told, ten of the Dancer's 1966 foals eventually became stakes winners, an astounding 47.6 percent of the crop. (One wonders how many stakes winners Northern Dancer might have had with the books of one hundred mares or more seen by top stallions today; through most of his career, he serviced no more than thirty-five or thirty-six mares per year.)

Three of Northern Dancer's first crop would win stakes races as two-year-olds, an excellent 14 percent of his named foals. To be fair, two were not of a kind to cause much excitement: Dorothy Glynn won the Cinderella Handicap while racing in British Columbia while Eaglesham won the City of Miami Beach Handicap at Hialeah. But the third was a certain flashy chestnut with a bad ankle.

Viceregal was never an entirely sound colt. The left ankle he had damaged as a yearling was a chronic problem; before his two-year-old season was over, his right foreleg had become troublesome as well. But he won eight of eight races, seven of them stakes, to rule as Canada's Horse of the Year as well as champion two-year-old colt.

Although he has not been as well remembered as some of Northern Dancer's later offspring, Viceregal exemplified the best qualities of his sire — speed, superb physical balance, and an indomitable will to win. Following his last race of the season, the Cup and Saucer Stakes, Viceregal limped away from the winner's circle with his vulnerable ankles battered; he had struck himself several times and been hit by another horse's hoof sometime during the race. Yet in the race itself, he had found the courage to come from ten lengths back to nail the pacesetter, Grey Whiz, by a neck. A stakes winner himself at two, Grey Whiz would win the following year's Breeders' Stakes.

Viceregal attempted to take the Triple Crown trail at three, but his first race that year proved to be his last. Racing at Keeneland in the six-furlong Whitney Purse on April 5, 1969, Viceregal closed well in the final yards to finish third, but jockey Craig Perret pulled the colt up immediately after the finish and hopped off. Veterinary examination proved that Viceregal had fractured the coffin bone in his left forefoot.

The disappointment must have been bitter to Taylor; years later, he would express the opinion that Viceregal might have been the best colt he ever bred. Others might well disagree, however, for in Northern Dancer's second crop was the magnificent Nijinsky II.

The result of the second mating between Northern Dancer and Flaming Page, Nijinsky was already a marked colt when he was sent to the Canadian Thoroughbred Horse Society annual yearling sale in September 1968. Thanks in no small part to Viceregal, Northern Dancer was proving too hot a commodity for his progeny to be handled through the Windfields sales, and the other Windfields stallions were also doing well. Thus, Taylor decided after 1967 that, rather than holding a private sale, he would send his young horses to the CTHS sale with reserve prices attached. If no one cared to open the bidding at Taylor's reserve, he would keep the yearling; otherwise, the youngster would be sold to the highest bidder. In keeping with the newly international nature of the CTHS sale, Laddie Dance and John Finney of the venerable Fasig-Tipton sales company were brought in to run the auction.

Taylor wound up keeping several high-reserve youngsters following the auction, among them Viceregal's full brother Vice Regent, whom Taylor valued at $100,000. But the Northern Dancer—Flaming Page colt was not among them. He had attracted the attention of Vincent O'Brien, European trainer for American platinum magnate Charles Engelhard. Originally sent to Canada to look over a *Ribot colt from the Windfields consignment for Engelhard, O'Brien had not liked the looks of the yearling. (His judgment was justified; the colt, later named Northern Monarch, ended up winning just three of nineteen starts, though he did place in two stakes events.) The big, handsome bay colt out of Flaming Page was another matter, however, and O'Brien advised Engelhard to purchase him instead. Engelhard took the advice and sent George Scott to purchase the Northern Dancer colt. The bidding went to $84,000, a Canadian record. Taylor's reserve was $60,000, so one presumes he was quite satisfied with the sale.

Among his many interests, Charles Engelhard was a patron of the arts. Accordingly, it probably surprised no one that he named his beautifully athletic new colt after the great ballet dancer Vaslav Nijinsky, who had believed that he would be reincarnated as a horse. The human Nijinsky could hardly have had a better namesake, for the equine Nijinsky proved as willful, temperamental, and talented as any human star that has ever graced a stage.

Shipped to O'Brien's training yard in Ireland, Nijinsky was a first-class bag of knots, each of which had to be untied with infinite care and patience. First he would not eat good oats, having been raised on a diet of processed feed; the day a shipment of his accustomed feed arrived from Canada was, of course, the day he decided oats might be acceptable after all. Then he began refusing to leave his stall to go to the yard, emphasizing his refusal by rearing; if gotten in motion, he would rear again every time the action paused.

Patience and persistence by O'Brien and his best exercise riders eventually got Nijinsky to settle into the routine of training and even to the races. Five times Nijinsky went to the post at two, including four starts in stakes events, and five times he won while hardly coming out of a canter. His last race at two was in the Dewhurst Stakes at Newmarket, traditionally considered a strong indicator for the following season's Classics, and his performance there brought him recognition as the best juvenile in England as well as in Ireland, where his previous four races had been run.

Despite the ease of Nijinsky's victories at two, however, he had his doubters. Many Europeans regarded Northern Dancer's Belmont loss as an indication that his progeny were not likely to relish the mile and a half of the Derby Stakes or its counterparts in France and Ireland. Those familiar with North American breeding could also point out that neither Flaming Page nor her sire Bull Page had ever won at twelve furlongs.

But facts on a catalog page meant nothing to Nijinsky. Following a season-opening win in the Gladness Stakes at The Curragh, Nijinsky went on to take the Two Thousand Guineas, the Derby Stakes, the Irish Sweeps Derby, the King George VI and Queen Elizabeth Stakes, and, almost as an afterthought, the St. Leger Stakes.

Nijinsky had swept all before him in England without ever being extended, and his St. Leger victory had made him the first winner of England's Triple Crown since *Bahram in 1935. Many experienced horsemen and Turf writers were hailing him as the best horse seen in England since World

War II — high praise indeed, since the English Turf had been graced by two extraordinary horses in unbeaten *Ribot and the magnificent *Sea-Bird in the years since the war. A further assessment of the horse's merit was provided by his syndication for $5.44 million, then a world record, prior to the St. Leger. And the man who perhaps knew him best as a racehorse, Lester Piggott — one of the great jockeys of English racing history and Nijinsky's regular rider — said of him, "I was never more impressed with a horse."

Yet the St. Leger marked a turning point in Nijinsky's career. He had come down with ringworm — a fungal infection of the skin — following the King George VI and Queen Elizabeth Stakes and had missed some work due to his skin's being too tender to tolerate a saddle. This was not originally of much concern as O'Brien had not planned to race him again until two months later in the Prix de l'Arc de Triomphe. Even when the schedule was changed to include the St. Leger, few worried about the work Nijinsky had missed, so superior to his potential rivals had he proven.

Nijinsky did win the St. Leger easily despite the fact that he was probably not fully fit. But Lester Piggott, in a distant echo of Tesio's comments regarding Nearco's staying ability, later expressed the opinion that the fourteen-furlong-plus distance of the St. Leger was really farther than Nijinsky truly stayed and had taken a good deal out of him. Vincent O'Brien recorded that Nijinsky lost thirty pounds during the race.

Nijinsky had also shown increasing signs that his high-strung nerves were feeling the strain of racing. He had lathered up badly before the Irish Derby and was totally unprepared when he was all but mobbed in the walking ring prior to the Arc. By the time he reached the start for the Arc, he was lathered and quivering, expending much-needed energy far too soon. It cost him dearly, for at the race's finish he just failed to stand off the French champion three-year-old, Sassafras. His normal acceleration was nowhere to be seen, and he was exhausted following the race as he had never been before.

The Arc had originally been slated as Nijinsky's last race, but Charles Engelhard could not bear the thought of his champion leaving racing with a loss. Accordingly, Nijinsky was entered for the ten-furlong Champion Stakes at Newmarket two weeks later. The effort was futile. Although Nijinsky looked splendid in the walking ring, he had probably not recovered from the draining effort in the Arc, and he became visibly frayed under the shouting and applause that followed him from the walking ring to the course. Once again, he lacked his usual turn of foot and could not catch front-running Lorenzaccio, who beat him a length and a half.

That was it for Nijinsky. As provided for in the terms of his syndication, he was sent to Claiborne Farm in Kentucky with a record of eleven wins and two seconds from thirteen starts and the title of English Horse of the Year for 1970. (It was at this time that his name was changed to "Nijinsky II," as there was already a horse registered in the United States under the name of Nijinsky.) A few months later, in March 1971, Charles Engelhard died.

******

Nijinsky was one of only four stakes winners from Northern Dancer's second crop but was not the only champion, for the crop also contained Fanfreluche. A smallish bay filly with a temperament reminiscent of Canterbury Pilgrim, Fanfreluche emulated her sire by winning Horse of the Year honors at three in Canada as well as becoming Northern Dancer's first American champion (she was co-champion three-year-old filly with Office Queen, whom she had defeated in the Alabama Stakes).

As good as she was on the racetrack, Fanfreluche was even better as a broodmare. Five of her eighteen foals became stakes winners, and her first-born, L'Enjoleur (by Buckpasser), continued the legacy of his dam and maternal grandsire by becoming a Canadian Horse of the Year. Another son, Medaille d'Or (by Secretariat), was a Canadian juvenile champion, and a daughter, La Voyageuse (by Tentam), won Canadian titles as champion three-year-old filly, handicap mare, and sprinter. The combined exploits of her progeny earned Fanfreluche honors as Canada's Broodmare of the Year in 1978.

Fanfreluche was also the subject of a bizarre crime. Stolen from Claiborne Farm in June 1977 while in foal to Secretariat, she vanished for five and a half months. Nothing was ever heard from the horsenapper(s); popular speculation held that they might have been Quebec separatists with a grudge against Fanfreluche's owner, Jean-Louis Lévesque, who was a staunch supporter of Canadian unity despite being Quebec-born. (Later, a Kentuckian named William Michael McCandless was arrested and convicted for the crime, but he never disclosed his motive.) Aside from ransom, a thief could not have hoped to realize any profit from the mare herself or from her unborn foal; as Claiborne president Seth Hancock put it, without the appropriate papers, she was only "a bay mare in foal to a chestnut stallion."

Improbably, Fanfreluche turned up alive at a farm near Tompkinsville, Kentucky. The farm owner, Larry McPherson, had no idea who the mare was; she had been brought to him by a neighbor who found her running loose along a nearby back road. McPherson had christened her "Brandy" and had been letting his wife use the mare as a riding horse. Not only was Fanfreluche actually in fairly good condition, but she was still in foal. A few months later, safely back at Claiborne, she gave birth to a healthy colt, who was appropriately named Sain Et Sauf — French for "safe and sound."

Although Sain Et Sauf never amounted to much, Fanfreluche produced his full brother, Breeders' Futurity (gr. II) winner D'Accord, the following year (1979). D'Accord, who was his dam's last stakes winner, and L'Enjoleur became useful regional sires in New York and Ohio, respectively, and Medaille d'Or gained a unique place of his own by managing to continue the male line of Secretariat through his son Tour d'Or. A leading regional sire in Florida, Tour d'Or died in early 2005 without a worthy successor.

Fanfreluche was named Canada's Broodmare of the Year in 1978, and her daughters have done their part to carry on her name. Her descendants include the top-level racehorses Holy Roman Emperor, Erupt, Aube Indienne, Combatant, and Sherwood Forest; the champion Argentine sire Lode; and the champion Australian sires Flying Spur and Encosta de Lago.

******

The year 1970 proved excellent for Northern Dancer, for in addition to the titles won by Nijinsky and Fanfreluche, Dance Act, a chestnut gelding out of *Queen's Statute, became the second champion from Northern Dancer's first crop by being crowned Canada's champion handicap male, a title he would repeat in 1971. Yet another champion emerged in 1970, this one from Northern Dancer's third crop as Minsky, a full brother to Nijinsky, was named champion two-year-old male in Ireland.

By this time, Northern Dancer was no longer in Canada. In 1963 Taylor had established a new division of Windfields on seven hundred acres near Chesapeake City, Maryland. The new farm was just across the road from Mrs. Richard C. du Pont's Woodstock Farm, where Nearctic stood from 1967 until his death in 1973 as the property of a syndicate headed by Taylor and Mrs. du Pont. Taylor apparently began with the intention of using the new Windfields division solely as a training center but, as was usual with Taylor, things had a way of expanding beyond the original plans. In 1968, a stallion barn with all the necessary amenities was added, and Northern Dancer was moved there in December of the same year.

Ostensibly, the move was to improve the horse's accessibility to the best mares, but in truth, the drive from Kentucky to Maryland was little if any shorter than the drive to Oshawa, Canada, and necessitated a trip across the Appalachian Mountains to boot — not the easiest of hauls with a loaded horse trailer, though the trip grew easier as the American interstate highway system continued to improve and expand. The true reason for the move may have had more to do with the fact that Maryland offered substantial tax incentives for the Thoroughbred breeding industry as well as the opportunity to train Northern Dancer's progeny right at the farm, which could not be done at the National Stud Farm. Taylor felt that training at the farm rather than at the track would be beneficial for his young horses, and the tax breaks surely appealed to his business sense. Besides, he simply liked building new things.

(As it turned out, the training center never worked out as well as planned and was phased out. By the early 1980s, Windfields' Maryland division had expanded to some 2,600 acres and encompassed two major sections: the eight-hundred-acre Maryland Stallion Station, where the Windfields stallions lived and visiting mares were boarded, and Windfields Farm Maryland, where Taylor's own mares were kept and the yearlings destined for the sales ring were prepped.)

In the meantime, the sons and daughters of Northern Dancer kept right on running. Lauries Dancer was Canada's champion three-year-old filly and Horse of the Year in 1971, and a third member of the Dancer's first crop became a champion that year when One for All earned honors as Canada's champion grass horse by winning the Canadian International Championship and the Niagara Handicap. Small wonder Northern Dancer's stud fee had risen from the original $10,000 to $15,000 for his first season in Maryland, then to $25,000 live foal for 1971. Years later those rates would be considered cheap indeed.

******

In 1970 a Northern Dancer colt out of the good race mare Goofed was being offered at the Newmarket yearling sale — the youngster's second trip through the sales ring, as he had earlier brought $35,000 at the 1969 Keeneland November mixed sale. Almost a replica of his sire, he was a stocky bay with a blaze face. But if anything, he was even smaller than Northern Dancer, and Vincent O'Brien, who had enjoyed such success with Nijinsky, was among the potential buyers and agents to bypass the little colt. After all, Nijinsky had been tall and rangy, not in the least like his sire in physique; perhaps he had been atypical of his sire in his ability, as well. The examples of Canterbury Pilgrim, Selene, and Hyperion notwithstanding, the prejudice against small horses remained strong, and this colt was *small*.

Champion French trainer Alec Head was one of the few who saw past the colt's size to his excellent balance and symmetry. The trainer bought the little bay for 15,000 guineas — the equivalent of $37,800 — on behalf of Madame Pierre Wertheimer. The colt was given the name Lyphard, a spelling variation on the name of the ballet dancer Serge Lifar.

Winner of the Prix Herod at two, Lyphard showed enough in the spring of his three-year-old season to be among the favorites for the 1972 Derby Stakes but was undone at Tattenham Corner, the bend into the final straight, where he ran extremely wide and lost a dozen lengths or more. Head attributed the colt's behavior to an undescended testicle, which caused pain when the colt was asked to turn left at speed. (The testicle later descended to the normal position in the scrotum by the time Lyphard went to stud, justifying Head's decision not to have it surgically removed.)

Lyphard recovered from the debacle at Epsom to win the seven-furlong Prix de la Foret and one-mile Prix Jacques le Marois, both against older runners. He also ran second to Sallust in the Prix du Moulin de Longchamp at a mile, establishing himself as one of the best milers of his time. His exploits helped break down the European prejudice against small horses — at least when those horses were sired by Northern Dancer — although lingering doubts remained as to whether "typical" sons and daughters of Northern Dancer could succeed at the distances of the great European Classic races.

Lyphard was followed in Europe by Northern Taste, a small blaze-faced chestnut who was out of Nearctic's half sister Lady Victoria (by Victoria Park) and was, thus, closely inbred to *Lady Angela. Winner of two group III events as a juvenile in France, Northern Taste emulated Lyphard by winning the Prix de la Foret (Fr-I) as a three-year-old in 1974. Unlike Lyphard, who won at up to about ten and a half furlongs, Northern Taste did not stay beyond a mile but was a determined runner within that distance despite his small stature. He went to stud in Japan after the conclusion of his racing career and became one of the greatest sires in that nation's history, leading the Japanese sire list ten times and gaining a great reputation as a broodmare sire as well.

Northern Dancer sired seven stakes winners from his 1972 crop, headed by 1974 Prix Morny (Fr-I) winner Broadway Dancer and 1976 Matchmaker Stakes (gr. IT) winner Dancers Countess. Six more stakes winners emerged from the 1973 crop, but they were quickly overshadowed by the 1974 crop, one of the best of Northern Dancer's career. Ten stakes winners emerged from that crop, the most since the Dancer's initial crop in 1966, and among them was The Minstrel, whose feats would destroy any lingering prejudice against "the little Dancers" and set off an international bidding war for the progeny of Northern Dancer.

Small and stocky like his sire, The Minstrel had to overcome another prejudice as well. A golden chestnut, he was what English horsemen commonly call "flashy," with a broad white blaze and four white stockings. In popular lore, such horses were suspected of lacking courage — "all show and no substance," as the saying goes — but The Minstrel was about to prove that, in his case at least, the old saw did not apply.

Vincent O'Brien came to the 1975 Keeneland July select yearling sale specifically to buy The Minstrel for the partnership of Robert Sangster and

John Magnier but had to work hard to sell himself on the animal's physical appearance: "I was definitely concerned about his height," he later admitted. The pedigree was another story, for the colt's dam Fleur was a Victoria Park half sister to Nijinsky. Whatever his misgivings, O'Brien ended up paying $200,000 for the colt, one of the sale's higher prices. It would prove a bargain.

Though he was closely related to Nijinsky — in horsemen's terminology, the two animals were three-parts or three-quarters brothers — The Minstrel proved as unlike Nijinsky in temperament as he was in appearance. He was an eager worker and determined to get to the front of every set he worked with. There were no bouts of rearing, no finickiness about food. And if he lacked Nijinsky's splendid ease of motion, he still had plenty of talent, going unbeaten in three starts at two. His four-length victory over Saros in the 1976 Dewhurst Stakes (Eng-I) earned him a rating of eight stone, thirteen pounds (125 pounds) on the English Free Handicap, eight pounds below champion J. O. Tobin.

The following year, The Minstrel set the seal on Northern Dancer's status as a Classic sire in emphatic fashion. Although he lost both the Two Thousand Guineas and the Irish Two Thousand Guineas — the latter a race he might have won had he not been impeded during the running — he captured the Derby Stakes by a neck over Hot Grove after a punishing drive over the last two furlongs. The Irish Sweeps Derby followed in somewhat easier fashion, and then came the King George VI and Queen Elizabeth Diamond Stakes (Eng-I). This time, the son of Northern Dancer had the lead coming down the homestretch and had to dig down for everything he had to stave off five-year-old Orange Bay. In a truly lion-hearted effort, The Minstrel shoved his blazed face past the finish pole just in front of his equally game rival.

The Minstrel was originally slated to end his career in the 1977 Prix de l'Arc de Triomphe (Fr-I), where he would have faced O'Brien's other star trainee, Alleged. Circumstances, however, intervened. (Alleged would go on to win the race and in 1978 would win the Arc again, becoming one of only six horses to win the Arc twice up to that time.) E.P. Taylor, seeing in The Minstrel the heir apparent to Northern Dancer, had been a driving force in the colt's syndication for nine million dollars — a world record for a

Thoroughbred stallion — shortly after the King George VI and Queen Elizabeth Diamond Stakes, buying eighteen of the thirty-six shares himself. An outbreak of contagious equine metritis in the United Kingdom and France threatened to shut down all importations of European-based horses to the United States, and The Minstrel ended up being hustled aboard an airplane and shipped to Maryland, his racing career over. The Minstrel arrived just prior to the September 9 embargo placed by the United States government on shipments of horses from Europe until the outbreak had run its course.

Taylor may have hoped that The Minstrel would assume his sire's mantle as his greatest successor, but he was to be disappointed. Although The Minstrel did very well at stud, getting more than 11 percent stakes winners from foals, he was not the equal of Nijinsky or Lyphard, and overall his fillies were more impressive than his colts. Nor did he outlive his sire, dying from complications of laminitis on September 3, 1990. His male line was dogged by equal ill-luck. Champions L'Emigrant and Bakharoff proved disappointing as sires, as did Breeders' Cup Mile (gr. IT) winner Opening Verse. The Minstrel's branch of the Northern Dancer sire line fared better in Brazil, where his stakes-placed sons Midnight Tiger and Minstrel Glory both ranked among the leading sires.

For a brief time, it appeared as if the male line of The Minstrel could be sustained in the Northern Hemisphere through his group/grade I-winning son Palace Music, whose son Cigar was the American Horse of the Year in 1995 and 1996. A mediocre runner on grass, Cigar blossomed when switched to the dirt late in his four-year-old season and launched a sixteen-race win streak that tied the modern North American record for consecutive victories established by the great Citation. (The record was later tied by the Louisiana-based filly Hallowed Dreams.) Cigar's streak included ten grade I events (the top rating assigned to races in North America), including the 1995 Breeders' Cup Classic, and he also won the 1996 Dubai World Cup. Although he lost three of his last four races, he was never disgraced in any of them against top competition and went to stud as one of the hottest prospects in years.

But a great stud career was not to be; Cigar proved completely and irreversibly sterile. From 1999 until his death in 2014, he resided at the

Rising Star

Kentucky Horse Park's Hall of Champions, a living memorial to the greatness passed down by one of Northern Dancer's gamest sons.

******

The Minstrel marked a turning point in Northern Dancer's stud career, based as much on who his connections were as on his own accomplishments. The second Derby winner sired by Northern Dancer, The Minstrel had sold Vincent O'Brien on the merits of the Dancer's progeny regardless of shape or size. Equally important, he had also convinced Robert Sangster.

Heir to the Vernons football pools fortune, Sangster had money, a love of fine horses, and a steely-eyed determination to own whatever horseflesh caught his fancy. And the Northern Dancers had caught his fancy in a major way. Over the next decade, he would lead a European charge into the American bloodstock market that would send prices for well-bred, well-conformed American youngsters into the same dizzying upward spiral that Canada had experienced a few years earlier thanks to E.P. Taylor and Northern Dancer — only on a nearly unimaginable scale.

Northern Dancer didn't know it, but he was about to become the most valuable commodity in the world.

Nearctic, sire of Northern
Dancer, as a racehorse (bottom)
and as a stallion (below).
Northern Dancer's dam,
Natalma (right), as a yearling.

E.P. Taylor (above, right) with trainer Horatio Luro; Windfields racing manager Joe Thomas (left); and Windfields trainer Pete McCann (below).

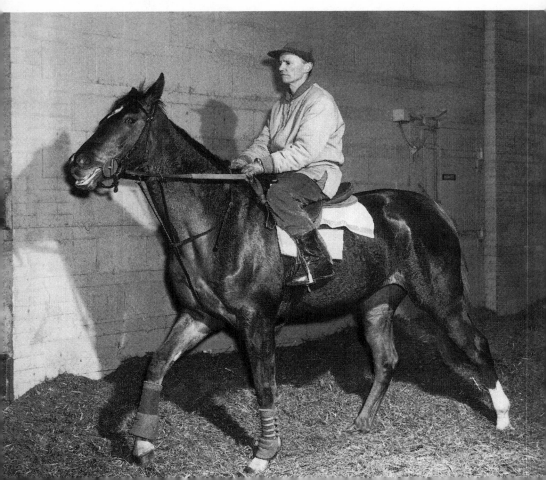

Northern Dancer wins the Remsen to cap his two-year-old season (bottom). On the Kentucky Derby trail, the Dancer takes the Flamingo (below) and Florida Derby (right) before heading to Kentucky.

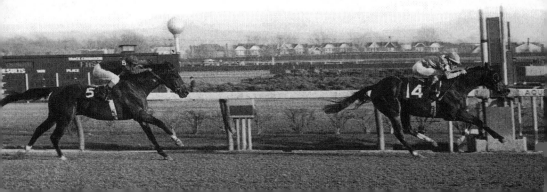

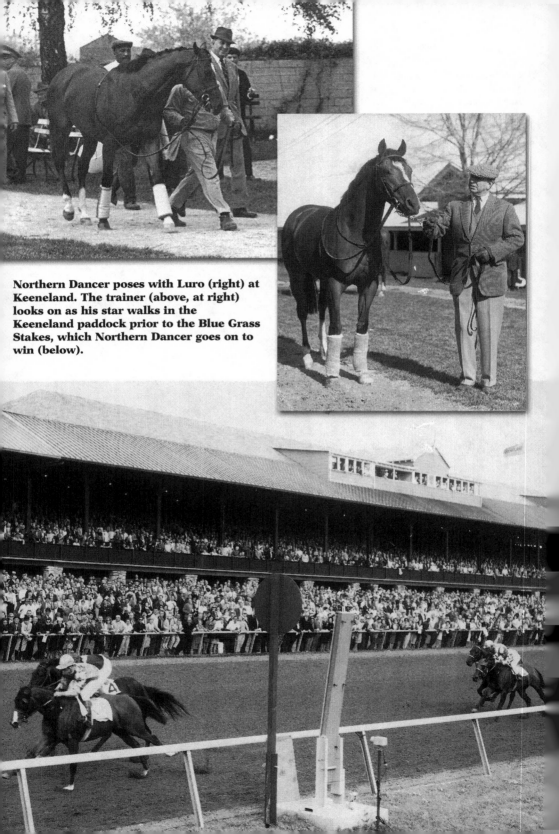

Northern Dancer poses with Luro (right) at Keeneland. The trainer (above, at right) looks on as his star walks in the Keeneland paddock prior to the Blue Grass Stakes, which Northern Dancer goes on to win (below).

Northern Dancer (above, inside) holds off Hill Rise to win the Kentucky Derby, then is led into the winner's circle by Taylor.

The Taylors and Luro greet Bill
Hartack and Northern Dancer
in the Pimlico winner's circle
(right) after the Canadian colt
wins the Preakness (below).
After a loss in the Belmont,
Northern Dancer returns home
to win the Queen's Plate
(above).

After retiring from racing, Northern Dancer enters stud at Windfields Farm in Canada and is later moved to the Windfields Maryland division.

Northern Dancer parades at Windfields Maryland.

Nijinsky II, as a yearling at the suburban Toronto division that was part of Windfields at the time (below), and winning the 1970 Epsom Derby (above).

Lyphard (above, outside), winning the 1972 Prix Jacques le Marois, and (below) at stud in 1988 at Gainesway Farm in Kentucky.

Nureyev, selling as a yearling for $1.3 million at the 1978 Keeneland July sale (below), and as a stallion in 1994 at Walmac International in Kentucky.

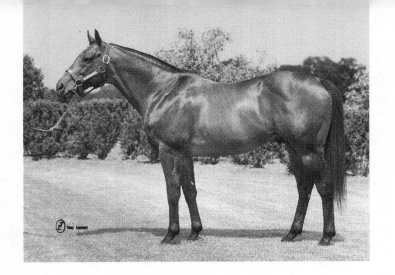

Dixieland Band (above) and Vice Regent (below) are both members of the "century club" of stallions to sire a hundred stakes winners or more. Vice Regent's son, Deputy Minister (right), is a two-time U.S. leading sire.

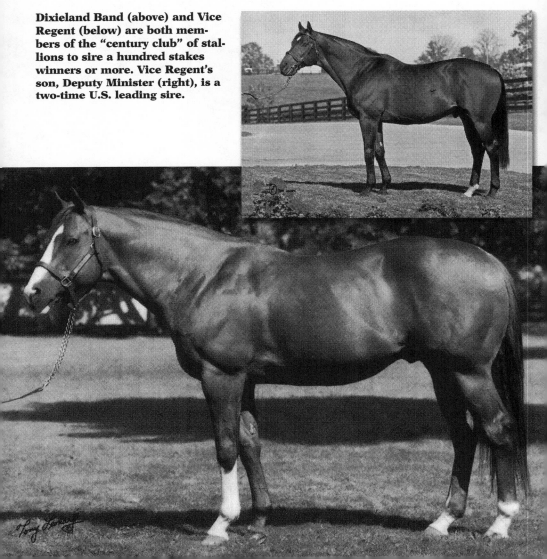

Dominant father-son duos: Danzig (above) and his son, Danehill (right), and Storm Bird (below) and his son, Storm Cat (below, right).

Sadler's Wells, winning the 1984 Irish Two Thousand Guineas (above), and as a perennial leading sire at Coolmore in Ireland.

Northern Dancer's outstanding daughters include Danseur Fabuleux (above), the dam of champions Arazi and Noverre, and Dance Number (below), a stakes winner and dam of champion Rhythm.

More of Northern Dancer's top
daughters: Fanfreluche (left),
a Canadian Horse of the Year
and outstanding producer;
Northernette (below, on outside),
a full sister to Storm Bird and a
Canadian champion racehorse
and stakes producer; and
Broadway Dancer (bottom),
a champion in France.

King of the World

Now comfortably middle-aged, Northern Dancer had long since settled into a routine in his Maryland home. He had no way of know-
ing about the continued successes of his progeny. Not only had
The Minstrel been crowned 1977 Horse of the Year in both England and
Ireland, but Try My Best had been named champion two-year-old in both
countries; in Canada, the three-year-old championships went to
Northernette (female) and Dance in Time (male).

As if racing success were not enough, Northern Dancer's sons were also
beginning to show the ability to pass the magic on. Lyphard, whose daughter Durtal had gotten him off to a fine start by being crowned 1976 English
champion juvenile filly, led the French general sire list in 1978; in that year,
his daughters Reine de Saba and Dancing Maid were champions in France
and England, respectively.

Lyphard was in Kentucky by then; like The Minstrel, he had been sent to
the United States just ahead of the equine metritis ban. But the foals he had
sired in France prior to his departure were still running. In 1979 his daughter Three Troikas won the Prix de l'Arc de Triomphe (Fr-I), earning Horse
of the Year honors in France. In the same year Lyphard's Irish-bred son
Monteverdi became his first champion colt, being named champion two-
year-old male in both England and Ireland after winning the Dewhurst
Stakes (Eng-I) and the National Stakes (Ire-II).

Nijinsky was equally impressive in Europe, though he himself was based
in Kentucky. His first crop contained Green Dancer, who became his sire's

first Classic winner by taking the 1975 Poule d'Essai des Poulains (French Two Thousand Guineas). His daughter Cherry Hinton was named 1977 champion two-year-old filly in England, and in 1978 the stallion had another top-class son in Ile de Bourbon, whose victory in that year's King George VI and Queen Elizabeth Diamond Stakes (Eng-I) lifted him to the three-year-old male championship in England. Niniski followed in 1979, winning that year's Irish St. Leger and Prix Royal-Oak (French St. Leger); in the same year, Princesse Lida won the Prix de la Salamandre (Fr-I) and with it a title as France's champion juvenile filly. To crown all, Golden Fleece followed in his sire's footsteps by taking the 1982 Derby Stakes in an impressive performance.

The successes of Lyphard and Nijinsky were, to some extent, expected; both were first-rate racehorses out of mares that excelled both on the track and in the paddocks, and both received books of high-class mates to start their stud careers. The Minstrel, too, benefited from a fine harem and promptly began producing the expected results, getting 1983 Poule d'Essai des Poulains winner L'Emigrant in his second crop. What was less expected was that Northern Dancer's lesser sons would also begin proving themselves as sires.

The beautiful Viceregal, alas, was not one of them. After disappointing in Canada, he was sold to France and eventually wound up in Japan, where his son Gold City was the leading Japanese juvenile of 1986. Viceregal was not a complete failure by any means: his French-bred daughter Kaiserblume was 1982 champion three-year-old filly in Germany; his son Esclavo, also sired during Viceregal's stay in France, was the 1978 champion German juvenile; and several of his Canadian daughters turned out to be good producers. But Viceregal's career paled beside that of Vice Regent, the full brother that E.P. Taylor had valued at $100,000 against $60,000 for Nijinsky.

Plagued by injury during his brief racing career, Vice Regent was no Nijinsky on the track. Nonetheless, he was given a chance at stud in Canada due to his brother's accomplishments. He made the most of it. Standing his first season in 1972, he sired Canadian champion older mare Christy's Mount and stakes winners Kirkfield Park and Military Bearing from his first small crop. His third crop contained 1978 Queen's Plate winner Regal

Embrace, and by then he was on his way as a perennial leading Canadian sire. And in 1981 he proved he could sire horses capable of winning on the highest levels in North America when his son Deputy Minister became both Canadian Horse of the Year and American champion two-year-old male, the colt's victories including the grade I Young America Stakes and Laurel Futurity. Vice Regent eventually begot 105 stakes winners from 685 named foals, ranking him among Northern Dancer's best sons at stud.

Vice Regent died in 1995, but Deputy Minister carried on ably until his death in 2004, leading the American general sire list in 1997 and 1998. His son Touch Gold, who won the 1997 Belmont Stakes, sired the first-class filly Composure and the crack sprinting colt Midas Eyes, both grade I winners, in his first crop. Awesome Again, whose upset victory in the 1998 Breeders' Cup Classic (gr. I) capped an unbeaten season and gave Deputy Minister the sire championship that year, has also sired two first-class horses in 2004 American Horse of the Year Ghoszapper, who entered stud in 2006, and Toccet, a brilliant juvenile who ranked second only to unbeaten Vindication among American juveniles of 2002 after winning the Champagne Stakes (gr. I) and the Hollywood Futurity (gr. I).

Deputy Minister's best sire son was Silver Deputy, who showed marked ability in two starts in Canada before being forced into retirement by injury. The sire of two-time Canadian champion filly Deputy Jane West in his first crop, Silver Deputy later begot Canadian champions Scotzanna, Deputy Inxs, Archers Bay, Poetically, and Larkwhistle as well as two-time champion American filly Silverbulletday. The sire of eighty-eight stakes winners, he also sired the dams of two-time American champion female sprinter Groupie Doll and two-time Argentine champion sire Roman Ruler.

Another interesting Deputy Minister son is Dehere, the champion American juvenile of 1993. After getting off to a good but not spectacular start as a shuttle sire in the United States and Australia, the horse was sold to Japan in 1999. (He continued to shuttle to Australia, where he has sired several group I winners including champion filly Belle Du Jour.) Dehere was not an outstanding success in Japan, but the American-bred offspring that reached racing age in his absence included the popular filly Take Charge Lady, winner of the Spinster Stakes (gr. I) in 2002 and 2003. Later a Broodmare of the Year, Take Charge Lady helped lift Dehere to second on the American general sire list in 2002, and the horse was repatriated to Ashford Stud in Kentucky in late 2005. He died in 2014, having sired eighty stakes winners.

Northfields was another of Northern Dancer's lesser sons who made a name for himself by the early 1980s. Roughly of grade II class as a racehorse, the half brother to champion European miler Habitat sired 1976 Irish Two Thousand Guineas winner Northern Treasure and English group III winner Oats in his first crop and the following year, he had the multiple group winners Nanticious and North Stoke. Northjet emerged as France's champion miler in 1981, and No Pass No Sale became his sire's second Classic winner by capturing the 1985 Poule d'Essai des Poulains. Northfields was sold to South Africa in 1983 for $2.1 million, but the daughters he left behind would make him the leading English broodmare sire of 1992.

Horsemen were quickly learning that no son of Northern Dancer could be written off at stud until tried. Northern Jove, a minor stakes winner, became a useful sire whose career was punctuated by grade I winners Candy Eclair (1978 U.S. champion two-year-old filly), Wings of Jove, Northern Tempest, Equalize, and Jovial (GB). Barachois, a minor stakes winner but a full brother to Fanfreluche, sired a fair number of small stakes winners and the hardy gelding Win, a two-time grade I winner in the mid-1980s. Northern Taste (*see Chapter 11*) became the most successful sire ever seen in Japan until the advent of Sunday Silence, who benefited greatly by being mated to Northern Taste's daughters. Be My Guest, a group II winner but rated well below the best European runners of his generation, became England's champion sire in 1982, when he was represented by Irish Derby winner Assert and One Thousand Guineas winner On the House, both members of his first crop. He later sired Go and Go (Ire), winner of the 1990 Belmont Stakes. Multiple grade II winner Dance Spell died young but nonetheless got six stakes winners including 1982 Alabama Stakes (gr. I) winner Broom Dance. Unraced Staff Writer, a useful regional sire, got into the act by siring Timely Writer, winner of four grade I stakes races in 1981–1982.

As if all this were not enough, Northern Dancer's runners kept coming. White Star Line ranked among the best American sophomore fillies of 1978 with wins in the Kentucky Oaks, Delaware Oaks, and Alabama Stakes, all grade I events. Northern Baby took down the 1979 Champion Stakes (Eng-I). And Storm Bird, a $1-million sales yearling, emulated Try My Best by becoming the champion juvenile in England and Ireland in 1980, though a planned start in the Two Thousand Guineas evaporated after a disgruntled Ballydoyle employee chopped off the hair from Storm Bird's mane and tail. Traumatized by the bizarre attack, Storm Bird became ill and never recovered his two-year-old form, finishing unplaced in his only start at three. Syndicated for a record $30 million after his two-year-old season, Storm Bird followed Nijinsky, Lyphard, and The Minstrel to stud in the United States.

******

Northern Dancer's magic combination of bequeathing both racing ability and sire power was irresistible in the sales ring, where his sons and grandsons were fueling an unprecedented boom in yearling sale prices. In 1967, when the first Northern Dancer yearlings had come to auction (both public and Taylor's pre-priced sale), seven had sold for a total of $268,500, averaging $38,357. In 1978 a single Northern Dancer colt sold for more than four times the amount that all seven 1967 Northern Dancer sales yearlings had brought put together. The colt's name was Nureyev, and the $1.3 million that Greek shipping magnate Stavros Niarchos paid for him at the Keeneland July sale (outbidding — who else? — Robert Sangster) made this son of Northern Dancer the second most expensive yearling bought at public auction up to that time. Only Canadian Bound, a 1975 son of Secretariat out of the stakes-winning mare Charming Alibi, had sold for more — he had brought $1.5 million — and he had proven a complete disappointment, failing to win in four starts before going on to what would be an equally disappointing stud career.

Nureyev, however, did not disappoint, though he started only three times. His sole start at two, a win in the Prix Thomas Bryon (Fr-III), was sufficiently impressive to rank him second among French juveniles. The following year the colt won the Prix Djebel easily and then scored a neck victory over Known Fact in the Two Thousand Guineas, only to be disqualified for

interference with third-place finisher Posse. Although Nureyev was officially unplaced as a result of the stewards' decision, the fact remains that
he finished ahead of two first-class milers; Known Fact later took the
measure of the older champion Kris in the Queen Elizabeth II Stakes (Eng-
II) and was highweighted among milers in England that year, while Posse
also defeated older males in taking the Sussex Stakes (Eng-I).

Although Nureyev came out of the Guineas sound enough, he came down
with a minor illness that prevented him from being considered for any of
the later Classics and was eventually retired without having started again.
So impressive had he been in his brief career, however, that he was crowned
champion miler in France off his lone official victory. He was syndicated for
a reported $14.2 million, an astounding sum for a horse that was not offi-
cially a Classic winner.

Meanwhile, the sales figures for Northern Dancer yearlings continued to
increase, along with the prices for yearlings by his best sons. In 1979 the
North American yearling market topped its previous highest gross by more
than $38 million, and Northern Dancer's sales yearlings averaged $327,813;
that same year, Nijinsky's thirteen sales yearlings averaged $390,769. The
next year Northern Dancer's thirteen sales yearlings averaged $537,308,
while a colt by his son Lyphard went for a record $1.7 million. (Stavros
Niarchos, who bought the Lyphard colt, was not as lucky with this purchase
as with Nureyev; the colt, named Lichine, did become a minor stakes winner but made no great mark as a sire in France and was transferred to
Spain after the 1993 breeding season.)

A triangle of factors was driving the boom in auction prices. One, of
course, was Northern Dancer himself. One was Robert Sangster, whose
success with The Minstrel had fueled a seemingly bottomless appetite for
Northern Dancer yearlings and whose wealth seemed nearly unlimited.
And one was a quiet man with a passionate love of good racehorses and
wealth even greater than Sangster's: Sheikh Mohammed bin Rashid al
Maktoum, the third son of the ruler of oil-rich Dubai.

Two exceptional Northern Dancer colts headed almost everyone's short
lists at the 1981 Keeneland July sale. One was out of 1970 Canadian Oaks
winner South Ocean and, thus, a full brother to Storm Bird; the other was
the first foal of 1977 Kentucky Oaks (gr. II) winner Sweet Alliance. The

lines were drawn for the first of many battles between Sangster and his partners and associates and the newly aggressive oil money from the Middle East.

The South Ocean colt went first, and the bidding rapidly developed into a two-party skirmish between the Sangster consortium and Sheikh Mohammed. It must have been a new experience for Sangster, who was accustomed to running off much of the competition when it became known that he had his sights set on a particular horse; very few people had the wealth to seriously challenge his bidding power, and still fewer had the determination to outduel him. But in the quiet sheikh from Dubai, Sangster had met his match. Every bid he made was countered without hesitation, and both the excitement in the sales pavilion and the tension between the opponents mounted as the price soared up past one million dollars, two million, three million. The duel ended only after the price reached a new record: $3.5 million, more than twice the record set with Lichine the year before. Sangster and associates had won, or perhaps lost, for the colt, named Ballydoyle, was a huge disappointment as a racehorse and no better as a sire. The one-time $3.5 million yearling was last recorded by The Jockey Club as covering mares in 2000 in California at a fee of $1,000.

(Sangster fared much better with another Northern Dancer colt of 1980, Lomond. A half brother to 1977 American Triple Crown winner Seattle Slew, Lomond was purchased privately by Sangster for $1.5 million from breeders Warner L. Jones, William Farish, and W.S. Kilroy. After winning the 1983 Two Thousand Guineas, Lomond enjoyed a useful stud career during which he sired the 1988 Irish St. Leger winner Dark Lomond and the 1992 Irish One Thousand Guineas winner Marling.)

Having secured his primary target, Sangster was apparently not as interested in the Sweet Alliance colt, which went to Sheikh Mohammed for $3.3 million as the Arab prince outdueled American breeder William Farish. Two years later Sheikh Mohammed had the satisfaction of seeing this colt, Shareef Dancer, win the Irish Derby and the King Edward VII Stakes (Eng-II) on the way to being named champion three-year-old male in both England and Ireland. Unfortunately, Shareef Dancer proved one of the more disappointing sires among Northern Dancer's good sons, but he did get an excellent filly in Possessive Dancer, winner of the 1991 Oaks d'Italia and Irish Oaks. He also sired Italian champion juvenile Glory of Dancer, later a sire in India, and 1996 Premio Parioli (Italian Two Thousand Guineas) winner Dancer Mitral.

Shareef Dancer's most important producing daughter was group II winner Colorado Dancer (Ire), the dam of Dubai Millenium. Considered the horse of a lifetime by owner Sheikh Mohammed, Dubai Millennium won nine of his ten starts including the 1999 Prix Jacques le Marois (Fr-I) and Queen Elizabeth II Stakes (Eng-I) and the 2000 Dubai World Cup (UAE-I) and Prince of Wales's Stakes (Eng-I). European champion miler at three and both European champion older male and Horse of the Year in the United Arab Emirates, Dubai Millenium died of grass sickness midway through his first breeding season. Fifty-six foals were produced from his only crop, among them the 2005 Irish Two Thousand Guineas winner and top European sire Dubawi, whose second dam is a daughter of Lyphard's great son Dancing Brave.

******

A man has to be a pretty fair gambler to give $3.5 million for an untried yearling that may prove either a champion or a cull. But such a risky investment paled beside the gamble proposed by French veterinarian Laslo Urban in the fall of 1981. Acting on behalf of a European syndicate, Dr. Laslo tendered a bid of $40 million for Northern Dancer himself. Ounce for ounce, this placed Northern Dancer's value as higher than that of gold or platinum.

At first glance, this might not seem a gamble at all; the horse was the world's foremost sire and in good health. But Northern Dancer was no longer young. At twenty years old — he would be twenty-one before the next breeding season commenced — he was still both virile and fertile, but how long could he continue? Most Thoroughbred stallions either die or are pensioned due to declining fertility in their early to mid-twenties.

With Edward Taylor having been incapacitated by a stroke the preceding year, it fell to his son Charles Taylor to handle the situation. Charles found Urban's proposal a delicate one because of his family's personal attachment to Northern Dancer; neither he, his mother, nor Joe Thomas — by now a trusted family friend as well as an employee — were in favor of selling, both because of their feelings about the horse and because of their concern about how well the aging stallion could adapt to a change of venue. As the younger Taylor contacted syndicate members and apprised them of the situation, however, he was surprised to find that a number of them were seriously interested in the offer, which after all represented a handsome profit on shares that had originally cost $75,000 each; the Urban offer effectively raised Northern Dancer's value per share to $1.25 million.

In the end, Windfields management decided to remain neutral regarding its nine shares in the horse. If the twenty-three other shareholders wished to sell, they would go along, but they would not actively encourage the sale.

Eighteen shareholders voted for the sale; five voted against, and after the votes were taken, Windfields threw in its nine votes with those opposed. Taylor wired back to Urban that Northern Dancer *in toto* was not for sale, but provided the names and addresses of shareholders who had indicated they were willing to sell. In theory, Urban and his syndicate could have purchased the available shares, provided the offer for any given share was not matched by an existing shareholder. But once it became apparent that there was no way to purchase all of Northern Dancer, the Europeans backed away. Urban's only comment to the press was that he did not understand how the offer could have been refused.

Those who knew Northern Dancer knew how.

******

As generous as $40 million might seem for a twenty-year-old stallion, events were to prove that the offer was probably far below the horse's real value, which continued to appreciate at an incredible rate. Northern Dancer's eleven 1981 sales yearlings averaged $1.26 million; at the end of that year, two hundred of his progeny had generated an aggregate of more than $42 million in the sales ring. (Roughly half of Northern Dancer's 645 foals eventually went through the auction ring; the other half were either retained by their breeders or sold privately.)

The rise in Northern Dancer's stud fee paralleled the cost of his youngsters. Since his syndication in 1970, few breeding rights had been available on the open market, but by 1982 Windfields was regularly asking — and getting — at least $250,000 for one of the handful of breeding rights it sold annually, with no guarantee that the service would actually produce a foal; if Northern Dancer covered the mare, the contract was fulfilled regardless of results. To put the value placed on Northern Dancer's services in perspective, consider that in 1982, only twenty American stallions stood for fees of $100,000 or more, and five of those were Northern Dancer's own sons; another was a grandson.

As Robert Sangster once said, "There are two kinds of horses — Northern Dancers and the rest."

Northern Dancer's 1982 sales yearlings were relatively quiet, averaging "only" $857,188 in the sales ring, less than 70 percent of the previous year's average. But Northern Dancer's wild ride in the American bloodstock market was to get even wilder in 1983, fueled by Shareef Dancer's Irish Derby win and Lomond's victory in the Two Thousand Guineas. Dance Number and Spit Curl added grade I wins to their sire's tally that year. Yet the racetrack performances of Northern Dancer's sons and daughters were overshadowed by events in the sales ring.

My Bupers had not won in thirteen starts, but she was a proven broodmare. Her first foal, My Juliet, had been crowned champion sprinter in the United States in 1976. None of her other foals had reached such a standard, but her 1980 foal by Lyphard, Lyphard's Special, had been a promising juvenile in England (he would go on to win the group III September Stakes). And her 1982 colt by Northern Dancer was exceptionally handsome. Given the prices being paid for virtually anything by Northern Dancer, there was no telling what this colt might fetch at the 1983 Keeneland July sale, but one thing was almost certain: when the bidding ended, he would be owned by either Robert Sangster and his associates or by Sheikh Mohammed of Dubai.

The atmosphere at the Keeneland sales pavilion on July 19, 1983, was electric. Although Keeneland officials had requested that the general public refrain from attending the sale, rumors had run wild and the sales pavilion was packed with spectators anticipating a rare spectacle. When the My Bupers colt was led out, they got all they had anticipated, and perhaps more.

A tense silence gripped the pavilion, broken only by the auctioneer's introduction of the colt and his pedigree. Then the bidding was opened at one million dollars, a sum that would have been nearly unthinkable a decade earlier. For this colt, it was merely a prelude to an all-out war between two of the wealthiest men on earth.

As anticipated, other bidders began dropping out rapidly as the price soared and soared — past four million, past five million. The former world record of $4.25 million, jointly held by sons of Nijinsky II and Northern Dancer, was long gone. At $5.2 million, so were all the bidders other than the two principals. And the price continued to rise.

By six million, the Sangster group was consulting within itself before every bid; they were past their agreed limit. But Sheikh Mohammed stood quietly while his chief bloodstock adviser, Colonel Richard Warden, countered every bid the Sangster group made. Tension mounted in the faces of the Sangster people, yet they refused to give up the fight, even in the face of a growing suspicion that this time, Sheikh Mohammed would not be denied. Eight million … nine million … $9.6 million, offered by Warden.

There was a brief pause. "Ten million," countered Philip Payne-Gallwey, as spokesman for the Sangster group.

The audience sat in stunned silence as the bid registered. A slight delay ensued as the electronic display board was reset; with a limit of seven digits, it could not accommodate an eight-digit bid and had to be set back to zero. When the board was ready, the auctioneer turned back to Sheikh Mohammed. His face remained impassive, but his mind was apparently made up; Warden did not hesitate in continuing to bid on his employer's behalf, upping the ante to $10.2 million.

Sangster wanted to continue. Perhaps the issue was no longer money, or even the colt; the battle of wills may itself have become the object. But he could marshal his group to no more. The auctioneer's hammer came down, and the audience rose to its feet in a spontaneous standing ovation as Sheikh Mohammed signed the purchase ticket.

He had won, but he had also lost. Named Snaafi Dancer, the son of My Bupers would go down as the most expensive complete bust in history, for he never raced and was a failure at stud. It was Northern Dancer who came out the clear winner from one of the most dramatic nights in auction history, for the sale of Snaafi Dancer helped boost Northern Dancer's sales average for the year to $1,768,281, more than double the 1982 figure.

******

Following an effortless win in the 1984 Two Thousand Guineas, El Gran Senor was hailed as the best son of Northern Dancer since Nijinsky II. He was at that time unbeaten in six starts following a juvenile season in which he had emulated Try My Best and Storm Bird as the champion juvenile in both England and Ireland.

Yet he failed in his primary objective, the Derby, and the reason was yet another son of Northern Dancer. El Gran Senor had assumed the lead inside the two-furlong pole and seemed poised to glide to victory when up came Secreto, pounding away as if his life depended on getting home first. He seemed sure to fall short as El Gran Senor, feeling the whip for the first time in his career, quickened his lovely floating stride. But Secreto churned on relentlessly, and when the whip cracked across El Gran Senor's haunches a second and a third time, there was no response; the champion had given everything he had to give, and Secreto just nailed him in the shadow of the finishing post. The official verdict was a short head. So compelling were both colts' performances that the connections of both were accorded the traditional Derby winner's privilege of an invitation to the Royal Box.

El Gran Senor and Secreto went separate ways thereafter, with El Gran Senor redeeming his narrow loss at Epsom by winning the Irish Derby, his last race. Retired to stud as a four-year old, he began his stud career with everything that might be desired for a young stallion: excellent conformation, racing performance of the highest class, impeccable pedigree, and the finest of connections. Unfortunately, he lacked one thing: normal fertility. Yet in spite of his handicap, he became a good stallion until pensioned at the age of nineteen. His best sons were Rodrigo de Triano, winner of the 1992 Two Thousand Guineas and Irish Two Thousand Guineas, and Lit de Justice, the American champion sprinter of 1996.

Neither Rodrigo de Triano nor Lit de Justice has proved a good sire, and El Gran Senor's most important contribution has been through his daughters, headed by his grade I-winning daughter Toussaud. One of only a handful of mares to produce four or more group or grade I winners, Toussaud was named Broodmare of the Year in 2002, the year before her son Empire Maker won the Belmont Stakes.

Secreto did not start again after his Derby upset. At stud, he had only a moderate reputation and was shipped to Japan at age eleven, faring no better there as his only Japanese-bred runner of much note was Tamuro Cherry, generally considered the best Japanese juvenile filly of 2001. His Kentucky-sired offspring included the Italian juvenile filly champions Miss Secreto (1988) and Secrage (1992) and the 1991 Two Thousand Guineas winner Mystiko, who did not prove a successful sire.

Almost unnoticed by comparison with the dramatic performances of El Gran Senor and Secreto were Northern Dancer's third and fourth Classic winners of the year, the Irish Two Thousand Guineas winner Sadler's Wells and the Prix de Diane Hermes winner Northern Trick. Yet their victories, combined with those of El Gran Senor and Secreto, gave Northern Dancer a total of five European Classic wins in one year, a feat that had not been accomplished by a sire since St. Simon swept the five English Classics with Diamond Jubilee, Winifreda, and La Roche in 1900. The incredible series of Classic wins was not lost on bloodstock buyers, who that year paid a total of $46,485,000 for fourteen Northern Dancer yearlings at auction — an average of $3,320,357.

The most expensive of the lot was Imperial Falcon, for whom Robert Sangster and his associates paid $8.25 million. A half brother to 1980 Canadian Horse of the Year Glorious Song and 1983 American champion juvenile Devil's Bag, Imperial Falcon showed promise in Ireland in two starts at three but did not last long enough to show more than that. After a stint at stud in Kentucky, Imperial Falcon began drifting down the stallion ranks and, after several moves, ended up in Michigan. Sheikh Mohammed fared no better; his most expensive purchase that year, a $7.1 million colt named Jareer, won only one of nine starts and likewise proved a stud failure.

******

The year 1984 was the high water mark for Northern Dancer as a commercial sire. The following year twelve Northern Dancer yearlings sold for an average of $1,515,053. Although the demand for Northern Dancer's services was stronger than ever — a single no-guarantee season to the stallion reportedly went for one million dollars in 1985 — the bottom was beginning to drop out of the yearling market. Events such as the spectacular sale of Seattle Dancer, Seattle Slew's half brother by Nijinsky II, who went to Robert Sangster and partners for a record $13.1 million at the 1985 Keeneland July sale, masked the fact that the market was losing strength at all but the most elite levels.

The primary culprits in the top-heavy structure were the sharply rising costs of breeding and raising a yearling and overproduction. The high prices for the very top level of yearlings drove stud fees up across the board but were not reflected in the prices for more modest animals, which were being produced in incredible numbers — more than 50,000 foals a year in 1985–1987. When the stock market took a sharp correction in 1987 and the number of people willing to pay six or seven figures for a sales yearling dropped drastically, the collapse in the bloodstock industry was even more painful and complete than that of Wall Street. It would be nearly a decade before the bloodstock market made a significant recovery — in no small part driven by the increasing appetite of Japanese investors for American Thoroughbreds — and it would never again approach the heady heights of 1983–1985, when the sons and daughters of Northern Dancer made him the king of the bloodstock world.

The King Is Dead...

While Northern Dancer did not collapse like the bloodstock market, he, too, was slowing down. He had five stakes winners in his 1982 crop and eight more in his 1983 crop, but none were of Classic caliber and only three were grade or group I winners — an excellent performance for any other stallion, but a decline compared to the dazzling three-year-olds of 1984. Ajdal, a foal of 1984, provided a late flash of brilliance by becoming England's champion sprinter in 1987, but by then, Northern Dancer was no longer in service.

Northern Dancer had always been an exceptionally virile stallion, but as he aged, the fierce determination to reach the breeding shed at any cost had burned down to mere indignation that he was not permitted to breed every mare brought to the farm. Gone were the days when even a closed stall and a chain clipped to his halter could barely restrain him when he realized that another stallion was being taken to breed; he still protested with squeals and obvious sexual excitement, but he was no longer a threat to climb over his stall door. Once he had hollered and plunged his way to the breeding shed, often going the distance on his hind legs; now he merely pranced and snorted. And in 1987, the fire had faded further, to the point where he could not always sustain an erection even when brought out to breed a mare.

A less visible problem became apparent by mid-April of that year: Northern Dancer had managed to impregnate only four of the twenty-four mares bred to him. Lab examination of his semen revealed a very low sperm count, but the results only confirmed what Charles Taylor's intuition had already told him.

"It just seemed to me like his heart wasn't in it," Taylor later recalled.

Thus it was that, in April 1987, Northern Dancer was officially retired from breeding. Just two colts constituted his final crop in 1988, and one, Northern Park, topped the 1989 Keeneland July yearling sale at $2.8 million; he later became a stakes winner. It was an appropriate ending to one of the most amazing stud careers of modern times. From 645 named foals, Northern Dancer begot 411 winners, of which 147 were stakes winners. Twenty-six were named champions or highweights in the United States, Canada, or Europe. And, at the time of his death, some 120 of his sons were standing in locations all over the world.

Northern Dancer had done more than establish himself as a great sire; he had also established a new type among modern Thoroughbreds: a small to medium-sized horse with the powerful muscling and symmetry of a top gymnast, superb balance, and often a goodly measure of their forefather's fiery spirit. Even today, the "Northern Dancer type" can be picked out among descendants of the Dancer. Big or small, they have the look of their ancestor, and in the eyes of many, this has become the look of a champion.

******

The twilight of Northern Dancer's life was paralleled by the downfall of the American yearling market, the decline of Windfields, and the fading away of E.P. Taylor, who never recovered from the stroke that had incapacitated him in 1980. When Taylor died on May 14, 1989, he was the breeder of record of more than three hundred stakes winners, though in truth, control of Windfields' breeding program had long since been shared between Charles Taylor and Joe Thomas and then between the younger Taylor and Joe Hickey after Thomas' death from cancer in 1984.

Although Windfields remained a major player in the sales ring and continued to race homebreds, it no longer dominated Canadian racing as it once had. Part of this can be credited to E.P. Taylor's vision and persistence in drawing new owners and breeders into the game. By the 1980s Windfields was competing with several major outfits including those of

Kinghaven Farm, Conn Smythe, and Sam-Son Farms, all of which had ben-efited greatly from access to bloodlines developed by Windfields. But part of the problem could be traced to the fact that the farm's operations had simply become too spread out. Instead of most of its horses being trained by one home trainer, Pete McCann, the horses were now scattered among a dozen public stables, where they could not easily be overseen and evalu-ated by the farm's management; instead of retaining half its homebreds, the vast majority were now consigned for sale, and the ones retained for home racing were generally not the most fashionably bred. Further, the mainte-nance of two separate breeding farms over a thousand miles apart was proving no light task.

Eventually, the Windfields management, headed by Charles Taylor, decid-ed that the Windfields operations were too far-flung to be properly man-aged, and the Maryland property was sold. A portion was retained, howev-er, with the intent of allowing the aging Northern Dancer to live out his days in familiar surroundings.

The days slowed down to a leisurely pace for Northern Dancer; as Joe Hickey put it, he had gone from "sultan to smoking jacket and slippers." His days were spent eating, sleeping, and patrolling his paddock; even in his old age, he still showed the territorial behavior of a wild stallion, and groom Bill Husfelt knew better than to presume he could enter the paddock and bring the stallion back to the barn without incident. Sometimes Northern Dancer would stop and stare into the distance, gazing at something that eluded human sight; sometimes he would still rear and scream, though what he challenged, no one knew.

Perhaps he sometimes missed the mares. But for the most part he seemed contented and remarkably ageless, with an arthritic right knee, a deepening dip in the back, and a bit of gray about the temples and muzzle the only clues to his advanced years.

The end came with surprising suddenness. On November 15, 1990, the old stallion developed colic. Charles Taylor was apprised of the horse's con-dition, and medical treatment was initiated. The horse seemed to respond and by midnight was no longer in acute distress. But at 6:00 a.m., Taylor was awakened by an urgent phone call: the colic had returned, and Northern Dancer was in great pain. Alan McCarthy, the farm veterinarian, could offer little hope. Had the stallion been younger, surgery might have been considered, but his advanced age and a heart condition that had developed several years earlier made it a real possibility that Northern Dancer might not even survive the van ride to a veterinary hospital capable of handling the surgery, much less the strain of being subjected to general anesthesia. And he was suffering terribly.

There was really no decision to be made, only an acceptance of the inevitable. Charles Taylor gave the order to end Northern Dancer's misery, and at 6:15 a.m., the fatal dose of sedative was administered. Within the hour, the news was breaking across Canada, leading the headlines on every television and radio news broadcast and topping the front page in the newspapers. Windfields was inundated with telegrams, letters, and phone calls, many of the latter tearful to the point of choking, as though Canada had lost a favorite son. And, in truth, it had.

Arrangements had long since been made with the Canadian Department of Agriculture to return Northern Dancer to his native land on his death. All that remained was to transfer the stallion's body to the oak casket that had been built to receive it and to secure the necessary papers for crossing the border. When all was ready, Northern Dancer began his last journey. Charles Taylor, Bernard McCormack (who had succeeded Joe Thomas as head of Windfields' general operations), and Windfields veterinarian Patrick Hearn met the funeral van at the border and escorted it back to Oshawa.

It was nearly midnight when the cortege pulled in at Windfields, and cold and black as only a rainy northern night in November can be. Nonetheless, the entire Windfields staff had turned out to welcome Northern Dancer home and see him laid to rest in the heart of the farm where he had been born. The simple granite marker adorning his grave can still be seen in the horse cemetery on the Windfields estate, and for many years a nearby rose bush every spring trailed deep red roses over his resting place, in memory of a victory wreath won long ago by the little colt with the great heart.

Legacy

F ew horses have ever left such a rich legacy as did Northern Dancer. Unlike ordinary stallions, who are fortunate if they beget one or two sons able to carry on their lines, the question with Northern Dancer was not whether he would leave an enduring male line but how many branches it would have. By the time of his death, Nijinsky II, Lyphard, The Minstrel, Vice Regent, Nureyev, Be My Guest, Northern Taste, Danzig, Sadler's Wells, and Storm Bird had all sired sons with race records guaranteed to earn them solid chances at stud, and many more were on the way.

Northern Dancer did not leave a clear-cut successor to his throne; yet this was not for lack of heirs but because he had too many great sire sons for any one to dominate all the rest. Of the many fine stallions he sired, Nijinsky II, Lyphard, Nureyev, Sadler's Wells, Danzig, Dixieland Band, and Storm Bird will be profiled in later chapters, for their accomplishments are too far-reaching to be confined to a few brief paragraphs. Others have already had their stallion careers briefly profiled in connection with discussion of their racing careers. But many other sons of Northern Dancer deserve at least brief mention; some, indeed, would be considered among the best sire sons of almost any other stallion.

Even some of Northern Dancer's least likely sons have had their moments of brilliance. Among them was Compliance, a 1978 colt out of Sex Appeal and, thus, a full brother to champions El Gran Senor and Try My Best. He proved virtually useless as a racehorse, failing to win in three starts although he did run third in a small stakes in Ireland. His form may well have been compromised by a nasty temperament, which probably would have made him a gelding had he been a son of any other horse but Northern Dancer.

Given a chance at stud in New York, Compliance highlighted his stud career by siring two remarkable full brothers out of the Bold Arian mare Broadway Joan: Fourstardave, the beloved "Sultan of Saratoga" who won races at the old Spa for eight consecutive seasons, and Fourstars Allstar, who became the first American-based horse to win a European Classic when he captured the 1991 Irish Two Thousand Guineas. Fourstars Allstar eventually became a National Hunt sire in Ireland, while Fourstardave, a gelding, died in retirement at the age of seventeen.

Night Shift, a 1980 full brother to Fanfreluche, proved only slightly better than Compliance as a racehorse, managing to win one minor race in seven starts. He retired to stud in England in 1985 with modest expectations but in 1990 made headlines with his daughter In the Groove. Winner of three group I events that year including the Irish One Thousand Guineas, In the Groove attracted more and better mares to her sire. He took advantage of his improved opportunities by siring such good horses as 1999 Prix de Diane winner Daryaba, English and Irish sprint highweight Northern Goddess, and grade or group I winners Align, Azamour, Creaking Board, Listening, Lochangel, Nicolotte, and Night Style in a career that included stints in England, the United States, and Australia.

With two wins and five placings (including a third in the Grand Prix de Vichy, Fr-III) from fourteen starts, Sovereign Dancer was also far from a top-flight racehorse. Given a chance at stud because of his royal pedigree — his dam, the Bold Ruler mare Bold Princess, is one of the nine stakes winners produced from the remarkable matron Grey Flight — Sovereign Dancer delivered with a solid career that was highlighted by four first-class sons: Gate Dancer, the 1984 Preakness winner; Itsallgreektome, 1990 champion turf male; Priolo, a multiple group I winner in France; and Louis Quatorze, the 1996 Preakness winner.

Unfortunately, none of Sovereign Dancer's sons proved able to succeed their sire, who died in 1994, though he did leave a mark on breeding through Leo Castelli, the 1987 Peter Pan Stakes (gr. II) winner. Exported to Russia after the 1989 breeding season, Leo Castelli was promptly repatriated after his first crop, foaled in 1989, produced four 1991 stakes winners including the aptly named Soviet Sojourn, a multiple grade III-winning filly. Alas, Leo Castelli was never able to live up to the promise his first crop had shown following his return to Kentucky, but Soviet Sojourn became the dam of Indian Charlie, the 1998 Santa Anita Derby (gr. I) winner and a well-regarded young sire. Leo Castelli also got several stakes winners while in Russia, including the 1994 Russian Derby winner, Gul.

******

Unlike Compliance, Night Shift, and Sovereign Dancer, Fairy King had not proven himself to be an indifferent racehorse prior to going to stud. He was an unknown quantity, having fractured a sesamoid during his only start. But as a 1982 full brother to Sadler's Wells, the young classic winner who was just then beginning his own stud career, Fairy King was given a chance to make good at stud by Philip Myerscough, son-in-law of renowned Irish trainer Vincent O'Brien.

O'Brien, who had conditioned both Sadler's Wells and Fairy King, thought that Fairy King had real talent despite his abbreviated racing career. His judgment was perhaps vindicated by Fairy King's performance as a stallion, for there is no question that Fairy King was able to sire horses with considerable ability. He reached his peak in 1996 when his three-year-old son Helissio earned championship honors by defeating older males in the Grand Prix de Saint-Cloud (Fr-I) and the Prix de l'Arc de Triomphe (Fr-I). The colt added the Prix Ganay (Fr-I) and a repeat score in the Grand Prix de Saint-Cloud at four before being sold to Japanese interests for stud duty. Based in large part on Helissio's exploits, Fairy King was leading sire in France in 1996.

Fairy King died in 1999, the year his son Oath won the Derby Stakes and his grandson Island Sands (by 1994 Irish Two Thousand Guineas winner Turtle Island) won the Two Thousand Guineas. Neither Helissio nor Oath (who followed Helissio to Japan at the conclusion of his racing career) has proven a consistent sire, and Fairy King's heir at stud proved to be Encosta de Lago, an Australian group I winner who led the Australian general sire list twice and, as of 2023, has led the Australian broodmare sire list four times.

Legacy

Fairy Bridge, the dam of both Fairy King and Sadler's Wells, might have had yet another top sire son by Northern Dancer to her credit had the fates decreed otherwise. Her 1983 foal by the Dancer, Tate Gallery, ranked among the best juveniles in Ireland in 1985, when he won the National Stakes (Ire-I). Unfortunately, he was killed in a plane accident in 1990, leaving behind one first-class runner in Lyric Fantasy. Affectionately known as the "Pocket Rocket," the diminutive filly won the 1992 Queen Mary Stakes (Eng-III) at five furlongs against other juvenile fillies, then defeated all-aged competition in the five-furlong Nunthorpe Stakes (Eng-I), a rare feat indeed and one that earned her honors as Europe's champion juvenile filly.

******

Given the results obtained by some Northern Dancer sons that were quite indifferent racehorses, it should hardly be surprising that good results continue as one moves up the ladder of racing class among the Dancer's sons. Topsider, however, was something of a surprise in type; bred from the tough staying mare Drumtop in 1974, he proved a sprinter, scoring his sole stakes victory in the six-furlong Sport Page Handicap. Nonetheless, he proved quite a good sire in spite of his modest racing accomplishments, perhaps not least because of his descent from the same female family that includes Sadler's Wells, Nureyev, and Fairy King. Topsider's daughter North Sider was the 1987 American champion older female, while his son Salse, the 1988 Prix de la Foret (Fr-I) winner and champion three-year-old male in France, proved a successful sire in Europe. Salse died in 2001 but sired the Classic winners Classic Cliche (1995 St. Leger), Luso (1995 Derby Italiano), and Air Express (1997 German and Italian Two Thousand Guineas; unfortunately, he died in 2000). Another Topsider son, the Italian group I winner Assatis, is the sire of Wing Arrow, twice Japan's champion dirt horse.

Fabulous Dancer, a multiple group III winner in France, was at least equal to Topsider as a sire, as he was the leading French sire of 1992. Unlike some sires whose success is due to the earnings of one or two championship-caliber runners, Fabulous Dancer earned his title through the exploits of several good but not spectacular runners, led by group II winner Fabulous Hostess. He did sire two champions: Lady Winner, French champion older female of 1990, and Fabulous La Fouine, Japan's champion three-year-old filly in 1996. Generally speaking, Fabulous Dancer's fillies were better than his colts, and none of his sons were able to carry on as sires.

Like Fabulous Dancer, Unfuwain, a 1985 son of the fine racer and producer Height of Fashion (Fr), was also a good sire whose reputation was based primarily on his daughters. A half brother to the 1989 Two Thousand Guineas and Derby Stakes winner Nashwan (by Blushing Groom [Fr]), Unfuwain was rated the best English three-year-old of 1988 despite not winning a Classic or, for that matter, any event above group II status. He proved a good sire before his death at age seventeen, getting the Irish Oaks winners Bolas, Petrushka, and Lailani; the One Thousand Guineas winner Lahan; and the English Oaks winner Eswarah. His best son was Alhaarth, winner of the 1995 Dewhurst Stakes (Eng-I) and sire of the 2004 Two Thousand Guineas winner Haafhd.

The 1979 Champion Stakes (Eng-I) winner, Northern Baby, also sired a first-class daughter in 1995 American champion turf mare Possibly Perfect, as well as getting a Classic-winning son in 1989 St. Leger Stakes winner Michelozzo. Nonetheless, despite a quite useful career as a sire of flat racers, Northern Baby is perhaps best known as a steeplechase sire thanks to his gelded sons Highland Bud (1989 American champion steeplechaser) and Warm Spell (1994 American champion steeplechaser).

******

Although it sometimes seemed as though every champion son of Northern Dancer became a top-class stallion, this was not always the case. Sometimes conformation was the culprit, as it seems to have been with Try My Best. Although a champion juvenile and champion miler in his own right and a full brother to the excellent El Gran Senor, Try My Best was markedly back at the knee, and transmission of this defect seems to have been one reason for his inconsistency as a sire. To call him a failure, as some have done, is not quite fair; after all, he did sire thirty stakes winners from his 407 foals and was champion sire in Italy twice. Nonetheless, only one approached the class of his sire: Last Tycoon (Ire). Champion sprinter in England and France at three, Last Tycoon was considered to stay barely five furlongs but, with a cleverly rated ride, managed to stretch his speed to win the 1986 Breeders' Cup Mile (gr. IT) by a head over another Northern Dancer grandson, Palace Music (by The Minstrel).

On paper, Last Tycoon should have stayed much further — his dam is a daughter of 1971 Derby Stakes winner Mill Reef — and his best progeny have generally proved capable of staying at least a mile and often more. Champion sire in Australia in 1993/94 — the same year his gelded son Mahogany was Horse of the Year there — Last Tycoon sired top-class progeny all over the world while shuttling among Ireland, Australia, and Japan. They include three-time European group I winner Ezzoud; Bigstone, a four-time European group I winner; 1996/97 New Zealand Horse of the Year O'Reilly, a four-time champion sire in his native land; and Taipan, who twice won the twelve-furlong Europa-Preis (Ger-I). Marju, another group I winner by Last Tycoon, did fairly well at stud in Ireland and sired champions Indigenous, Pawnee Rhythm, Soviet Song, and Viva Pataca.

******

Such sons as Night Shift, Sovereign Dancer, Fabulous Dancer, Fairy King, Topsider, Try My Best, and Unfuwain would collectively be enough to establish a reputation as a good sire of sires for almost any stallion. The irony is that among the sons of Northern Dancer, they are almost afterthoughts; the great ones are yet to be discussed.

Princes of the Blood

I t is appropriate that any discussion of Northern Dancer's great sire sons should begin with Nijinsky II, the first of the Dancer's sons to gain international acclaim and the first to hint at Northern Dancer's prowess as a sire of sires. Unfortunately, Nijinsky II did not long survive his sire, dying in 1992 at Claiborne Farm, where he had stood throughout his career. He had done well to live as long as he had, for he had suffered from chronic laminitis since 1984, and it is a testament to the quality of care provided him at Claiborne that he was able not only to live fairly comfortably but also to continue as a breeding stallion during the years following his initial illness.

During his career Nijinsky II sired 155 stakes winners, a huge number in an era when neither books of one hundred or more mares nor shuttling to the Southern Hemisphere was commonplace. He has had even greater success as a broodmare sire, leading the American broodmare sire list in 1993 and 1994, and is considered one of the best modern influences for stamina.

Nijinsky II's early successes in Europe have already been mentioned in Chapter 12. In America, Nijinsky II provided the Northern Dancer male line with its first Kentucky Derby winner when his son Ferdinand, magnificently ridden by none other than Bill Shoemaker, wove his way through fifteen rivals to win going away in 1986. The following year Ferdinand captured Horse of the Year honors with a narrow victory over 1987 champion three-year-old male Alysheba in the Breeders' Cup Classic (gr. I). Ferdinand was retired to Claiborne Farm in 1988 after failing to win another stakes as a five-year-old but proved a failure at stud and was sent to Japan. He fared no better in his adoptive country, and a media uproar broke out when it was discovered that the stallion had been sent to a slaughter facility in late 2002. Some good came from the sad fate of Ferdinand, however; since his death, a number of other aging sires have been repatriated from Japan to live out their days as pensioners at retirement facilities in the United States.

In 1986 Nijinsky II was represented by another outstanding runner when his son Shahrastani won the English and Irish derbys and earned champion three-year-old honors in Ireland. His successes played a major role in making Nijinsky II the leading sire in England that year. Shahrastani would not prove a successful sire, however, and it would fall to 1983 Prix du Jockey-Club winner and French champion three-year-old male Caerleon to become the leading son of Nijinsky II in Europe. The leading English sire of 1988 and 1991, Caerleon is best remembered as the sire of Generous (Ire), who won the 1991 English and Irish derbys but did not live up to the high expectations held for him as a sire while standing in England, Japan, and New Zealand.

Green Dancer, Nijinsky II's first Classic winner when he won the French Two Thousand Guineas in 1975, led the French general sire list in 1991. That year his son Suave Dancer won the Prix du Jockey-Club and the Prix de l'Arc de Triomphe (Fr-I) on the way to honors as France's champion three-year-old male. Unfortunately, Suave Dancer was killed by lightning in 1999 without leaving a top sire son, and neither Italian champion juvenile Will Dancer nor American multiple grade I winner Greinton (GB) proved successful as sires. Green Dancer did get one champion sire in Oak Dancer, who led the Argentine general sire list in 1990 but did not leave a son to succeed him.

Nijinsky II's son Niniski, though considered something of a plodder (he won the 1979 Irish and French St. Legers), also did quite well as a sire in Europe. His best son, Hernando, won the 1993 Prix du Jockey-Club and finished second in the 1994 Prix de l'Arc de Triomphe but was more successful as a sire of broodmares than as a sire of winners, leading the 2022 French broodmare sire list.

Another top son of Niniski, Lomitas, was the German champion three-year-old male and Horse of the Year of 1991 after winning three group I events that year. Now at stud in England, his best progeny include the 1999 Deutsches Derby (Ger-I) winner Belenus, the 2003 Oaks d'Italia winner Meridiana, and 2001 German Horse of the Year Silvano. The last-named horse was a well-traveled sort whose record includes wins in the 2001 Arlington Million (gr. IT), Singapore Cup (Sin-I), and Queen Elizabeth II Cup (HK-I). Sent to stud in South Africa, he has been champion sire there five times as of 2023.

Nijinsky II's other Classic winners had spotty sire records, either from lack of opportunity or from failure to capitalize on the chances they had. English Derby winner Golden Fleece died after siring only two crops. The 1981 Irish Two Thousand Guineas winner Kings Lake was disappointing and ended up being sent to Germany; 1985 Two Thousand Guineas winner Shadeed sired 1992 Queen's Plate winner Alydeed and European champions Sayyedati and Shadayid in an uneven career. Lammtarra, winner of the Derby Stakes, the King George VI and Queen Elizabeth Stakes (Eng-I), and the Prix de l'Arc de Triomphe in an unbeaten four-race career, went to Japan after only one stud season in Europe and was not a success there before being repatriated to England and pensioned in 2006. His one top-class runner, his daughter Melikah, echoing the successes of Nijinsky II and Northern Dancer in the American sales rings of the 1980s, became the highest-priced yearling ever sold through the Deauville sale in France when she fetched ten million French francs in 1998; she later won a stakes and finished second in the 2000 Irish Oaks and third in the Epsom Oaks.

Still, Classic winners make up only a small fraction of the sons of even the best stallions, and Nijinsky II has enjoyed success as a sire of sires with some of his other sons. Royal Academy, winner of the 1990 Breeders' Cup Mile (gr. IT) sired 167 stakes winners, including two-time Irish St. Leger winner Oscar Schindler, 1997 One Thousand Guineas winner Sleepytime, 1998 Poule d'Essai des Pouliches winner Zalaikya, and champions Eyeofthetiger and Top Hat. The 1992 U.S. champion turf male and multiple Canadian champion Sky Classic, primarily a sire of late-maturing types, has sixty-five stakes winners to his credit, including 1999 Canadian Horse of the Year and champion grass male Thornfield. Baldski, a first-class regional sire in Florida who died in 1993, sired forty-nine stakes winners including the exceptionally fast filly Chaposa Springs. Stack, an allowance winner in the mid-1980s, was champion sire three times in Peru.

Other sons have had their moments, if not consistent success. Sportin' Life, a minor stakes winner, was far from a top-class sire but did get 1987 Belmont Stakes winner Bet Twice, who unfortunately did not do well at stud before dying at age fifteen. Manzotti, a multiple grade III winner, sired the consistent filly Two Altazano, winner of the 1994 Coaching Club American Oaks (gr. I). The beautifully bred Whiskey Road (out of two-time American champion filly Bowl of Flowers) also got a "big horse," this being the globe-trotting Strawberry Road, whose exploits included championship honors in his native Australia and a title as champion older male in Germany. In a loss to the breed, Strawberry Road died in 1995 at the age of sixteen after siring American champion fillies Escena and Ajina and the high-class turf runner Fraise. The last-named horse proved a stud failure in Japan and was eventually donated to a riding school before being returned in 2005 to the United States, where he died later that year.

Although the Nijinsky II branch of the Northern Dancer sire line appears to be on the wane, Nijinsky II is likely to remain a tremendous influence on the distaff side of pedigrees for a long time to come. Among his top-producing daughters are multiple grade II winner Number, dam of 1989 Grand Criterium (Fr-I) winner Jade Robbery, 1996 William P. Kyne Handicap (gr. III) winner Chequer, and 1994 Derby Trial (gr. III) winner Numerous, the last-named a sire of some standing in Argentina; Oh What a Dance, dam of 1994 American champion three-year-old filly Heavenly Prize and 1998 Matron Stakes (gr. I) winner Oh What a Windfall; Ruby Slippers, dam of 1992 American champion sprinter Rubiano and granddam of 2004 Wood Memorial Stakes (gr. I) winner and three-time American champion sire Tapit; Wasnah, dam of 1995 English highweight miler Bahri and 1996 Champagne Stakes (Eng-II) winner Bahhare; and Snuggle, dam of 1993 Belmont Stakes winner Colonial Affair.

******

Lyphard was another Northern Dancer son whose early reputation was based on his accomplishments in Europe (*see Chapter 12*). His yearlings remained popular with European buyers even after his relocation to Kentucky from France, and no wonder; of the forty stakes winners he had sired by mid-1983, thirty-five had earned black type in Europe. By the early 1980s, however, Lyphard was beginning to show some strength in North America as well, though predominantly as a turf sire, a pattern that continued throughout his stud career.

One can debate for hours on whether Dancing Brave or Manila was the best of Lyphard's 115 stakes winners. Coincidentally, both were foaled in 1983. Dancing Brave, a European champion, won eight of ten starts including the Two Thousand Guineas and the Prix de l'Arc de Triomphe, the latter in a breathtaking run; yet he lost perhaps the two most important starts of his career, finishing second by a half-length to Shahrastani (by Nijinsky II) in the Derby and unplaced behind winner Manila in the Breeders' Cup Turf (gr. IT).

To base a comparison of the two colts on the Breeders' Cup Turf, in which Dancing Brave was probably past his best form, would not be quite fair, but there is no question that Manila was an exceptional runner in his own right. The 1986 U.S. champion turf horse, he had come into the Breeders' Cup Turf off scores over older males in the United Nations Handicap (gr. IT) and Turf Classic (gr. IT). The following year Manila added a repeat victory in the United Nations and a win in the Arlington Million (gr. IT) before being forced to the sidelines by injury.

Unfortunately, Manila proved a disappointing stallion and is now at stud in Turkey, while his best son, multiple grade I winner Bien Bien, died relatively young and did not impress during his brief career at stud. Dancing Brave was much the better of the two as a sire, though he was exported to Japan before his 1990 crop could prove its merit. That crop included Wemyss Bight, winner of the Irish Oaks; White Muzzle, winner of the Derby Italiano; and Commander in Chief, winner of the English and Irish derbys.

Both Commander in Chief and White Muzzle followed their sire to Japan, and Lyphard's male-line descent in Europe is primarily through his multiple group III-winning son Bellypha (Ire), a good sire whose grandson Linamix became the first fifth-generation descendant of Northern Dancer to win a Classic race by taking the 1990 Poule d'Essai des Poulains. Linamix also became the first fifth-generation descendant of Northern Dancer to head the sire list of a major racing nation when he led the French general sire list in 1998, the year his son Sagamix won the Prix de l'Arc de Triomphe, and repeated his French sire championship in 2004.

Another of Lyphard's European-based sons, Alzao, was an even lesser racehorse than Bellypha. Although he was also a group III winner, his sole win at that level was in the Premio Ellington (Ity-III), where the competition was considered a little easier than in England or France. Despite his modest racing credentials, Alzao, whose dam, Lady Rebecca, is a half sister to 1965 Preakness winner and good sire Tom Rolfe, became a very good sire, his progeny including 1996 Irish One Thousand Guineas winner Matiya, 1998 English Oaks winner Shahtoush, 1998 Irish Oaks winner Winona, and 2000 Oaks d'Italia winner Timi.

Al Nasr (Fr), a group I winner in his native land, had some success on both sides of the Atlantic while standing in Kentucky: his son Nasr El Arab was a multiple grade I winner in California while another son, Zaizoom, won the 1987 Derby Italiano. Neither Nasr El Arab nor Zaizoom made any significant mark at stud, and while Al Nasr is the maternal grandsire of one very good runner in 1996 Metropolitan Handicap (gr. I) winner Honour and Glory, he was not otherwise an outstanding broodmare sire. Another French-bred son of Lyphard who had at least modest success while standing in the United States was Lyphard's Wish, who won the 1980 United Nations Handicap (gr. IT) and then begot the grade I winners Derby Wish and Spellbound and the good steeplechaser Declare Your Wish before being exported to Japan as a ten-year-old.

Lyphard's American-bred sons had little impact, although he sired some first-class runners in Dahar, Ends Well, and Au Point. The last-named was the only Lyphard son to win a grade I race on dirt (the 1983 Dwyer Stakes) and might have been expected to escape the usual American bias against turf runners as sires but wound up standing in Louisiana. Ends Well also became a regional sire, in his case in New York, while Dahar was exported to Japan in 1994, the year after his son Buckhar won the Washington, D.C., International Mile (gr. IT). Dahar also sired the New Zealand-bred group I winners Daacha, Des's Dream, and Stony Bay and the top Venezuelan runner Veterano.

Lyphard had better fortune with multiple Canadian champion Rainbows for Life, who was bred by leading Canadian breeder Sam-Son Farm. After attracting little patronage during his initial season (1994) in Kentucky, Rainbows for Life stood several seasons in Ireland and then was moved to Eastern Europe. He became a champion sire in the Czech Republic and Slovakia, having led the sire list three times in the former country and once in the latter.

Lyphard was one of the first Northern Dancer-line stallions to have a significant impact in South America thanks to his son Ghadeer. A group III winner in Italy, Ghadeer proved an extraordinary sire in Brazil before his death in 2005, leading that country's general sire list eight consecutive times from 1990/91 to 1997/98. Unfortunately, his best son, Falcon Jet — a Horse of the Year and a top sire in Brazil — died in 2000 after only seven seasons at stud, but his daughters carried on his name in splendid fashion, earning Ghadeer fourteen titles as Brazil's leading broodmare sire. An example of his ability as a broodmare sire is Riboletta (Brz), winner of the 1998 Grande Premio Diana (Brazilian Oaks) in her native country and American champion older female in 2000.

Lyphard, who led the French general sire list in 1978 and 1979 and the American general sire list in 1986, was also an exceptional broodmare sire and led the French broodmare sire list in 1985 and 1986. Among the important horses produced from his daughters are Bering, winner of the 1986 Prix du Jockey-Club and a useful sire; Candy Stripes, only stakes-placed on the racetrack but an important sire in Argentina (and sire of 2005 U.S. champion turf male Leroidesanimaux); Regal State, a group I winner in France and the dam of 2003 Breeders' Cup Classic winner Pleasantly Perfect; 1987 French champion juvenile Common Grounds; and Cee's Tizzy, a leading regional sire in California and the sire of two-time Breeders' Cup Classic winner Tiznow.

Lyphard proved the longest-lived of all Northern Dancer's major sons, dying on June 10, 2005, at the ripe old age of thirty-six. Perhaps the most like his sire in size and conformation, he was also much like him in personality — a feisty little peacock who loved being the center of attention and could strut like a runway model if he had an appreciative audience. His spunky attitude, combined with a basically kind nature and a love of being petted, made him a great favorite with visitors to Gainesway Farm, where he stood throughout the American phase of his stud career and where he now lies buried.

******

Standing at Walmac International in Kentucky, Nureyev proved one of Northern Dancer's most versatile sire sons, his progeny ranging from blazing-fast sprinters to top twelve-furlong performers. Among the best of his early runners were 1987 U.S. champion turf male Theatrical (Ire), winner of the Breeders' Cup Turf and a successful sire; Miesque, a multiple champion on both sides of the Atlantic and dam of French classic winners East of the Moon and Kingmambo, the latter an important sire; and Zilzal, 1989 English champion three-year-old male and Horse of the Year.

Like Lyphard, Nureyev tended to sire horses that did their best running on turf and was not perceived as likely to make a sire of sires in the United States. Theatrical, however, received good early support from his owner, Allen Paulson, and he proved to be one of those rare turf horses who prove capable of siring good dirt runners as well as grass performers. The sire of eighty-two stakes winners, he was also a rather atypical son of Nureyev in his proclivity for siring stamina-oriented types rather than milers. None of his sons proved to be a good stallion, but the 106 stakes winners produced from his daughters include English Channel, the American champion grass horse of 2007 and a successful sire of turf horses.

Aside from Theatrical and Zilzal, other top Nureyev sons foaled during the 1980s include Soviet Star (1987 Poule d'Essai des Poulains), Stately Don (1987 Secretariat Stakes and Hollywood Derby, both grade I events on turf), Polar Falcon (1991 Ladbroke Sprint Cup, Eng-I), and Alwuhush, who won two group I events in Italy and the Carleton F. Burke Stakes (gr. IT) in the United States as a four-year-old in 1989. However, neither Alwuhush nor Stately Don proved a consistent sire. Polar Falcon, who died in 2001, did better, begetting three-time English champion broodmare sire Pivotal, while Soviet Star's group I-winning sons Ashkalani and Starcraft (the latter a champion in Australia) were unable to succeed him.

Nureyev's stud career nearly came to an untimely end early in 1987, when the stallion fractured a hind leg in a paddock accident. Despite immediate surgery and the best of post-operative care, the horse's life hung in the balance for five months as he went through one crisis after another: damaged screws in the repaired leg, infection at the operation site, colitis, respiratory infection, exhaustion. But slowly, aided by devoted care and by the fierce will inherited from his sire, Nureyev began to recover. Walmac's resident veterinarian John Howard knew Nureyev was back when, in October 1987, Nureyev lashed out with the once-broken hind leg, breaking Howard's arm. In spite of the pain, Howard could only laugh.

By December, Nureyev was ready to move in to his own private stallion barn, complete with a personal breeding court. And on April 1, 1988, a mare appropriately named Histoire (Fr) was led into Nureyev's court and successfully covered, marking the stallion's return to service. The result of that mating, the filly Oumaldaaya, became a group II winner in Italy.

Nureyev eventually died at the age of twenty-four in 2001 after a battle with cancer but not before having the most spectacular season of his stud career in 1997. That year he was represented by the brilliant Prix de l'Arc de Triomphe winner Peintre Celebre, who demolished a field considered exceptional even by the standards of Europe's premier all-aged race; English Oaks winner Reams of Verse; champion French miler Spinning World, winner of the Breeders' Cup Mile; and Atticus, who set a world record for the mile on the turf in the Arcadia Handicap (gr. IIT) and came back later in the season to win the Oaklawn Handicap (gr. I) on dirt.

Two more top Nureyev sons emerged in 1999: Fasliyev, the season's European champion juvenile male, and Stravinsky, the top-rated sprinter in England and Ireland. Although Fasliyev got off to a fast start at stud as the best European first-year sire of 2003, he was not able to sustain that success, and Stravinsky and Peintre Celebre also failed to live up to the hopes held for them as stallions. On the other hand, Nureyev's daughters have proven valuable broodmares, and Nureyev led the English broodmare sire list in 1997. In no small part, this was thanks to the accomplishments of his maternal grandson Desert King (by Danehill and, thus, closely inbred to Northern Dancer), who swept the Irish Two Thousand Guineas and Irish Derby that season and earned honors as Irish champion three-year-old male. Other top runners out of Nureyev mares include the aforementioned

Kingmambo and East of the Moon, 2001 Japanese Horse of the Year Jungle Pocket, 2008 American champion three-year-old male Big Brown, 2001 Japanese champion older female To the Victory, and 1993 Canadian Triple Crown winner and Horse of the Year Peteski.

******

Sadler's Wells was almost the forgotten horse among Northern Dancer's extraordinary batch of runners in 1984 despite his victory in the Irish Two Thousand Guineas. At stud, he was something else again. After winning his first English sire title in 1990 and finishing second among English sires in 1991, he led the English sire list thirteen consecutive times from 1992 to 2004. Sadler's Wells was also champion sire in France in 1993, 1994, and 1999.

The great stallion notched his first Classic victories as a sire when his son Old Vic captured the Prix du Jockey-Club and Irish Derby in 1989. The brilliant filly Salsabil followed in 1990, taking the One Thousand Guineas, Oaks, and Irish Derby; then came Intrepidity, who captured the 1993 Oaks, and Barathea, who took the 1993 Irish Two Thousand Guineas to emulate his sire. Sadler's Wells next sired Moonshell, the 1995 Oaks victress, and Dance Design, who captured the 1996 Irish Oaks.

Ebadiyla, a top staying filly, gave Sadler's Wells a second consecutive victory in the Irish Oaks in 1997 and also won that year's Prix Royal-Oak (French St. Leger) against all-aged competition, while Entrepreneur won the 1997 Two Thousand Guineas. Then came 1998, in which the progeny of Sadler's Wells scored four Classic successes: Dream Well in the Prix du Jockey-Club and Irish Derby; King of Kings in the Two Thousand Guineas; and Kayf Tara in the Irish St. Leger. In addition, Kayf Tara captured England's longest group I event, the historic Ascot Gold Cup.

Sadler's Wells' runners added four more classic scores in 1999, when Kayf Tara repeated in the Irish St. Leger; Saffron Walden won the Irish Two Thousand Guineas; and Montjeu emulated Old Vic and Dream Well by completing the Prix du Jockey-Club–Irish Derby double, adding the Prix de l'Arc de Triomphe for good measure. No Classic winners emerged in 2000, but Sadler's Wells' offspring made up for that in 2001 by getting five Classic wins, equaling the feats of St. Simon in 1900 and Northern Dancer in 1984. The 2001 Classic winners sired by Sadler's Wells included his first Derby Stakes winner, Galileo, who also won the Irish Derby; St. Leger winner Milan; and Imagine, who won the Irish One Thousand Guineas and Irish Oaks.

Two-time U.S. champion turf male High Chaparral (2002 English and Irish derbys) and 2002 Irish One Thousand Guineas winner Gossamer were next in the parade of Classic winners for Sadler's Wells; 2003 brought three more such winners in Yesterday (Irish One Thousand Guineas), Refuse to Bend (Two Thousand Guineas), and Brian Boru (St. Leger). After a three-year drought, the stallion closed his tally as a Classic sire with Alexandrova, who won the 2006 Oaks Stakes and Irish Oaks. All told, Sadler's Wells sired the winners of thirty-two events generally considered Classics in England, France, and Ireland. Even given the fact that Sadler's Wells covered books of well over one hundred mares per season during most of his career, this is an extraordinary record.

Of all of Northern Dancer's sons, Sadler's Wells may have come closest to matching him as a sire of sires. His son El Prado (Ire), the 1991 Irish champion juvenile, led the American general sire list in 2002, and has been succeeded by 2004 American champion turf male Kitten's Joy, a two-time American champion sire, and by multiple grade I winner Medaglia d'Oro, who has ranked seven times among the top ten American sires through 2022. Another son, 1990 Breeders' Cup Turf winner In the Wings, enjoyed a solid stud career highlighted by 1996 American champion turf male Singspiel, who likewise became a good sire.

Fort Wood, winner of the 1993 Grand Prix de Paris (Fr-I), is another of Sadler's Wells' sons to establish a reputation as a fine sire. Based in South Africa, he led the general sire list in that country in 1999 and ranked among the top ten sires on another thirteen occasions. He also led the South African broodmare sire list twice. An even better Sadler's Wells son in the Southern Hemisphere was multiple group II winner Dushyantor, a three-time champion sire and (as of January 2024) an eight-time champion broodmare sire in Chile.

Sadler's Wells saved his best for last in Europe with a one-two punch headed by 1999 European champion three-year-old male Montjeu. The French champion sire of 2005, Montjeu racked up a fine record in England

and Ireland as well and appears to have left a worthy successor in 2012 European champion three-year-old male Camelot.

As good as Montjeu was, he was eclipsed by 2001 European champion three-year-old male Galileo, who took over where his sire left off. Produced from the great broodmare Urban Sea (a winner of the Prix de l'Arc de Triomphe during her own racing days), Galileo dominated the European sire standings for over a decade before his death in 2021, leading the English general sire list ten times, the French general sire list twice, and the Irish general sire list twelve times. He has already led the broodmare sire lists in England, France, and Ireland multiple times each and, to top everything else, he begot a successor to his crown in unbeaten Frankel, the highest-ranked racehorse in the world in 2011–2012 and a champion sire in England and France.

As great a sire as he was, Sadler's Wells may have an even greater long-term influence on the breed through his daughters. As of January 2024, mares sired by Sadler's Wells have produced 435 stakes winners around the world, and the stallion has earned broodmare sire titles in England, France, Ireland, and the United States as well as finishing in the top ten among maternal grandsires in Germany, Italy, and Japan. His youngest daughters will be passing out of production in the next five to ten years, but every black-type runner they produce between now and then will only cement their sire's place as one of the greatest sires in the history of the Thoroughbred.

Princes of the Blood (Part II)

A common denominator among Nijinsky II, Lyphard, Nureyev, and Sadler's Wells is that their primary successes as sires have for the most part been in Europe and/or on the turf. We now turn to sons of Northern Dancer that have had marked success in North America and on dirt, beginning with Danzig.

A 1977 bay colt out of Pas de Nom, Danzig brought $310,000 as a yearling at the 1978 Fasig-Tipton Saratoga sale — a relatively modest price for a good-looking Northern Dancer colt. His dam, however, was not fashionably bred (Admiral's Voyage—Petitioner), and though Pas de Nom became a nice stakes winner at two and three, the market appeal of her pedigree may be judged by the fact that she fetched only $4,700 as a yearling.

Be that as it may, Danzig quickly showed he had talent. Turned over to Hall of Fame trainer Woody Stephens for training, Danzig won his juvenile debut by eight and a half lengths. But a knee chip forced him to the sidelines after his impressive maiden victory, and he went lame again after two brilliant allowance wins at three. X-rays revealed the beginnings of a slab fracture of the knee, ending the colt's racing career.

That left owner Henryk de Kwiatkowski with a dilemma. Danzig clearly had exceptional ability but had not earned a stakes win, limiting his marketability as a stallion prospect. Fortunately, Danzig had a strong advocate in Woody Stephens, who considered the colt one of the finest prospects he had ever trained. Given Stephens' strong endorsement of the colt's talent, Seth Hancock of Claiborne Farm was willing to take a chance on the fragile speedball and arranged a syndication for him at $80,000 per share.

As with Northern Dancer, those who bought shares in Danzig when they first became available were the lucky ones. Danzig's first crop hit the ground running in 1984, when his son Chief's Crown won the inaugural Breeders' Cup Juvenile (gr. I) and with it the title of champion two-year-old male. At three Chief's Crown was among the leaders of his generation, winning four grade I events and placing in all three Triple Crown races.

Although not the equal of his sire as a stallion, Chief's Crown sired English champion juvenile Grand Lodge, 1994 Derby Stakes winner Erhaab, and 1997 U.S. champion turf male and Canadian Horse of the Year Chief Bearhart. Grand Lodge, in turn, became a popular shuttle sire in Ireland and Australia before shattering a knee in a paddock accident in September 2003. Complications forced his euthanization that December, but he sired 2002 European champion older male Grandera and 2000 European champion three-year-old male Sinndar before his untimely demise.

Erhaab and Chief Bearhart were less successful in carrying on the male line of Chief's Crown although Chief Bearhart did sire 2004 Japanese champion juvenile male Meiner Recolte. But a lesser son of Chief's Crown, 1997 Jim Beam Stakes (gr. II) winner Concerto, became a useful sire in Florida and was represented in 2005 by Wood Memorial Stakes (gr. I) winner Bellamy Road, the beaten favorite for the Kentucky Derby after a breathtaking seventeen-length romp in the Wood.

Polish Navy was among Danzig's best-bred sons — his dam Navsup is a half sister to Buckpasser — and he ran up to his blue blood on the racetrack, winning the 1986 Champagne Stakes (gr. I) and the 1987 Woodward Stakes (gr. I). Although not a particularly successful sire, he did get the 1992 Secretariat Stakes (gr. IT) winner Ghazi and the 1993 Kentucky Derby winner, Sea Hero. The latter was a somewhat delicate sort that trainer Mack Miller described as being "more like a filly than a colt — you couldn't train him that hard." But Sea Hero, though inconsistent, had a knack for winning big races, his other major triumphs including the Champagne Stakes at two and the Travers Stakes at three. He was unable to live up to his splendid pedigree (out of Broodmare of the Year Glowing Tribute) as a sire and was exported to Turkey.

Neither of Danzig's other American Classic winners — the 1992 Preakness winner Pine Bluff and the 1986 Belmont winner Danzig Connection — proved top sires although both had some solid runners. A worse fate befell Lure, the brilliant two-time Breeders' Cup Mile (gr. IT) winner: he proved markedly subfertile. Nonetheless, Lure managed to continue his branch of Danzig's male line through his son Orpen, a group I-winning juvenile in France and a champion sire and broodmare sire in Argentina.

The 1996 European champion sprinter Anabaa surprised many when his first-crop son Anabaa Blue stayed well enough to win the 2001 Prix du Jockey-Club, then at 2,400 meters (it was shortened to 2,100 meters in 2005). The sire of eighty-eight stakes winners, including Australian champion sprinter Yell, Anabaa also became a three-time champion broodmare sire in France. Another champion sprinter by Danzig, 1990 English Horse of the Year Dayjur, narrowly missed a shot at an American sprint championship when he jumped shadows down the stretch of the Breeders' Cup Sprint (gr. I), allowing the champion sprint mare Safely Kept to come back and win the race by a neck. His twenty-seven stakes winners were headed by 2005 Brazilian champion miler Eyjur and the group I-winning juvenile Hayil, both poor sires.

Several of Danzig's more modest sons have been useful sires including Belong to Me, Honor Grades (a half brother to 1992 Horse of the Year A.P. Indy), Polish Numbers, and Ascot Knight. Lost Soldier has also come into the spotlight as the sire of the brilliant sprinter Lost in the Fog, the 2005 American champion sprinter who, sadly, fell victim to cancer as a four-year-old.

Danzig's best son at stud in the United States has been 2007 King's Bishop Stakes (gr. I) winner Hard Spun, the sire of 102 stakes winners through January 2024 and the broodmare sire of 2017 American champion two-year-old male Good Magic, sire in turn of 2023 Kentucky Derby winner Mage. Even so, the best of all Danzig's sire sons have both been based abroad. The elder of the two, the high-class sprinter Green Desert, sired ninety-four stakes winners while standing in England and continued his line in Europe through 2003 European champion sprinter Oasis Dream and group I winners Invincible Spirit and Cape Cross. The last-named horse, in turn, sired 2009 European Horse of the Year Sea the Stars, a half brother to Galileo that has sired 115 stakes winners through January 2024. Another son of Green Desert, Volksraad, was only a minor winner as a racehorse but led the New Zealand general sire list seven times. And no discussion of Danzig's influence would be complete without mention of his son Desert Sun, sire of three-time Australian Horse of the Year and four-time New Zealand Horse of the Year Sunline — surely one of the greatest mares of all time.

Danzig's best son at stud by far, however, was the closely inbred Danehill, whose dam Razyana is a granddaughter of Natalma. While Danehill certainly had the credentials for a reasonable chance at stud — he won the 1989 Ladbroke Sprint Stakes (Eng-I) — he was successful beyond anyone's wildest expectations. The second Northern Dancer-line horse to become leading sire in Australia (following in the hoofprints of Last Tycoon, who was Australian leading sire for 1993/94), he led the Australian general sire list nine times. He was also a great success in Europe (he was leading sire in France in 2001 and 2002 and led both the English and European sire lists in 2005) and became the first sire to be represented by three hundred stakes winners when his daughter Nevis won the Bacardi Breezer Toy Show Quality Stakes at Randwick, Australia, on August 20, 2005. According to The Jockey Club Information Services, his final tally was 347 stakes winners worldwide.

Danehill's landmark accomplishment was admittedly aided and abetted by the huge books he served in both the Northern and Southern hemispheres (he is credited with having sired 2,499 foals of racing age), but there is far more to his success than sheer numbers; he sired champions or Classic winners in Australia, Canada, New Zealand, England, Ireland, France, and the United States. He died in 2003 at the regrettably early age of seventeen but is the sire of Australian champion sires Redoute's Choice, Flying Spur, and Exceed and Excel; two-time Argentine champion sire Catcher in the Rye; and the important European sires Danehill Dancer and Dansili, among others.

As might be expected from a horse with such great success as a sire, Danzig has been well represented as a broodmare sire. Perhaps the most celebrated North American runner among the 213 stakes winners produced from his daughters was 2000 Kentucky Derby winner Fusaichi Pegasus, but Danzig is also the maternal grandsire of American champion sire and broodmare sire Distorted Humor; of grade I winner and important sire Arch; of Queen's Plate winners Scatter the Gold (2000) and Dancethruthedawn (2001); and of multiple Canadian champion Soaring Free. Outside North America, Danzig's daughters were responsible for Japanese champions Believe, Grass Wonder, and Nishino Flower and for 1995 Irish St. Leger winner Strategic Choice.

******

Dixieland Band, although a multiple grade II winner, was one of Northern Dancer's less spectacular sons on the racetrack. Nonetheless, he was one of the most reliable as a sire, with 111 stakes winners to his credit. His best include European champion stayer Drum Taps, 2000 Prix de Diane winner Egyptband, and 2004 Oaks d'Italia (Ity-I) winner Menhoubah. He was pensioned in 2008 and died in 2010.

Although Dixieland Band had the ability to get occasional runners of the very highest class, his reputation as a stallion stemmed from his consistency in getting solid rather than spectacular runners year in, year out. In this, he appears to reflect the family of his dam, 1977 Matchmaker Stakes (gr. I) winner Mississippi Mud (by Delta Judge). This family has thrown up a fair number of good horses through the years, but one has to go three generations back along Mississippi Mud's female line to find another top-class runner; this was Misty Isle, winner of the 1940 Matron Stakes.

Dixieland Band probably lost his best chance to found an enduring branch of the Northern Dancer male line when his multiple grade I-winning son Dixie Union died at age 13, leaving behind 2012 Belmont Stakes winner Union Rags (an inconsistent sire) and forty-seven other stakes winners. Another Dixieland Band son worthy of mention is Dixieland Heat, who from modest opportunities sired Xtra Heat, a brilliant sprint filly who was named 2001 champion three-year-old filly. As tough as she was talented, Xtra Heat raced into her five-year-old season, winning twenty-six of her thirty-five starts.

In the long run, it appears that Dixieland Band will have his greatest long-term impact through his daughters. The 2004 American champion broodmare sire is the maternal grandsire of 213 stakes winners as of August 2023.

Princes of the Blood (Part II)

His maternal grandson Monarchos won the 2001 Kentucky Derby, and other top runners produced from his daughters include multiple grade I winners Southern Image, Society Selection, Exotic Wood, First Samurai, and Dream Supreme.

******

Storm Bird, a 1978 colt out of South Ocean, entered stud in 1982 and proved a good stallion. He was pensioned in 1999 and died in 2004. His best runners were Indian Skimmer, the 1987 Prix de Diane winner; Bluebird, a champion sprinter in Ireland; Summer Squall, winner of the 1990 Preakness Stakes; Balanchine, winner of the 1994 English Oaks and Irish Derby; and grade/group I winners Prince of Birds, Classy Mirage, Personal Hope, Pacific Squall, and Storm Cat.

Both Bluebird and Summer Squall became good sires. Bluebird, a successful shuttle sire in Ireland and Australia, was pensioned in November 2004 but did not leave an obvious successor at stud. He is perhaps best known in the United States as the sire of Yellow Ribbon Invitational Stakes (gr. IT) winner Aube Indienne (Fr) and multiple grade II winner Blues Traveller (Ire), while in Europe he begot the group I-winning sprinters Dolphin Street (Fr) and Lake Coniston (Ire). His best Australian progeny include 1992 VATC One Thousand Guineas (Aus-I) winner Azzurro, South Australian Derby winner (Aus-I) Blue Murder, and VATC Oakleigh Plate (Aus-I) winner Singing the Blues.

Summer Squall, a half brother to 1992 Horse of the Year A.P. Indy, was troubled by fertility problems through much of his stud career but nonetheless sired Charismatic, who earned Horse of the Year honors in 1999 after winning the Kentucky Derby and Preakness and finishing a courageous third on a broken leg in the Belmont. Summer Squall also sired 1996 champion juvenile filly Storm Song. He was pensioned in February 2004, fifteen months after Charismatic's sale to Japanese interests. (Charismatic, a poor sire, was pensioned and returned to the United States in 2016, dying the following year.)

Storm Bird also had success as a broodmare sire, with his daughters producing such top runners as 1994 U.S. champion juvenile filly Flanders, 1995

Kentucky Derby and Belmont winner Thunder Gulch, 2003 U.S. champion three-year-old filly Bird Town, and 2004 Belmont winner Birdstone.

But it is Storm Cat who has ensured Storm Bird a lasting place in blood-stock annals. Winner of the 1985 Young America Stakes (gr. I), Storm Cat missed becoming that year's American juvenile champion by a scant nose, the margin of his defeat by Tasso in the Breeders' Cup Juvenile. After one win and one unplaced run at three, Storm Cat retired to stud at owner William T. Young's Overbrook Farm.

Storm Cat rapidly proved a tremendous influence for speed, precocity, and gameness and became the unquestioned king of the American commercial market during the 1990s and 2000s. His progeny ran equally well on both dirt and turf and generally came to hand quickly; with the right mare, Storm Cat also proved capable of getting Classic horses and good older runners. His son Tabasco Cat won the 1994 Preakness and Belmont before becoming a solid if rather unappreciated sire (he was sent to Japan in late 2000 and died there of an apparent heart attack in March 2004) while Good Reward won the 2005 Manhattan Handicap (gr. IT) over ten furlongs as a four-year-old. Cat Thief, though inconsistent, could also handle ten furlongs well enough to win the 1999 Breeders' Cup Classic as a three-year-old. With horses like these on his resume, it is no wonder that Storm Cat became the leading American sire of 1999 and 2000.

In 2004, Storm Cat earned his seventh title as champion juvenile sire in the United States, surpassing the great Bold Ruler, who won that title six times. He became known as a great sire of sires, though for many of his more popular sons, their apparent success has as much to do with huge books as it does with the overall quality of what they sire. Nonetheless, Storm Cat sired champion sires or broodmare sires in Argentina (Bernstein, Pure Prize), Chile (Easing Along, Seeking the Dia, Tumblebrutus), and the United States (Giant's Causeway), a good record by virtually any sire's standards short of Northern Dancer himself.

In 2001 Hennessy, the 1995 Hopeful Stakes (gr. I) winner, became the first of Storm Cat's sons to earn a sire championship when he headed the list of American juvenile sires based largely on the exploits of his son Johannesburg. A handsome, well-balanced bay, Johannesburg won the Phoenix Stakes (Ire-I), Prix Morny (Fr-I), Middle Park Stakes (Eng-I), and

Breeders' Cup Juvenile. He was voted champion juvenile in both Europe (earning national championships in England, Ireland, and France, as well) and the United States but failed to show his juvenile form in three starts at three and was retired. He was an inconsistent stallion but succeeded in handing on his male line through his multiple grade I-winning son Scat Daddy (a two-time champion sire in Chile) to Justify, winner of the American Triple Crown in 2018 and, as of January 2024, a hot young sire who was America's champion juvenile sire in 2023.

Storm Cat's best son on the racecourse was 2000 European Horse of the Year Giant's Causeway, who earned three American sire titles before his death in 2018 and was also champion broodmare sire that year. His best son at stud was 2004 European champion juvenile male Shamardal, who was a champion sire of juveniles in England and Ireland and begot a solid successor in dual French Classic winner Lope de Vega.

Aside from the accomplishments of his male line, Storm Cat (who was pensioned in 2008 and died in 2013) left a legacy through his daughters, whose foals made him a three-time American champion broodmare sire. 2004 American champion sprinter Speightstown, a leading sire in his own right, is probably the most important horse produced from Storm Cat's daughters, but the stallion is also the maternal grandsire of champions Churchill, Close Hatches, Folklore, Gleneagles, Hail Glory, Happily, Honor Code, Randy Cat, and Shared Belief.

The most dominant sire of his time on the track, Storm Cat also dominated the commercial market in a manner not seen since Northern Dancer's heyday. The sire of a record ninety-one yearlings that sold for a million dollars or more at auction, he reached his peak in the sales ring in 2005. At that year's Keeneland September sale, a Storm Cat colt out of multiple grade I winner Tranquility Lake brought a sale-record $9.7 million, evoking memories of the days when Robert Sangster and Sheikh Mohammed dueled over Seattle Dancer, Snaafi Dancer, and Imperial Falcon — especially since the record-setting colt was purchased by Sheikh Mohammed. And the underbidder? Coolmore Stud, the managing director of which is John Magnier, a long-time partner and associate of Robert Sangster.

******

Over thirty years have passed since Northern Dancer's death, and all of his sons are now gone as well; even most of his grandsons have passed from the scene. Yet the Northern Dancer sire line shows no signs of fading or narrowing to just one or two major branches. Although challenged in North America by the Raise a Native sire line (primarily through the descendants of Raise a Native's son Mr. Prospector), and in Japan by the descendants of Halo through Sunday Silence, no sire line compares to that of Northern Dancer for influence around the world. The Dancer's male-line descendants include:

- Eight of the top twenty American sires of 2023
- Sixteen of the top twenty English sires of 2023, including four of the top five
- Eight of the top twenty Brazilian sires of 2022/23
- Eleven of the top twenty Argentine sires of 2023
- Fourteen of the top twenty Chilean sires of 2023
- Thirteen of the top twenty Australian sires of 2022/23
- Thirteen of the top twenty New Zealand sires of 2022/23
- Twelve of the top twenty South African sires of 2022/23

There is hardly a country where Thoroughbreds are raised that has not felt the influence of Northern Dancer, and not just in the major racing nations. Wherever men and Thoroughbreds have gone, the blood of Northern Dancer has gone also.

The Dancer has gone, but the dance goes on.

The Dancer's Daughters

Northern Dancer's daughters were not quite so outstanding as his sons; however, there were some excellent individuals among them, both as racers and as broodmares, and they have done much to spread the Dancer's genes further in the Thoroughbred population. Space does not permit enumeration of all the accomplishments of Northern Dancer's daughters, but the following survey (in alphabetical order) may serve to provide a picture of the impact that the Dancer's daughters have had on the modern Thoroughbred.

Ballet de France (1981 bay filly, out of Fabulous Native) won the C.L. Weld Park Stakes (Ire-III) as a juvenile. Her fourth foal was Muhtarram, a champion in Ireland at age four and in Italy at age five. Ballet de France also produced Profit Column, a grade III winner and dam of the grade III winner Final Round. Through another daughter, Pronghorn, Ballet de France is the second dam of Italian group III winner Omaticaya.

Barbs Dancer (1971 chestnut filly, Periodista) was stakes-placed on the track but was much better as a broodmare. Her son by Mr. Prospector, Eillo, won the inaugural Breeders' Cup Sprint (gr. I) and was named U.S. champion sprinter in 1984. Unfortunately, Eillo died a month after the Breeders' Cup from complications of colic, but his half sister Czar Dancer (by Czaravich, by Nijinsky II) is the dam of 1996 Top Flight Handicap (gr. I) winner Flat Fleet Feet. Another half sister, the Dr. Fager mare Ellie Milove, is the second dam of 2002 King's Bishop Stakes (gr. I) winner Gygistar.

The Dancer's Daughters

Cool Mood (1966 chestnut filly, Happy Mood) won the 1969 Canadian Oaks. Her stakes-winning daughter Passing Mood (by Buckpasser) is the dam of five stakes winners, including 1989 Canadian Triple Crown winner With Approval and 1997 Belmont Stakes winner Touch Gold. The latter horse is the result of close inbreeding as his sire, Deputy Minister, is a grandson of Northern Dancer. Another daughter of Cool Mood, Shy Spirit (by Personality), is the dam of four stakes winners including 1990 Canadian Triple Crown winner Izvestia. Shy Spirit's daughter Playful Spirit (by Bold Hour) is the granddam of 1998 Santa Anita Oaks (gr. I) winner Hedonist, whose sire Alydeed is by Shadeed, by Nijinsky II. Other top descendants of Cool Mood include grade I winners Healthy Addiction (2006 Santa Margarita Invitational Handicap), Brilliant Speed (2011 Toyota Blue Grass Stakes), and My Sweet Addiction (2015 Vanity Handicap).

Dance Number (1979 bay filly, Numbered Account) won the 1983 Beldame Stakes (gr. I). As a broodmare, she produced 1989 American champion juvenile male Rhythm and grade III winner Get Lucky, both by Mr. Prospector. Not For Love, a stakes-placed full brother to Rhythm and Get Lucky, was a useful sire in Maryland, while Get Lucky produced 2010 Vosburgh Handicap (gr. I) winner Girolamo and grade III winners Accelerator and Daydreaming, all by A.P. Indy. Dance Number is also the granddam of 2010 Kentucky Derby winner Super Saver, 2006 Haskell Invitational Stakes (gr. I) winner Bluegrass Cat, and 2014 Man o' War Stakes (gr. I) winner Imagining. Another daughter of Dance Number, Oscillate (by Seattle Slew), is the dam of stakes winner Mutakddim (by Seeking the Gold), the Argentine champion sire of 2006.

Danseur Fabuleux (1982 bay filly, Fabuleux Jane) was group III-placed in France. She struck gold with her second foal, a small colt by Blushing Groom (Fr). Named Arazi, the little chestnut proved himself the best juvenile in France in 1991 with six stakes victories, three at group I level. He then crossed the Atlantic to turn in a breathtaking performance in the Breeders' Cup Juvenile (gr. I), winning by five lengths pulling up.

Few horses could have lived up to the hype generated by Arazi's juvenile campaign, and Arazi was not one of them. He finished unplaced as the favorite in the 1992 Kentucky Derby after undergoing surgery for a knee chip over the winter and never recovered the brilliance of his two-year-old form, though he did win the Prix du Rond-Point (Fr-II) later in the year. He was a disappointing sire but begot one very good horse in Congaree, a multiple grade I winner.

Danseur Fabuleux is also the dam of Noverre (by Blushing Groom's son Rahy), who won the 2001 Poule d'Essai des Poulains but was later disqualified after testing positive for methyprednisolone, a medication that trainer Saeed bin Suroor said was being used to treat an arthritic condition. Later in the year, the colt earned a group I victory for keeps by winning the Sussex Stakes.

Dokki (1986 bay filly, Alluvial) never raced but produced two grade 1 winners in the Seattle Slew filly Sleep Easy and her three-parts brother Aptitude (by A.P. Indy, by Seattle Slew). The former won the 1995 Hollywood Oaks (gr. I), while the latter won the 2001 Hollywood Gold Cup (gr. I) and the Jockey Club Gold Cup (gr. I), the latter race by ten lengths.

Drama School (1966 chestnut filly, *Stalino) was a good three-year-old in Canada, winning the 1969 Star Shoot Stakes and Selene Stakes. Her 1973 colt by Buckpasser, Norcliffe, took two legs of the Canadian Triple Crown by winning the 1976 Queen's Plate and Prince of Wales Stakes. Norcliffe's half sister Vaguely Dramatic (by *Vaguely Noble) is the granddam of 1993/94 Argentine champion two-year-old male El Sultan, a multiple group I winner.

Falafel (1973 bay filly, *Queen's Statute) made no impact on the racecourse but produced two colts who showed their best form in Europe. The first, Again Tomorrow (by Honest Pleasure), was an inconsistent runner but scored one of his four wins from twenty-seven starts in the 1985 Premio Parioli (Italian Two Thousand Guineas). The other, Brief Truce (by Irish River [Fr]), won three stakes, including the 1992 St. James's Palace Stakes (Eng-I), and was third in the 1992 Irish Two Thousand Guineas and Breeders' Cup Mile (gr. IT).

Northern Meteor (1975 dark bay or brown filly, Patelin) won the California Oaks before founding a brilliant but ill-fated family. Her son A Phenomenon ranked among the best sprinters of his generation, winning the 1983 Vosburgh Stakes (gr. I) but died as a four-year old, while a daughter, Seattle Meteor (1988 Spinaway Stakes, gr. I), produced nothing of significant merit among her nine foals.

Bad luck also dogged the offspring of Northern Meteor's best producing daughter, Meteor Stage. After producing the Puerto Rican group II stakes winner Full Stage and multiple grade III winner Stage Colony, Meteor Stage hit the jackpot with the Pleasant Colony filly Pleasant Stage. The 1991 champion juvenile filly, Pleasant Stage died at three of anaphylactic shock after a routine administration of intravenous vitamins. The family received some recompense when Pleasant Stage's full sister Meteor Colony produced 2001 Grey Breeders' Cup Stakes (Can-I) winner Changeintheweather. Another full sister to Pleasant Stage, Colonial Play, won the 1998 Orchid Handicap (gr. II) and is the dam of multiple grade I winner Marsh Side.

Northern Sea (1974 bay filly, Sea Saga) won the 1977 Test Stakes (gr. III). Her stakes-placed son Southern Halo (by Halo) was the most sensational sire in Argentine history, leading that country's general sire list from 1994 through 2001 and again in 2003. His American-bred son More Than Ready became an important international sire, and Southern Halo led the Argentine broodmare sire list sixteen times.

Southern Halo has not been Northern Sea's only contribution to her breed. Her daughter by Smarten, Excellent Lady, is the dam of the popular California gelding General Challenge (by General Meeting), a multiple grade I winner, and of the 2000 Oak Leaf Stakes (gr. I) winner Notable Career (by Avenue of Flags).

Pacificus (1981 bay filly, Pacific Princess) was a modest winner in England, taking two of her eleven starts. Sent to Japan, she produced back-to-back Horses of the Year in Biwa Hayahide (1993) and Narita Brian (1994), the latter a winner of the Japanese Triple Crown. She is also the granddam of multiple group II winner Last Impact.

Really Lucky (1978 chestnut filly, Realty) won the listed Prix de Saint-Cyr in France and produced Ravinella, winner of a Classic double in the 1988 One Thousand Guineas and Poule d'Essai des Pouliches. The 1987 champion juvenile filly in both France and England and the 1988 champion three-year-old filly in France, Ravinella is by Mr. Prospector and is a full sister to Line In The Sand, winner of the 1992 Louisiana Derby (gr. III).

Royal Statute (1969 bay filly, *Queen's Statute) was a minor winner but proved a fine broodmare, producing three graded or group winners including 1982 English champion three-year-old filly Awaasif, herself the dam of three graded or group winners. The best of them, Snow Bride, won the 1989 Oaks Stakes on the disqualification of Aliysa and, in turn, to the cover of Nijinsky II, produced unbeaten Lammtarra, winner of the 1995 Derby Stakes.

Sleek Dancer (1968 bay filly, Victorine) never raced but produced three stakes winners: 1978 Monmouth Oaks (gr. I) winner Sharp Belle (by Native Charger); three-time stakes winner Northern Prospect (by Mr. Prospector), a useful sire; and Sue Babe, a full sister to Northern Prospect. Sue Babe, in turn, produced the 1987 Irish Derby winner Sir Harry Lewis to the cover of Alleged. Another daughter of Sleek Dancer, Sleek Belle (by *Vaguely Noble) produced four stakes winners including grade III winner Witwatersrand, herself the dam of 1994 Yushun Himba (Japanese Oaks) winner Chokai Carol.

Wild Applause (1981 bay filly, Glowing Tribute) won the 1984 Diana Handicap (gr. II) and Comely Stakes (gr. III) and is among the best broodmares sired by Northern Dancer with four graded winners to her credit including 1990 Futurity Stakes (gr. I) winner Eastern Echo. Her grade II-winning son Roar (by Forty Niner) led the Argentine sire list in 2004 and was represented by eleven group I winners that year, headed by the dual Classic winner Forty Marchanta. Wild Applause's grade II-winning daughter Yell (by A.P. Indy) is the granddam of multiple grade 1 winner Elate and grade II winner Tax.

******

If the Dancer's daughters do not quite have the sterling record of his sons, they still have an honorable history. All told, they produced 229 stakes winners and made their sire the leading American broodmare sire of 1991. Taken by themselves, they would earn Northern Dancer a respected place in bloodstock annals; combined with the contributions of Northern Dancer's sons, they underscore Northern Dancer's reputation as the type of breed-shaping sire whose like we may see perhaps once a century.

Was Northern Dancer Great?

As a stallion, there is no question of Northern Dancer's greatness. At first, his lone sire championship in the United States and four championships in England may seem good but not all that impressive; Bold Ruler, after all, led the U.S. sire list eight times, while St. Simon led the English sire list nine times and Hyperion led it six times. Why should Northern Dancer, as good as he was, be considered the peer or even the superior of these great sires?

Consider, first, the sheer quality of Northern Dancer's output. Of his 645 registered foals, 147 became stakes winners — more than 23 percent — and twent-six were recognized as champions or highweights in England, France, Ireland, Italy, the United States, or Canada. He begot three English Derby winners, four Irish Derby winners, three Two Thousand Guineas winners, one Irish Two Thousand Guineas winner, one St. Leger winner, and one Prix de Diane winner — a remarkable record in the European Classics for a sire physically based in North America.

(Even given the incredible European appetite for Northern Dancer's best yearlings in the late 1970s through the 1980s, it seems surprising that Northern Dancer had much less spectacular success in North America than in Europe. The reason for this may lie in conformation and constitution. Many of Northern Dancer's progeny were somewhat sickle-hocked, with hind legs that angled forward at the hock more than is considered ideal. Such legs, unless extreme, do not seem to hinder performance on the undulating grass courses of Europe, where agility and the ability to keep changing stride smoothly to cope with uneven footing are more important than the ability to deliver the sustained powerful stride necessary for American dirt racing. As Joss Collins of the British Bloodstock Agency noted, many of the Northern Dancers also seemed better suited to the European style of training up to a particular race than to the American style of trying to maintain a horse at or near peak fitness for extended periods while racing every few weeks.)

There is no question that Northern Dancer's record is comparable with the greatest sires of the breed, yet it does not necessarily exceed them. St. Simon sired 25 percent stakes winners, including the winners of seventeen Classic races; Bold Ruler sired 23 percent stakes winners; Hyperion, 22 percent. All could fairly be said to have been the greatest sires of their respective days.

But Northern Dancer's claim to preeminence is in the great stallions he has sired; as was once said of the Godolphin Arabian, "his pedigree is written in his sons." Collectively, Northern Dancer's sons led the English sire list sixteen times, the American sire list four times, the Japanese sire list ten times, and the French sire list nine times. Further, they passed the magic on. Sons of Northern Dancer's sons were leading sires in Argentina, Australia, Brazil, England, France, South Africa, and the United States, and the list of countries where Northern Dancer-line stallions are wielding influence continues to grow.

As a Classic influence, Northern Dancer has been little short of amazing. Since Gate Dancer broke the ice in 1984, twenty-two Northern Dancer-line horses have won American Triple Crown races. Since 2000, twenty runnings of the English Derby have gone to the Northern Dancer line, as have twenty runnings of the Irish Derby and fourteen editions of the Prix du Jockey-Club in the same period. Similar patterns are seen in the other English, French, and Irish Classics, which have become increasingly dominated by descendants of the little bay stallion from Canada. As for Northern Dancer's native land, twenty runnings of the King's Plate (run as the Queen's Plate during the reign of Queen Elizabeth II, 1952–2002) have been taken by his direct descendants.

It is in the ongoing excellence of his sire line that Northern Dancer is perhaps unrivaled in Thoroughbred history. St. Simon and Hyperion were both great sires of sires, yet today their sire lines are on the verge of extinction. Bold Ruler's line has largely constricted to the descendants of his great-grandson A.P. Indy. Even Northern Dancer's great ancestor Phalaris, while the male-line ancestor of some 90 percent of modern Thoroughbreds, has the vast majority of his descendants through one grandson: Nearco. But as of this writing, Northern Dancer's line continues to flourish widely through the Danzig, Sadler's Wells, and Storm Cat branches, with the Try My Best branch very much alive in Australasia and Nureyev maintaining a presence in France through his great-grandson Siyouni, a two-time sire champion in that country.

It may be that at some future time, the Northern Dancer sire line will suffer one of the same two fates that have eventually befallen every other sire line: virtual extinction, or survival through only one or two major branches founded by horses that themselves merit the title of "supersire." But for now, the Northern Dancer sire line is the most dominant international sire line on the planet, and it all began with a small bay colt that no one seemed to want.

******

While no one debates Northern Dancer's greatness as a sire, his merit as a racehorse has been open to more question. The general consensus seems to be that he was a very good racehorse rather than a truly great one. But is this fair?

On the surface, his record would seem to support the general consensus. He was a versatile performer who could handle any surface at distances up to ten furlongs, and his record of fourteen wins, two seconds, and two thirds from eighteen starts compares favorably with those of many of the sport's greats. By all accounts, his agility and acceleration were exceptional, and one must remember that he had not necessarily come to his full powers by the end of his career; only two of his starts were made after his actual third birthday. Yet he never possessed the shattering brilliance of a Man o' War or a Secretariat, and nearly half his starts were made in Canada, where the competition was weaker than at the major American tracks.

Northern Dancer's stamina has long been a subject for debate. Horatio Luro seems to have considered him essentially a miler, getting longer

distances on class; yet it is a curious fact that of his eight starts at nine furlongs or longer, Northern Dancer lost only one: the Belmont, and there are
partisans (mostly Canadian) who still insist that he should have won even
that. Other observers (mostly American), while conceding that the colt was
brilliant up to ten furlongs, note him as having failed to stay the Belmont
distance. The best that can be said from a bare reading of the race chart is
that he had a clear shot at Quadrangle with a furlong to go and failed to nail
him or even hold the place. Whether his failure to handle the distance can
be laid to tactics, injury, or an innate lack of stamina will probably be debated for as long as the horse is remembered.

It is on sheer heart that Northern Dancer can stake a claim to greatness,
for the fact remains that after the Summer Stakes — only the third start of
his career — he battled one physical problem after another and probably
was never entirely sound. Both the quarter crack and the splint in his left
foreleg would have stopped many other horses, and the tendon strain that
ended his career probably began during the Belmont, when he was fighting
so gallantly to win at a distance that, whatever the reason, was beyond him
that day. How much he actually suffered and how much his performance
was affected by his injuries we will never know, for those who knew him
well all agreed that the Dancer was the kind of horse that would try to run
through any injury, any problem.

As it was, the memory of a courageous little horse and his fiery will to win
have stayed with at least one man through more than half a century, beyond
a career in which he rode such champions as Damascus, Riva Ridge, and
Fort Marcy.

"Next to Secretariat," says Ron Turcotte, "Northern Dancer was the greatest horse I ever rode."

Appendix

NORTHERN DANCER	Nearctic, 1954	Nearco, 1935	Pharos, 1920	Phalaris, 1913 — Polymelus / Bromus
				Scapa Flow, 1914 — **Chaucer** / Anchora
			Nogara, 1928	Havresac II, 1915 — Rabelais / Hors-Concours
				Catnip, 1910 — Spearmint / Sibola
		*Lady Angela, 1944	Hyperion, 1930	**Gainsborough**, 1915 — Bayardo / Rosedrop
				Selene, 1919 — **Chaucer** / Serenissima
			Sister Sarah, 1930	Abbots Trace, 1917 — Tracery / Abbots Anne
				Sarita, 1924 — Swynford / Molly Desmond
	Natalma, 1957	Native Dancer, 1950	Polynesian, 1942	Unbreakable, 1935 — *Sickle / *Blue Glass
				Black Polly, 1936 — *Polymelian / Black Queen
			Geisha, 1943	Discovery, 1931 — Display / Ariadne
				Miyako, 1935 — John P. Grier / La Chica
		Almahmoud, 1947	*Mahmoud, 1933	*Blenheim II, 1927 — Blandford / Malva
				Mah Mahal, 1928 — **Gainsborough** / Mumtaz Mahal
			Arbitrator, 1937	Peace Chance, 1931 — Chance Shot / Peace
				Mother Goose, 1922 — *Chicle / Flying Witch

Appendix Notes:

The inbreeding noted on the lists of Northern Dancer's stakes winners (page 202) and his stakes winners as broodmare sire (page 210) reflect inbreeding between sire and dam only.

Starting on page 218, stakes winners are listed for Northern Dancer's sons who sired 100 or more stakes winners. For active stallions, the lists are current through December 2005.

Appendix: Northern Dancer's Stakes Winners

HORSE	C/S/YOB	DAM	BROODMARE SIRE	STATUS
Cool Mood	ch.f. 1966	Happy Mood	*Mahmoud	SW
Dance Act	ch.g. 1966	*Queen's Statute	Le Lavandou (Fr)	SW
Dorothy Glynn	b.f. 1966	Save Time	War Admiral	SW
Drama School	ch.f. 1966	*Stalina	Stalino (GB)	SW
Eaglesham	ch.c. 1966	Pink Velvet	Polynesian	SW
Northern Bay	b.c. 1966	Wendasy	Your Host	SW
One for All	b.c.1966	Quill	*Princequillo	SW
Sno Where	ch.f. 1966	Wonder Where	Occupy	SW
True North	ch.g. 1966	Hill Rose	Rosemont	SW
Viceregal	ch.c. 1966	Victoria Regina	*Menetrier	SW
Fanfreluche	b.f. 1967	Ciboulette	Chop Chop	SW
Nijinsky II	b.c. 1967	Flaming Page	Bull Page	SW
Swinging Apache	b.c. 1967	Allegro	Chop Chop	SW
Zingari	ch.c. 1967	Prodana Neviesta	Reneged	SW
Aladancer	ch.f. 1968	Mock Orange	Dedicate	SW
Alma North	b.f. 1968	Spaws Arrow	Swaps	G1SW
Lauries Dancer	b.f. 1968	Its Ann	*Royal Gem II	SW
Minsky	ch.c. 1968	Flaming Page	Bull Page	SW
Northern Jove	ro.c. 1968	Junonia	Sun Again	SW
Northfields	ch.c. 1968	Little Hut	Occupy	SW
Barachois	ch.c. 1969	Ciboulette	Chop Chop	SW
Gay Northerner	b.f. 1969	Miss Kisco	Mr. Busher	SW
Grand Lachine	b.c. 1969	*Lachine II	Grey Sovereign (GB)	SW
Lyphard	b.c. 1969	Goofed	*Court Martial	SW
Nice Dancer	b.c. 1969	Nice Princess	*Le Beau Prince	G3SW
Champagne Charlie	ro.c. 1970	Shy Dancer	Bolero	G3SW
North of Venus	b.f. 1970	Fly by Venus	Dark Star	G3SW
Northern Fling	b.c. 1970	Impetuous Lady	Hasty Road	G3SW
Jacango	b.c. 1971	I Deceive	Bagdad	SW
Northern Gem	ch.f. 1971	*Bamboozle	Alcide (GB)	G2SW
Northern Taste	ch.c. 1971	Lady Victoria	Victoria Park	G1SW
Black Powder	b.c. 1972	Obeah	Cyane	SW
Broadway Dancer	b.f. 1972	*Broadway Melody	*Tudor Melody	G1SW
Dance d'Espoir	b.c. 1972	Julie Kate	Hill Prince	G3SW
Dancers Countess	b.f. 1972	Countess Belvane	*Ribot	G1SW
Dancing Liz	ch.f. 1972	Crimson Queen	Crimson Satan	SW
North of the Law	ch.c. 1972	*Queen's Statue	Le Lavandou (Fr)	SW
Northerly	b.c. 1972	Politely	*Amerigo	SW
Dance Spell	b.c. 1973	Obeah	Cyane	G2SW
Far North	b.c. 1973	Fleur	Victoria Park	G3SW
Gay Jitterbug	b.g. 1973	Gay Meeting	Sir Gaylord	G3SW
Laissez Passer	dk.b.c. 1973	Lindenlea	Double Jay	SW
Northern Affair	b.g. 1973	Affaire d'Amour	Summa Cum	SW
Yallah Native	b.c. 1973	Little by Little	Fisherman	SW
Be My Guest	ch.c. 1974	What a Treat	*Tudor Minstrel	G2SW
Dance in Time	b.c. 1974	Allegro	Chop Chop	SW
Giboulee	b.c. 1974	Victory Chant	Victoria Park	G3SW
Music of Time	ch.g. 1974	First Feather	First Landing	G3SW
Northern Ballerina	b.f. 1974	Floral Victory	Victoria Park	SW
Northern Sea	b.f. 1974	Sea Saga	*Sea-Bird	G3SW
Northernette	b.f. 1974	South Ocean	New Providence	G1SW
Rassendyll	ch.c. 1974	Zenda	Graustark	SW

INBREEDING MALE	INBREEDING FEMALE	FEMALE FAMILY
Mahmoud 4x2; Gainsborough 5x4		2-n Renaissance
none		22-b Mincian
Hyperion 4x4		9-f Rose Leaves
Hyperion 4x4; Phalaris 5x5	Scapa Flow 5 (Pharos) x 5 (Fairway)	10-d Epping Rose
Polynesian 4x2; Phalaris 5x5	Selene 5 (Hyperion) x 5 (Sickle)	1-h Noontide
Hyperion 4x4; Mahmoud 4x4		14-f Honora
none		5-g Remembrance
Discovery 5x4		20-b High Flyer
Discovery 5x3		8-d Cloak
Phalaris 5x5	Scapa Flow 5 (Pharos) x 5 (Fairway)	10-c Bellamia
none		4-g Doonwater
Phalaris 5x5	Selene 5 (Hyperion) x 5 (Pharamond II)	8-f Torpenhow
none		3-g Russet
none		2-n Donnetta
none		4-m Sanfara
Nearco 3x5; Hyperion 4x4x5		9-c Americus Girl
none		A1 Understudy
Phalaris 5x5	Selene 5 (Hyperion) x 5 (Pharamond II)	8-f Torpenhow
Mahmoud 4x4		25 Ancient
none		4-r Prinzessin
none		4-g Doonwater
Hyperion 4x4; Blenheim II 5x4		3-e Elisalexi
Nearco 3x4x4; Havresac 5x4; Blenheim II 5x5		19-b Sunshot
Phalaris 5x5; Gainsborough 5x5	Scapa Flow 5 (Pharos) x 5 (Fairway)	17-b Cerda
none		1-e Flittervil
none		21-a Slippers
Mahmoud 4x4		13 Helen Barbee
Discovery 5x4		1-l Ladasine
none		4-i Hour Glass
Nearco 3x4; Hyperion 4x5; Blenheim II 5x5		21-a Simon Lass
none	Lady Angela 3 (Nearctic) x 2 (Lady Victoria)	14-c Pretty Polly
Nearco 3x5		2-f Altoviscar
Nearco 3x5; Hyperion 4x5		12-g Helvia
none		2-h Shad Fly
Pharos 4x5		5-i Louli
none		A34 Noowa
none		22-b Mincian
Nearco 3x3; Hyperion 4x5		9 Tea Enough
Nearco 3x5		2-f Altoviscar
none		8-f Torpenhow
Nearco 3x5; Hyperion 4x4		16-h Fine Feathers
Blenheim II 5x5		A11 Arrowshaft
Hyperion 4x4; Blenheim II 5x3		5-f Miss Fiora
none		1-w Bellita
Pharos 4x5; Hyperion 4x4		8-c Cherokee Rose
none		3-g Russet
none		3-g Russet
Nearco 3x5		5-g Remembrance
none		5-d Virginal
Nearco 3x5; Native Dancer 3x4; Discovery 5x5		16-g Olympia
none		4-j Lovelight
Hyperion 4x5		1-k Rose Ronald

Appendix: Northern Dancer's Stakes Winners

HORSE	C/S/YOB	DAM	BROODMARE SIRE	STATUS
The Minstrel	ch.c. 1974	Fleur	Victoria Park	G1SW
Topsider	b.c. 1974	Drumtop	Round Table	SW
Fairy Dance	b.f. 1975	Hill Shade	Hillary	SW
La Dorga	ch.f. 1975	Directoire	Gun Bow	G3SW
Norsk	b.c. 1975	Doris White	Black Beard	SW
Northern Meteor	dk.b.f. 1975	Patelin	Cornish Prince	SW
Robin's Song	b.c. 1975	Little Red Robin	*Ribot	SW
Try My Best	b.c. 1975	Sex Appeal	Buckpasser	G1SW
White Star Line	b.f. 1975	Fast Line	Mr. Busher	G1SW
Countess North	ch.f. 1976	Impetuous Lady	Hasty Road	G3SW
Double Deceit	dk.b.f. 1976	Double Agent	Double Jay	SW
Fabulous Dancer	b.c. 1976	Last of the Line	The Axe II	G3SW
Feu d'Artifice	ch.f. 1976	Quadrillion	Quadrangle	SW
Imperial Fling	b.c. 1976	Royal Dilemma	Buckpasser	G3SW
Northern Baby	b.c. 1976	Two Rings	Round Table	G1SW
Salpinx	b.f. 1976	Suprina	*Vaguely Noble	G2SW
Disconiz	b.f. 1977	*Codorniz	*Cockrullah	G3SW
Gold Treasure	b.f. 1977	Treasure Chest	Rough'n Tumble	SW
Magesterial	b.c. 1977	Courting Days	Bold Lad	G2SW
Northern Ringer	b.c. 1977	Two Rings	Round Table	SW
Nureyev	b.c. 1977	Special	*Forli	G3SW
Stephanie Leigh	b.f. 1977	Quadruple	Fleet Nasrullah	SW
Swift Bird	b.f. 1977	Flood Light	Bold Lad	SW
Cresta Rider	dk.b.c. 1978	Thoroly Blue	Blue Prince	G2SW
Dance Bid	b.c. 1978	Highest Trump	Bold Bidder	G3SW
Discorama	b.f. 1978	Obeah	Cyane	G2SW
Northern Fable	b.f. 1978	Fairway Fable	Never Bend	G3SW
Really Lucky	ch.f. 1978	Realty	Sir Ivor	SW
Storm Bird	b.c. 1978	South Ocean	New Providence	G1SW
Yarmouk	ch.c. 1978	Taken Aback	Carry Back	SW
Dance Number	b.f. 1979	Numbered Account	Buckpasser	G1SW
Larida	ch.f. 1979	Kittiwake	*Sea-Bird	G2SW
Linda North	dk.b.f. 1979	Lindaria	*Sea-Bird	SW
Northeastern	ch.f. 1979	Miss Toshiba	Sir Ivor	SW
Northrop	b.c. 1979	Sand Buggy	Warfare	SW
Pilgrim	b.c. 1979	Fleur	Victoria Park	SW
Woodstream	ch.f. 1979	Rule Formi	*Forli	G1SW
Danzatore	b.c. 1980	Shake a Leg	Raise a Native	G2SW
Dixieland Band	b.c. 1980	Mississippi Mud	Delta Judge	G2SW
Eskimo	b.c. 1980	Dr. Mary Lou	Dr. Fager	SW
Glenstal	b.c. 1980	Cloonlara	Sir Ivor	G2SW
Hero's Honor	b.c. 1980	Glowing Tribute	Graustark	G1SW
Lomond	b.c. 1980	My Charmer	Poker	G1SW
Mysterieuse Etoile	b.f. 1980	Gulanar (Ire)	*Val de Loir	G3SW
Routine	ch.f. 1980	Chappaquiddick	Relic	SW
Salmon Leap	ch.c. 1980	*Fish-Bar	Baldric	G2SW
Shareef Dancer	b.c. 1980	Sweet Alliance	Sir Ivor	G1SW

INBREEDING MALE	INBREEDING FEMALE	FEMALE FAMILY
none		8-f Torpenhow
Nearco 3x4; Blenheim II 5x5		5-h Simon's Shoes
Hyperion 4x4	Selene 5 (Hyperion) x 5 (Hyperion) x 5 (Moonlight Run)	3-m Isadora
Nearco 3x5; Hyperion 4x4; Mahmoud 4x5; Discovery 5x5		5-f Miss Fiora
Hyperion 4x5; Blenheim II 5x4		1-c Chit Chat
Nearco 3x5; Mahmoud 4x4; Discovery 5x5		23-b Broom Flower
Pharos 4x5; Hyperion 4x5		8-g Ste Claire
Hyperion 4x5; Discovery 5x5		8-f Torpenhow
none		4-m Mary King
Discovery 5x4		1-l Ladasine
Discovery 5x3		18 Old Lady
Hyperion 4x5; Mahmoud 4x3; Phalaris 5x5; Gainsborough 5x5; Blenheim II 5x4x5	Scapa Flow 5 (Pharos) x 5 (Fairway)	2-f Altoviscar
Hyperion 4x4; Mahmoud 4x4		14-c Pretty Polly
Nearco 3x5; Discovery 5x5		23 Aroon
Nearco 3x5		17-b Lygie
Nearco 3x4; Hyperion 4x5x5	Almahmoud 3 (Natalma) x 4 (Cosmah)	2-d Dazzling
Nearco 3x4; Blenheim II 5x5		14-f Flitaway
none		21-a Solirena
Nearco 3x5; Mahmoud 4x5; Discovery 5x5		1-s Doxa
Nearco 3x5		17-b Lygie
Nearco 3x5; Hyperion 4x4		5-h Simon's Shoes
Nearco 3x4; Blenheim II 5x5		22-c Busy Girl
Nearco 3x5; Pharos 4x5; Mahmoud 4x5; Discovery 5x5		8-c Cherokee Rose
Pharos 4x5x5		8-h Ophirdale
Nearco 3x5; Hyperion 4x5; Discovery 5x5		13-c Frizette
Nearco 3x5		2-f Altoviscar
Nearco 3x4; Blenheim II 5x5		4-m Mary King
Hyperion 4x5; Mahmoud 4x5		1-n Pennula
none		4-j Lovelight
Hyperion 4x5; Blenheim II 5x5		22-b Crepuscule
Nearco 3x5; Hyperion 4x5		1-s Doxa
Native Dancer 3x4		4-m Martha Gorman
Native Dancer 3x4; Hyperion 4x5; Mahmoud 4x5		14-f Honora
Mahmoud 4x5		1-k Reine de Naples
Hyperion 4x5x4; Mahmoud 4x5		4-m Martha Gorman
none		8-f Torpenhow
Nearco 3x4; Hyperion 4x4; Blenheim II 5x5		14-f Honora
Nearco 3x5; Native Dancer 3x3		2-f Toucan
Hyperion 4x5x5; Discovery 5x5		4-m Martha Gorman
none		3-i Gallenza
Mahmoud 4x5		8-c Primavista
Hyperion 4x5		1-s Doxa
Nearco 3x5; Blenheim II 5x5		13-c Frizette
none		9-c Americus Girl
Nearco 3x4	Nogara 4 (Nearco) x 5 (Nearco) x 5 (Niccolo Dell'Arca)	3-o Jean's Folly
Hyperion 4x5; Blenheim II 5x5		8-c Primavista
Mahmoud 4x5		4-r Artless

Appendix: Northern Dancer's Stakes Winners

HORSE	C/S/YOB	DAM	BROODMARE SIRE	STATUS
Spit Curl	b.f. 1980	Coiffure	Sir Gaylord	G1SW
Sulemeif	ch.f. 1980	Barely Even	Crème dela Crème	G3SW
Ballet de France	b.f. 1981	Fabulous Native	*Le Fabuleux	G3SW
Concordene	ch.f. 1981	Nocturnal Spree (Ire)	Supreme Sovereign (GB)	SW
Dance Flower	b.f. 1981	Flower Princess	Majestic Prince	SW
El Gran Senor	b.c. 1981	Sex Appeal	Buckpasser	G1SW
Lucky North	b.c. 1981	Lucky Ole Me	Olden Times	SW
Northern Trick	ch.f. 1981	Trick Chick	Prince John	G1SW
Pink	b.c. 1981	Pink Valley	Never Bend	G3SW
Sadler's Wells	b.c. 1981	Fairy Bridge	Bold Reason	G1SW
Secreto	b.c. 1981	Betty's Secret	Secretariat	G1SW
Wild Applause	b.f. 1981	Glowing Tribute	Graustark	G2SW
Antheus	b.c. 1982	Apachee (Fr)	Sir Gaylord	G1SW
Herat	b.c. 1982	Kashan	Damascus	G2SW
Northern Aspen	b.f. 1982	Fall Aspen	Pretense	G1SW
Northern Plain	b.c. 1982	Highest Trump	Bold Bidder	G3SW
Savannah Dancer	dk.b.f. 1982	*Valoris II	*Tiziano II	G2SW
Air Dancer	b.f. 1983	It's in the Air	Mr. Prospector	SW
Chercheur d'Or	dk.b.c. 1983	Gold River (Fr)	Riverman	G3SW
Fioravanti	b.c. 1983	Pitasia (Ire)	Pitskelly	SW
Glow	dk.b.c. 1983	Glisk	Buckpasser	G2SW
Northern Eternity	b.f. 1983	Hopespringseternal	Buckpasser	SW
Starry Night	b.c. 1983	Cloud Castle	Graustark	SW
Tate Gallery	b.c. 1983	Fairy Bridge	Bold Reason	G1SW
Wassl Touch	b.c. 1983	Queen Sucree	*Ribot	SW
Ajdal	b.c. 1984	Native Partner	Raise a Native	G1SW
Alwasmi	b.c. 1984	Height of Fashion (Fr)	Bustino (GB)	G3SW
Arctic Eclipse	dk.b.f. 1984	Gulls Cry	*Sea-Bird	SW
Chapel of Dreams	ch.f. 1984	Terlingua	Secretariat	G2SW
Northern Boy	b.c. 1984	Minstrel Girl (Fr)	Luthier (Fr)	SW
Palace Dancer	b.c. 1984	Better Begin	Buckpasser	SW
Rambo Dancer	b.c. 1984	Fair Arabella	Chateaugay	G2SW
Fairy Gold	b.f. 1985	Fairy Bridge	Bold Reason	G3SW
Gloria's Dancer	ch.f. 1985	Forlene (Ire)	*Forli	SW
Nabeel Dancer	b.c. 1985	Prayers'n Promises	Foolish Pleasure	G2SW
Unfuwain	b.c. 1985	Height of Fashion (Fr)	Bustino (GB)	G2SW
Diana Dance	ch.f. 1986	Deceit	Prince John	G2SW
Local Talent	b.c. 1986	Home Love	*Vaguely Noble	G1SW
Puppet Dance	ch.f. 1986	Fairy Bridge	Bold Reason	SW
Shotiche	b.c. 1986	Nimble Folly	Cyane	G3SW
Warrshan	b.c. 1986	Secret Asset	Graustark	G3SW
Antisaar	b.c. 1987	Detroit	Riverman	G2SW
Ladyago	b.f. 1987	Queen of Song	His Majesty	SW
Primetime North	b.f. 1987	Rally Around	Hoist the Flag	SW
Rakeen	b.c. 1987	Glorious Song	Halo	G2SW
Razeen	b.c. 1987	Secret Asset	Graustark	SW
Wajd	ch.f. 1987	Dahlia	*Vaguely Noble	G2SW
Northern Park	b.c. 1988	Mrs. Penny	Great Nephew (GB)	SW

INBREEDING MALE	INBREEDING FEMALE	FEMALE FAMILY
Nearco 3x5; Hyperion 4x5; Discovery 5x5		5-g Remembrance
Nearco 3x5; Hyperion 4x5		10-d Queen Tii
Native Dancer 3x4		10-a Court Dress
Nearco 3x4; Hyperion 4x5; Mahmoud 4x5		1-w Marchetta
Nearco 3x5; Native Dancer 3x4		8-f Torpenhow
Hyperion 4x5; Discovery 5x5		8-f Torpenhow
none		21-a Solirena
none		4-m Mary King
Nearco 3x4; Blenheim II 5x5		16-c Noreen Agnes
Hyperion 4x5		5-h Simon's Shoes
Nearco 3x5x5; Discovery 5x5		4-d Tribonyx
Hyperion 4x5		1-s Doxa
Nearco 3x5		4-i Palette Knife
Mahmoud 4x5		1-l Mistrella
Hyperion 4x4x5		4-m Audience
Nearco 3x5; Hyperion 4x5; Discovery 5x5		13-c Frizette
Phalaris 5x5	Nogara 4 (Nearco) x 5 (Niccolo Dell'Arca)	5-h Simon's Shoes
Nearco 3x5x5; Native Dancer 3x4		4-k Spring Chicken
Nearco 3x5		22-d Our Lassie
Native Dancer 3x4		14-c Pretty Polly
none		1-s Doxa
Nearco 3x5		16-g Olympia
Hyperion 4x5		1-k Rose Ronald
Hyperion 4x5		5-h Simon's Shoes
Pharos 4x5; Phalaris 5x5	Almahmoud 3 (Natalma) x 3 (Cosmah); Selene 5 (Hyperion) x 5 (Pharamond II)	2-d Dazzling
Native Dancer 3x3		7 N.R.A.
Hyperion 4x5		2-f Altoviscar
Nearco 3x5; Native Dancer 3x4		1-c Chit Chat
Nearco 3x5; Discovery 5x5		8-c Cherokee Rose
Nearco 3x5; Hyperion 4x5		1-u Veldt
Hyperion 4x4		13-b Epitaph
Hyperion 4x5; Polynesian 4x4; Mahmoud 4x4		16-c Noreen Agnes
Hyperion 4x5		5-h Simon's Shoes
Hyperion 4x4		13-c Frizette
Polynesian 4x4; Mahmoud 4x5		16-h Fine Feathers
Hyperion 4x5		2-f Altoviscar
Discovery 5x4		18 Old Lady
Nearco 3x4x5; Hyperion 4x5		17-b Lygie
Hyperion 4x5		5-h Simon's Shoes
Nearco 3x5; Native Dancer 3x4		4-r Lady Hubbard
Hyperion 4x5		1-s Doxa
Nearco 3x5		16-c Prune
Hyperion 4x5x5		5-j Balancoire
none		5-h Simon's Shoes
Mahmoud 4x5x5	Almahmoud 3 (Natalma) x 4 (Cosmah)	12-c Fruitful
Hyperion 4x5		1-s Doxa
Nearco 3x4; Hyperion 4x5x5		13-c Frizette
Nearco 3x5; Hyperion 4x5; Phalaris 5x5	Sister Sarah 4 (Lady Angela) x 5 (Sybil's Sister); Scapa Flow 5 (Pharos) x 5 (Fairway)	25 Ancient

Appendix

Northern Dancer's Champions and Leading Sires

Dance Act
1970 Canadian handicap horse
1971 Canadian handicap horse

Viceregal
1968 Canadian two-year-old colt
1968 Canadian Horse of the Year

Fanfreluche
1970 U.S. three-year-old filly
1970 Canadian three-year-old filly
1970 Canadian Horse of the Year
1978 Canadian Broodmare of the
Year

Nijinsky II
1969 English two-year-old colt
1969 Irish two-year-old colt
1970 English three-year-old colt
1970 Irish three-year-old colt
1970 European Horse of the Year
1986 Leading Sire in England
1993, 1994 Leading Broodmare
Sire in United States

Lauries Dancer
1971 Canadian three-year-old filly
1971 Canadian Horse of the Year

Minsky
1970 Irish two-year-old colt
1971 Canadian three-year-old colt

Northfields
1992 Leading Broodmare Sire
in Uruguay
1999 Leading Broodmare Sire
in South Africa

Lyphard
1978 and 1979 Leading Sire
in France
1985 Leading Broodmare Sire
in France
1986 Leading Sire in the U.S.

Nice Dancer
1972 Canadian three-year-old colt

Northern Taste
1982-1989, 1991 Leading Sire
in Japan
1991, 1993, 1994, 2003-2005
Leading Broodmare Sire in Japan

Broadway Dancer
1974 French two-year-old filly

Be My Guest
1982 Leading Sire in England

Dance in Time
1977 Canadian three-year-old colt

Giboulee
1978 Canadian older horse

Northernette
1976 Canadian two-year-old filly
1977 Canadian three-year-old filly

The Minstrel
1977 English Horse of the Year

Topsider
2000 Leadng Broodmare Sire
in Slovak Republic

Try My Best
1977 English two-year-old colt
1977 Irish two-year-old colt
1978 Irish miler
1990, 1992 Leading Sire in Italy

Fabulous Dancer
1992 Leading Sire in France

Nureyev
1980 French miler
1987, 1997 Leading Sire
in France

Storm Bird
1980 English two-year-old colt
1980 Irish two-year-old colt

Woodstream
1981 Irish two-year-old filly

Danzatore
1982 Irish two-year-old colt

Dixieland Band
2004 Leading Broodmare Sire in United States

Glenstal
1998 Leading Sire in Hungary

Shareef Dancer
1983 English three-year-old colt
1983 Irish three-year-old colt

El Gran Senor
1983 English two-year-old colt
1983 Irish two-year-old colt
1984 English three-year-old colt
1984 English miler

Northern Trick
1984 French three-year-old filly
1984 French Horse of the Year

Sadler's Wells
1984 French miler
1990, 1991-2004 Leading Sire in England/Ireland
1990, 1993, 1994, 1999 Leading Sire in France
2001, 2004 Leading Broodmare Sire in France

Antheus
1986 Italian older horse

Ajdal
1987 English sprinter

Unfuwain
1988 French highweight distance horse

Northern Dancer's Classic Winners

Nijinsky II
1970 English Triple Crown (Two Thousand Guineas, Epsom Derby, St. Leger)
1970 Irish Derby

The Minstrel
1977 Epsom Derby
1977 Irish Derby

White Star Line
1978 Kentucky Oaks

Lomond
1983 Two Thousand Guineas

Shareef Dancer
1983 Irish Derby

El Gran Senor
1984 Two Thousand Guineas
1984 Irish Derby

Northern Trick
1984 Prix de Diane

Sadler's Wells
1984 Irish Two Thousand Guineas

Secreto
1984 Epsom Derby

Appendix: Northern Dancer's Stakes Winners as Broodmare Sire

HORSE	C/S/YOB	SIRE	SIRE OF SIRE	DAM
Qathif	dk.b.c. 1987	Riverman	Never Bend	Al Bayan
Viscosity	b.f. 1978	Sir Ivor	Sir Gaylord	Aladancer
Vigliotto	ch.c. 1984	Blushing Groom (Fr)	Red God	Aladancer
Ruling	b.g. 1986	Alleged	Hoist the Flag	All Dance
Carezza	ch.f. 1989	Caro (Ire)	Fortino II (Fr)	All Dance
Tap Dance City	b.c. 1997	Pleasant Tap	Pleasant Colony	All Dance
Duns Scotus	dk.b.c. 1977	Buckpasser	Tom Fool	Alma North
High Baroque (Ire)	b.g. 1983	High Estate (Ire)	Shirley Heights (GB)	Alpine Symphony (Ire)
Antique Mystique	b.f. 1984	Affirmed	Exclusive Native	Antique Value
Vega (Jpn)	b.f. 1990	Tony Bin (Ire)	Kampala (GB)	Antique Value
Maquereau (Jpn)	b.c. 1997	Tony Bin (Ire)	Kampala (GB)	Antique Value
Tikvah	b.c. 1975	Rambunctious	Rasper II	Aquatic Ballet
Snowy Dancer	dk.b.f. 1979	Snow Knight (GB)	Firestreak (GB)	Aquatic Ballet
Comarctic	dk.b.g. 1989	Commemorate	Exclusive Native	Arctic Fling
Armiger (GB)	ch.c. 1990	Rainbow Quest	Blushing Groom (Fr)	Armeria
Truth or Die	b.g. 1991	Proud Truth	Graustark	Baffling Ballerina
Muhtarram	b.c. 1991	Alleged	Hoist the Flag	Ballet de France
Profit Column	ch.f. 1993	Private Account	Damascus	Ballet de France
Applaud	ch.f. 1993	Rahy	Blushing Groom (Fr)	Band
Sauterne (GB)	ch.f. 1998	Rainbow Quest	Blushing Groom (Fr)	Band
Ruler's Dancer	ch.f. 1978	Irish Ruler	Bold Ruler	Barbs Dancer
Eillo	ch.c. 1980	Mr. Prospector	Raise a Native	Barbs Dancer
Relief Pitcher (Ire)	b.c. 1986	Welsh Term (Ire)	Welsh Pageant (Fr)	Bases Loaded
Anavarza Mazgali (Tur)	b.c. 2002	Dilum	Tasso	Bassara
D'Arros (Ire)	b.c. 1989	Baillamont	Blushing Groom (Fr)	Bella Senora
Napoli (GB)	b.f. 1991	Baillamont	Blushing Groom (Fr)	Bella Senora
Belle Chanson (Aus)	ch.f. 1986	Biscay (Aus)	Star Kingdom (Ire)	Belle Marais
Silk Prima Donna (Jpn)	b.f. 1997	Brian's Time	Roberto	Bound to Dance
Moere Admiral (Jpn)	ch.c. 2002	Brian's Time	Roberto	Bound to Dance
Belle Bleue (GB)	b.f. 1988	Blazing Saddles (Aus)	Todman (Aus)	Broadway Dancer
Belonger	dk.b.c. 1972	New Providence	Bull Page	Canadian Ballet
Cool Tania	gr.c. 1978	Ruritania	Graustark	Canadian Ballet
Alofje	b.f. 1979	Lord Durham	Damascus	Canadian Ballet
Kirowan	b.c. 1984	Posse	Forli (Arg)	Cape Race
Ryafan	b.f. 1994	Lear Fan	Roberto	Carya
Epicentre	b.c. 1999	Kris S.	Roberto	Carya
Newton's Law (Ire)	dk.b.c. 1990	Law Society	Alleged	Catopetl
Close Conflict	dk.b.c. 1991	High Estate (Ire)	Shirley Heights (GB)	Catopetl
Jordy's Baba	b.f. 1979	Raja Baba	Bold Ruler	Celeberty Dancer
Nyama	b.f. 1982	Pretense	Endeavour II (Arg)	Chorea
Mr. Nutcracker	b.c. 1983	Mr. Prospector	Raise a Native	Christmas Wishes
Rydin and Wishin	ch.c. 1986	Red Ryder	Raise a Native	Christmas Wishes
Baldomero (Ire)	b.f. 1985	Pas de Seul (GB)	Mill Reef	Clonavee
Halo Reply	ch.f. 1980	Halo	Hail to Reason	Cold Reply
Real Prize	ch.f. 1978	Torsion	Never Bend	Cold Trick
Cold Colony	b.g. 1988	Pleasant Colony	His Majesty	Cold Trick
General Ironside (GB)	gr.c. 1973	Sea Hawk II (Fr)	Herbager (Fr)	Come Dancing
Passing Mood	ch.f. 1978	Buckpasser	Tom Fool	Cool Mood
Westheimer	ch.c. 1981	Blushing Groom (Fr)	Red God	Countess North

STATUS	INBREEDING MALE	INBREEDING FEMALE
G2SW	Nearco 4x4	Lalun 3 (Never Bend) x 4 (Bold Reason)
SW	Princequillo 4x4, Mahmoud 4x5, Nearco 5x4, Sir Gallahad III 5x5	
G1SW	Nearco 4x4	
SW		
SW	Nasrullah 4x5, Nearco 5x4	
G1SW	Nasrullah 5x5, Polynesian 5x5	
SW		
G3SW	Native Dancer 5x4	
SW	Native Dancer 4x4	
SW	Hyperion 4x5, Nasrullah 5x5	
SW	Hyperion 4x5, Nasrullah 5x5	
SW	Hyperion 4x5, Pharos 5x5	
SW	Hype-rion 5x5, Pharos 5x5	
SW	Native Dancer 4x4, Nasrullah 4x5, Nearco 5x4	
G1SW	Native Dancer 5x4, Nearco 5x4, Menow 5x5	
SW	Hyperion 5x5x5	
G1SW		
G3SW		
G3SW	Nearco 5x4, Menow 5x5	Almahmoud 5 (Cosmah) x 4 (Natalma)
SW	Native Dancer 5x4, Nearco 5x4, Menow 5x5	
SW	Nearco 4x4	
G1SW	Native Dancer 3x4, Polynesian 4x5x4, Nearco 5x4, Bull Dog 5x5	
SW		
SW		
G3SW	Nearco 5x4, Mahmoud 5x5, Menow 5x5	
SW	Nearco 5x4, Mahmoud 5x5, Menow 5x5	
G1SW	Hyperion 4x5x5	
SW	Nasrullah 5x5	
SW	Nasrullah 5x5	
SW	Court Martial 4x4, Hyperion 5x5	
SW	Teddy 5x5	Plucky Liege 5 (Bull Dog) x 5 (Sir Gallahad III)
SW	Hyperion 5x5x5	
SW	Heliopolis 4x4, Hyperion 5x5x5	
SW	Hyperion 4x4, Fair Trial 5x4, Nearco 5x4	
G1SW		
G3SW		
SW	Bold Ruler 4x4, Prince John 4x4, Princequillo 5x5x5, Polynesian 5x5	
G1SW	Native Dancer 5x4, Princequillo 5x5x5, Nasrullah 5x5	
SW	Nearco 4x4	
SW	Hyperion 3x5	
SW	Native Dancer 3x4, Nearco 5x4, Reigh Count 5x5	
SW	Native Dancer 3x4, Nearco 5x4, Reigh Count 5x5	
G3SW	Nasrullah 4x5, Nearco 5x5x4	Nogara 5 (Naucide) x 5 (Nearco)
SW	Nearco 5x4	Almahmoud 3 (Cos-mah) x 4 (Natalma)
SW	Nearco 4x4	
SW	Hyperion 5x5	
G3SW	Blue Peter 5x4, Mahmoud 5x5	
SW		
G2SW	Nearco 4x4	

Appendix: Northern Dancer's Stakes Winners as Broodmare Sire

HORSE	C/S/YOB	SIRE	SIRE OF SIRE	DAM
Skate's Honor	b.g. 1987	Overskate	Nodouble	Courage Please
Upsetter (Jpn)	b.c. 1980	Dandy Lute (Fr)	Luthier (Fr)	Crazy Kilts
Mr. Le Mans (Jpn)	b.c. 1981	Intermezzo (GB)	Hornbeam (GB)	Crazy Kilts
Inzar	dk.b.c. 1992	Warning (GB)	Known Fact	Czar's Bride
Bride Maid (Tur)	b.f. 1997	Galetto (Fr)	Caro (Ire)	Czar's Bride
Sinmelenn (Fr)	b.c. 1982	Swing Easy	Delta Judge	Dame Margot
Chinese Gold	b.c. 1985	Lemhi Gold	Vaguely Noble (Ire)	Dame Windsor
Dance At Sea	dk.b.g. 1986	Smarten	Cyane	Dance At Home
Zinc Tamon O. (Jpn)	b.c. 1989	Cormorant	His Majesty	Dance At Home
Rhythm	b.c. 1987	Mr. Prospector	Raise a Native	Dance Number
Get Lucky	b.f. 1988	Mr. Prospector	Raise a Native	Dance Number
No Review	ch.f. 1985	Nodouble	Noholme II (Aus)	Dance Review
Dance Colony	b.f. 1987	Pleasant Colony	His Majesty	Dance Review
Another Review	ch.c. 1988	Buckaroo	Buckpasser	Dance Review
Cozzy Grey	gr.g. 1990	Cozzene	Caro (Ire)	Danceable
Happy Feet	ch.f. 1977	Silent Screen	Prince John	Danceful
Exclusive Story	ch.f. 1982	Exclusive Native	Raise a Native	Dancer's Saga
Colonial Saga	b.f. 1983	Pleasant Colony	His Majesty	Dancer's Saga
Pleasant Tango	dk.b.c. 1990	Pleasant Colony	His Majesty	Dancer's Saga
Paris Prince	ch.c. 1980	Exclusive Native	Raise a Native	Dancers Countess
Val Dansant	b.c. 1981	Val de l'Orne (Fr)	Val de Loir (Fr)	Dancing Doris
Term Limits	ch.f. 1991	Time for a Change	Damascus	Dancing Doris
Tea Box	ch.g. 1990	Fit to Fight	Chieftain	Dancing Gull
Fly Love	ch.f. 1991	Rahy	Blushing Groom (Fr)	Dancing Gull
Oraibi	ch.c. 1985	Forli (Arg)	Aristophanes (GB)	Dancing Liz
Dancing Gun	b.g. 1972	Gun Bow	Gun Shot	Dancing Puppet
Kirby Lane	gr.c. 1973	Native Charger	Native Dancer	Dancing Puppet
Arazi	ch.c. 1989	Blushing Groom (Fr)	Red God	Danseur Fabuleux
Noverre	b.c. 1998	Rahy	Blushing Groom (Fr)	Danseur Fabuleux
Regal Parade (Ire)	br.c. 1984	Hello Gorgeous	Mr. Prospector	Danseuse Classique
Zante (GB)	b.f. 1995	Zafonic	Gone West	Danthonia
Requete (GB)	b.c. 1999	Rainbow Quest	Blushing Groom (Fr)	Danthonia
Digamist	ch.c. 1985	Blushing Groom (Fr)	Red God	Disconiz
Sleep Easy	b.f. 1992	Seattle Slew	Bold Reasoning	Dokki
Aptitude	dk.b.c. 1997	A.P. Indy	Seattle Slew	Dokki
Halo Dotty	b.f. 1980	Halo	Hail to Reason	Dorothy Glynn
Norcliffe	b.c. 1973	Buckpasser	Tom Fool	Drama School
Master Christopher	ch.c. 1985	Master Willie (GB)	High Line (GB)	Eastern Prancer
Flamingo Paradise (GB)	ch.c. 1991	Rainbow Quest	Blushing Groom (Fr)	Fabula Dancer
Flamingo Road (Ger)	ch.f. 1996	Acatenango (Ger)	Surumu (Ger)	Fabula Dancer
Again Tomorrow	b.c. 1982	Honest Pleasure	What a Pleasure	Falafel
Brief Truce	b.c. 1989	Irish River (Fr)	Riverman	Falafel
L'Enjoleur	dk.b.c. 1972	Buckpasser	Tom Fool	Fanfreluche
Grand Luxe	ch.f. 1974	Sir Ivor	Sir Gaylord	Fanfreluche
La Voyageuse	dk.b.f. 1975	Tentam	Intentionally	Fanfreluche
Medaille d'Or	ch.c. 1976	Secretariat	Bold Ruler	Fanfreluche
D'Accord	b.c. 1979	Secretariat	Bold Ruler	Fanfreluche
Lakeshore Road	b.c. 1993	Alleged	Hoist the Flag	Farewell Partner
Secret Partner	ch.f. 1996	Rahy	Blushing Groom (Fr)	Farewell Partner
Lady Roberta	b.f. 1977	Roberto	Hail to Reason	Farouche
Mangayah	b.f. 1983	Spectacular Bid	Bold Bidder	Farouche
Worood	b.f. 1985	Vaguely Noble (Ire)	Vienna (GB)	Farouche
Tursanah	dk.b.f. 1986	Roberto	Hail to Reason	Farouche

STATUS	INBREEDING MALE	INBREEDING FEMALE
SW	Princequillo 5x4, Co-lombo 5x5	
G3SW	Mahmoud 5x5	
G2SW	Hype-rion 3x5, Nearco 5x4	Nogara 5 (Niccolo dell'Arca) x 5 (Nearco)
G3SW	Hail to Reason 4x3, Native Dancer 5x4	
SW		
G3SW		
SW	Nearco 4x4, Hyperion 5x5	
SW	Nearco 5x4	
SW	Hyperion 5x5x5	
G1SW	Native Dancer 3x4, Nasrullah 4x5, Nearco 5x4	
G3SW	Native Dancer 3x4, Nasrullah 4x5, Nearco 5x4	
G1SW	Hyperion 5x5	
G2SW	Hyperion 5x5, Nasrullah 5x5	
G1SW		
SW		
SW	Count Fleet 4x4	
SW	Native Dancer 3x4x5	
SW	Hyperion 5x5, Nearco 5x5	
SW	Hyperion 5x5, Nearco 5x5	
G2SW	Native Dancer 3x4, Case Ace 4x5	
SW		
SW	Swaps 4x4	
SW	Nearco 5x4	
SW	Nearco 5x4	Almahmoud 5 (Cosmah) x 4 (Natalma)
G2SW	Hyperion 3x5	
G2SW	Hyperion 3x5	
G1SW	Native Dancer 2x4, Discovery 4x5, Hyperion 4x5	
G1SW	Wild Risk 3x4, Nearco 4x4	
G1SW	Wild Risk 4x4, Nearco 5x4	Almahmoud 5 (Cosmah) x 4 (Natalma)
SW	Native Dancer 4x4	
SW	Northern Dancer 4x2, Native Dancer 5x4	Somethingroyal 5 (Secretariat) x 5 (Sir Gaylord)
SW	Native Dancer 5x4, Nearco 5x4	
G1SW	Nasrullah 3x4, Nearco 4x4x5	
G1SW	Polynesian 5x5, Princequillo 5x5	
G1SW	Buckpasser 4x3, Princequillo 5x5	
SW	Nearco 5x4	Almahmoud 3 (Cosmah) x 4 (Natalma)
SW		
G3SW	Hyperion 4x5x5, Donatello II 5x5	
G3SW	Raise a Native 4x4, Native Dancer 5x4x5, Nearco 5x4	
G2SW		
G1SW	Mahmoud 4x5, Nearco 5x5x4	
G1SW	Djebel 5x4, Nearco 5x4	
G1SW		
SW	Mahmoud 4x5, Nearco 5x4	
SW		
SW	Nearco 4x4	
G2SW	Nearco 4x4	
G3SW		
SW	Nearco 5x4, Menow 5x5	Almahmoud 5 (Cosmah) x 4 (Natalma)
G3SW	Nearco 5x5x4, Bull Dog 5x5	
SW	Nearco 5x4, Mahmoud 5x5	
SW	Nearco 3x4, Hyperion 4x5x5	
G3SW	Nearco 5x5x4, Bull Dog 5x5	

Appendix: Northern Dancer's Stakes Winners as Broodmare Sire

HORSE	C/S/YOB	SIRE	SIRE OF SIRE	DAM
Vivano	dk.b.f. 1989	Island Whirl	Pago Pago (Aus)	Fiddlesticks
It's Fine	b.f. 1980	Sham	Pretense	Finely
Fleet Image	b.f. 1971	Dancer's Image	Native Dancer	Fleet Run
Tremor	b.f. 1982	Tromos (GB)	Busted (GB)	Fleet Run
Leading Witness	b.f. 1977	Mr. Leader	Hail to Reason	Friendly Witness
Valuable Witness	b.c. 1980	Val de l'Orne (Fr)	Val de Loir (Fr)	Friendly Witness
Lynneseemeplease	b.f. 1994	Avies Copy	Lord Avie	Frost Fair
Fly Start (Ire)	b.f. 1979	Run the Gantlet	Tom Rolfe	Free French
Snow Lover	b.f. 1980	Knightly Sport	Sir Gaylord	Fur Boots
Great Substance	dk.b.c. 1978	Pretense	Endeavour II (Arg)	Gay Northerner
Crown Silver	gr.f. 1986	Spectacular Bid	Bold Bidder	Gold Treasure
Castle Gandolfo	ch.c. 1999	Gone West	Mr. Prospector	Golden Oriole
Sleek n Graceful	dk.b.g. 1988	Ack Ack	Battle Joined	Graceful Dancer
Ville d'Amore	ch.f. 1988	Irish River (Fr)	Riverman	Hanoof
Sasscat	b.c. 1986	Sassafras (Fr)	Sheshoon (GB)	Home From the Fair
Tupido	gr.c. 1988	Runaway Groom	Blushing Groom (Fr)	Home From the Fair
Robannier	b.c. 1991	Batonnier	His Majesty	Home From the Fair
Maskul	b.c. 1994	Lear Fan	Roberto	Hooriah
Hey Babe	dk.b.f. 1976	Roberto	Hail to Reason	Icy Blast
Cool Northerner	b.c. 1991	Dom Alaric (Fr)	Sassafras (Fr)	Imperturbable Lady
Inquisitor	b.c. 1992	Alleged	Hoist the Flag	Imperturbable Lady
Point Proven	b.g. 1994	Slew o' Gold	Seattle Slew	Imperturbable Lady
Swinging Jenny	b.f. 1990	Mt. Livermore	Blushing Groom (Fr)	Jenny Dancer
Solitary Dancer	b.c. 1996	Lively One	Halo	Jenny Dancer
Natala	b.f. 1986	Gentleman Gene	Maribeau	Jersey Dancer
(Natalma)				
Kirkwall (GB)	ch.c. 1994	Selkirk	Sharpen Up (GB)	Kamkova
Rambushka	b.f. 1986	Roberto	Hail to Reason	Katsura
L'Irlandaise	ch.f. 1982	Irish River (Fr)	Riverman	La Dorga
Endless Joy (Ire)	b.f. 1987	Law Society	Alleged	La Joyeuse
Favoured Nations (Ire)	b.c. 1988	Law Society	Alleged	Lady Lavery
North Prospect	ch.c. 1980	Mr. Prospector	Raise a Native	Lady Northcraft
Magic of Life	b.f. 1985	Seattle Slew	Bold Reasoning	Larida
Brave Tender	b.c. 1994	Gulch	Mr. Prospector	Larida
Reach the Gold	ch.c. 1990	Slew o' Gold	Seattle Slew	Leave Me Alone
Debo	b.f. 1984	Plugged Nickle	Key to the Mint	Lesley's a Dancer
Norquestor	dk.b.c. 1986	Conquistador Cielo	Mr. Prospector	Linda North
Majesterian	dk.b.c. 1988	Pleasant Colony	His Majesty	Linda North
Miss Tobacco	ch.f. 1996	Forty Niner	Mr. Prospector	Lisaleen
Raja's Revenge	b.c. 1983	Raja Baba	Bold Ruler	Look North
Lightning Look	b.f. 1984	Fluorescent Light	Herbager (Fr)	Look North
Maison Close	b.f. 1985	Spectacular Bid	Bold Bidder	Magdalena
Legal Case (Ire)	b.c. 1986	Alleged	Hoist the Flag	Maryinsky
Xwoni Xwoni	b.g. 1992	Track Barron	Buckfinder	Meteor Dancer
Northern Majesty	b.c. 1979	His Majesty	Ribot	Misukaw
Share the Fantasy	ch.f. 1980	Exclusive Native	Raise a Native	Misukaw
Tokatee	b.c. 1986	Seattle Slew	Bold Reasoning	Misukaw
Dantsu Dancer (Jpn)	b.f. 1992	Capote	Seattle Slew	Moon Light Miracle
Cajun Sauce	ch.g. 1985	Sauce Boat	Key to the Mint	Neopolitan
Candle Bright	dk.b.f. 1980	Irish Stronghold	Bold Ruler	Night Light
Playlist	b.f. 1983	Miswaki	Mr. Prospector	Night Light

STATUS	INBREEDING MALE	INBREEDING FEMALE
G3SW	Native Dancer 4x4, Hyperion 5x5	
G2SW	Hyperion 4x5	
SW	Native Dancer 2x4, Nearco 5x4	
SW		
SW	Nearco 5x4	
G2SW		
SW	Mahmoud 5x5	
SW	Count Fleet 5x5	
SW	Mahmoud 4x5, Nearco 5x4, Hyperion 5x5	
G3SW	Hype-rion 3x5x5	
SW	Nearco 5x4, Mahmoud 5x5	
G3SW	Native Dancer 4x4, Tom Fool 5x4	
SW	Nearco 5x4, Princequillo 5x4	
SW	Nearco 5x4	
SW	Nearco 4x4, Hyperion 5x5	
SW	Nearco 5x4, Mahmoud 5x5	
G3SW	Ribot 3x3, Hyperion 5x5	
SW		
SW	Nearco 5x5x4, Johnstown 5x5	
G3SW	Nearco 5x4	
SW	Princequillo 4x4	
SW	Princequillo 5x4	
SW	Nearco 5x4	
G3SW	Mahmoud 5x4x5	Almahmoud 4 (Cosmah) x 4 (Natalma)
SW	Cosmic Bomb 4x4, Nearco 5x4	Almahmoud 4 (Cosmah) x 5 (Cosmah) x 4
G2SW	Native Dancer 4x4, Hyperion 5x5	
SW	Nearco 5x5x4x5x5	
SW	Nasrullah 4x5, Nearco 5x4, Princequillo 5x5	
G3SW	Bold Ruler 4x4, Pol-ynesian 5x5, Princequillo 5x5	
SW	Summer Tan 4x4, Polynesian 5x5, Princequillo 5x5	
SW	Native Dancer 3x4, Nearco 5x4	
G1SW	Polynesian 5x5	
SW	Native Dancer 4x4x5, Roman 5x5	
SW		
SW		
G1SW	Native Dancer 4x4x5	
SW	Alibhai 4x5, Hyperion 5x5	
G3SW	Native Dancer 4x4, Nasrullah 5x5x5	
G3SW	Nearco 4x4	
SW	Menow 5x5	
SW	Nearco 5x4, Mahmoud 5x5	
G1SW	Princequillo 4x4	
SW	Native Dancer 4x4	
SW	Hyperion 4x5, Mahmoud 5x5, Pharos 5x5	
G1SW	Native Dancer 3x4	
G2SW	Polynesian 5x5	Striking 5 (Glamour) x 4 (Hitting Away), Marching Home 5 (Sailing Home) x 5 (Leading Home)
SW	Nasrullah 4x5, Nearco 5x4	
SW	Graustark 3x3, Princequillo 4x4	
SW	Nearco 4x5x4	
SW	Native Dancer 4x4	

Appendix: Northern Dancer's Stakes Winners as Broodmare Sire

HORSE	C/S/YOB	SIRE	SIRE OF SIRE	DAM
Little Bighorn (Ire)	b.c. 1985	Blakeney (GB)	Heathersett (GB)	Nip in the Air
Cypriata	dk.b.f. 2001	Seeking the Gold	Mr. Prospector	Northern Aspen
Teal (Saf)	ch.g. 1991	Foveros (GB)	Averof (GB)	Northern Banner
Eternity Star	dk.b.c. 1988	Majestic Light	Majestic Prince	Northern Eternity
Eternal Reve	ch.f. 1991	Diesis (GB)	Sharpen Up (GB)	Northern Eternity
Eternity Range	b.c. 1993	Majestic Light	Majestic Prince	Northern Eternity
Dreaming Away	ch.f. 1979	Sir Ivor	Sir Gaylord	Northern Gem
Colonial Flag	b.c. 1980	Hoist the Flag	Tom Rolfe	Northern Gem
Southern Arrow	dk.b.c. 1981	Smarten	Cyane	Northern Lake
Masake	b.f. 1988	Master Willie (GB)	High Line (GB)	Northern Lake
Orne	b.c. 1984	Val de l'Orne (Fr)	Val de Loir (Fr)	Northern Lullaby
A Phenomenon	dk.b.c. 1980	Tentam	Intentionally	Northern Meteor
Seattle Meteor	b.f. 1986	Seattle Slew	Bold Reasoning	Northern Meteor
Meteor Miracle	b.f. 1999	Twining	Forty Niner	Northern Meteor
Knightly Marvin	b.c. 1974	Knightly Manner	Round Table	Northern Niece
Great Northern Gal	b.f. 1979	Cormorant	His Majesty	Northern Niece
Onda Nova	b.f. 2001	Keos	Riverman	Northern Trick
Judicial	b.f. 1987	Law Society	Alleged	Northern Valley
Passagere du Soir (GB)	b.f. 1987	Rainbow Quest	Blushing Groom (Fr)	Northern Walker
May Combination	b.c. 1972	Right Combination	Round Table	Northern Willow
L'Alezane	ch.f. 1975	Dr. Fager	Rough'n Tumble	Northern Willow
Gold Crest	dk.b.c. 1982	Mr. Prospector	Raise a Native	Northernette
Scoot	dk.b.f. 1983	Mr. Prospector	Raise a Native	Northernette
Biwa Shinseiki (Jpn)	b.c. 1998	Forty Niner	Mr. Prospector	Oceana
Echoed Green	b.c. 1975	Gallant Man (GB)	Migoli (GB)	Odoriko
Philosophos (Ire)	b.g. 1986	High Top (Ire)	Derring-do (GB)	Pacificus
Biwa Hayahide (Jpn)	gr.c. 1989	Sharrood	Caro (Ire)	Pacificus
Narita Brian (Jpn)	dk.b.c. 1991	Brian's Time	Roberto	Pacificus
Biwa Takehide (Jpn)	b.c. 1995	Brian's Time	Roberto	Pacificus
Cee Nord	ch.f. 1983	Bold Dun-Cee	Bold Commander	Pomme du Nord
Fearless Pirate	b.g. 1994	Pirate's Bounty	Hoist the Flag	Radiant Glow
Ravinella	dk.b.f. 1985	Mr. Prospector	Raise a Native	Really Lucky
Line in the Sand	ch.c. 1989	Mr. Prospector	Raise a Native	Really Lucky
Zind (Ire)	b.c. 1990	Law Society	Alleged	Rose Red
Legal Right	b.g. 1993	Alleged	Hoist the Flag	Rose Red
Famous Partner	dk.b.f. 1978	Illustrious	Round Table	Royal Partner
Akureyri	b.c. 1978	Buckpasser	Tom Fool	Royal Statute
Awaasif	b.f. 1979	Snow Knight (GB)	Firestreak (GB)	Royal Statute
Royal Lorna	b.f. 1981	Val de l'Orne (Fr)	Val de Loir (Fr)	Royal Statute
Zalazl	b.c. 1986	Roberto	Hail to Reason	Salpinx
Sha Tha	dk.b.f. 1988	Mr. Prospector	Raise a Native	Savannah Dancer
Brier Creek	dk.b.c. 1989	Blushing Groom (Fr)	Red God	Savannah Dancer
Family Calling	b.c. 1994	Mr. Prospector	Raise a Native	Sense of Unity
Maniches	b.f. 1979	Val de l'Orne (Fr)	Val de Loir (Fr)	Shahadish
Local Problem	dk.b.g. 1989	Restless Native	Native Dancer	Shiver My Timbers
Over the Brink	dk.b.g. 1990	Overskate	Nodouble	Shiver My Timbers
Half a Year	ch.c. 1984	Riverman	Never Bend	Six Months Long
Winning Pact	b.c. 1991	Alydar	Raise a Native	Six Months Long
Sharp Belle	ro.f. 1975	Native Charger	Native Dancer	Sleek Dancer
Northern Prospect	b.c. 1976	Mr. Prospector	Raise a Native	Sleek Dancer
Sue Babe	b.f. 1978	Mr. Prospector	Raise a Native	Sleek Dancer

STATUS	INBREEDING MALE	INBREEDING FEMALE
SW	Hype-rion 4x5x5, Nearco 5x5x4	
SW	Native Dancer 4x4, War Admiral 5x5	
G1SW	Nearco 4x4	
G1SW	Native Dancer 4x4, Nearco 5x4, Menow 5x5	
G3SW	Native Dancer 4x4, Hyperion 5x5	
SW	Native Dancer 4x4, Nearco 5x4, Menow 5x5	
G3SW	Nearco 5x4x5, Mahmoud 4x5	
G2SW		
G1SW	Nearco 5x4, Fairway 5x5	
G3SW	Hyperion 5x5	
SW		
G1SW	War Relic 4x5	
G1SW	Bold Ruler 4x4, Nasrullah 5x5x5, Polynesian 5x5	
SW	Nasrullah 4x5, Native Dancer 5x4, Nearco 5x4	
SW	Nearco 4x4, Hyperion 4x5	
SW	Hyperion 5x5x5	
SW	Northern Dancer 4x2, Prince John 4x3, Nearco 5x4	
SW	Polynesian 5x5	
G2SW	Native Dancer 5x4, Nearco 5x4	
SW	Nearco 4x4	
G2SW		
G2SW	Native Dancer 3x4, Nearco 5x4	
G1SW	Native Dancer 3x4, Nearco 5x4	
SW	Nearco 4x4	
SW	Mahmoud 3x5	
SW	Nearco 5x4	
SW		
SW		
SW		
SW	Nearco 5x4, Mahmoud 5x5	
SW	Hyperion 5x5x5	
G1SW	Native Dancer 3x4, Nearco 5x4	
G3SW	Native Dancer 3x4, Nearco 5x4	
SW	Polynesian 5x5	
SW	Prince Rose 5x5, Tourbillon 5x5	
SW	Nearco 4x4	
G3SW		
G1SW	Hyperion 5x5, Pharos 5x5	
G3SW		
G2SW	Nearco 5x4x5	
G2SW	Native Dancer 3x4, Nearco 5x4	
G3SW	Nearco 4x4	
SW	Native Dancer 3x4, Nearco 5x4	
SW		
SW	Native Dancer 3x4, Discovery 4x5	
SW	Princequillo 5x4	
G2SW	Nearco 4x4	
G2SW	Native Dancer 3x4, Nearco 5x4, Teddy 5x5	
G1SW	Native Dancer 2x4, Unbreakable 4x4, Hyperion 4x5, Display 5x5	
SW	Native Dancer 3x4, Nearco 5x4, Unbreakable 5x4	
SW	Native Dancer 3x4, Nearco 5x4, Unbreakable 5x4	

Appendix: Northern Dancer's Stakes Winners as Broodmare Sire

HORSE	C/S/YOB	SIRE	SIRE OF SIRE	DAM
Cool Halo	dk.b.c. 1983	Halo	Hail to Reason	Slight Deception
Truancy	b.f. 1972	Outing Class	Nasrullah	Small Problem
Dewan and Only	ch.c. 1974	Dewan	Bold Ruler	Small Problem
Signal Tap	b.c. 1991	Fappiano	Mr. Prospector	South Sea Dancer
Scarlet Flutter (Fr)	b.f. 1983	Beldale Flutter	Accipiter	Southern Maid
Pelagos (Fr)	gr/ro.c. 1995	Exit to Nowhere	Irish River (Fr)	Southern Maid
Cool	b.c. 1981	Bold Bidder	Bold Ruler	Star in the North
Mountain Kingdom	b.c. 1984	Exceller	Vaguely Noble (Ire)	Star in the North
Heaven and Earth	b.c. 1988	Stop the Music	Hail to Reason	Star in the North
Instant Stardom	b.f. 1992	Pleasant Colony	His Majesty	Star in the North
Sable d'Or	ch.g. 1985	Glint of Gold (GB)	Mill Reef	Starlight Roof
Withallprobability	b.f. 1988	Mr. Prospector	Raise a Native	Sulemeif
Kadrmas	ch.g. 1992	Gulch	Mr. Prospector	Sulemeif
Wild Grouse	b.c. 1985	J. O. Tobin	Never Bend	Swift Bird
Mary McGlinchy	b.f. 1992	Pleasant Colony	His Majesty	Tara's Number
The Key Rainbow (Ire)	ch.c. 1992	Rainbow Quest	Blushing Groom (Fr)	Te Kani
Daros (GB)	dk.b.g. 1989	Damister	Mr. Prospector	Tikanova
Concurrent	b.g. 1995	Relaunch	In Reality	Tizara
Torrey Canyon	dk.b.c. 1989	Gone West	Mr. Prospector	Tovalop
Tossup	dk.b.f. 1993	Gone West	Mr. Prospector	Tovalop
Trouble Multiplied	dk.b.f. 1988	Regalberto	Roberto	Trudie's Dancer
Northern Master	gr/ro.c. 2000	Masterfully	Raise a Native	Trudie's Dancer
Stellaria	ch.f. 1986	Roberto	Hail to Reason	Victoria Star
Imperial March	ch.c. 1972	Forli (Arg)	Aristophanes (GB)	Victorian Dancer
Northern Blossom	ch.f. 1990	Snow Knight (GB)	Firestreak (GB)	Victorian Heiress
Wall Street	ch.c. 1993	Mr. Prospector	Raise a Native	Wajd
Nedawi (GB)	ch.c. 1995	Rainbow Quest	Blushing Groom (Fr)	Wajd
Fitful Skies (Ire)	dk.b.f. 2009	Dubawi (Ire)	Dubai Millennium (GB)	Wajd
Native Wizard	ch.c. 1983	Exclusive Native	Native Dancer	White Star Line
Whitehaven (GB)	b.f. 1987	Top Ville (Ire)	High Top (GB)	White Star Line
Eastern Echo	b.c. 1988	Damascus	Sword Dancer	Wild Applause
Blare of Trumpets	b.c. 1989	Fit to Fight	Chieftain	Wild Applause
Roar	b.c. 1993	Forty Niner	Mr. Prospector	Wild Applause
Yell	dk.b.f. 2000	A.P. Indy	Seattle Slew	Wild Applause
Long Icarus (Jpn)	b.c. 1995	Cacoethes	Alydar	Wintergrace
Johnny Dance	ch.c. 1978	Stage Door Johnny	Prince John	Witch Dance
Voo Doo Dance	ch.f. 1980	Stage Door Johnny	Prince John	Witch Dance
Estimraar (Ire)	ch.c. 1991	Bustino (GB)	Busted (GB)	Yaqut

STATUS	INBREEDING MALE	INBREEDING FEMALE
G3SW	Nearco 5x4	Almahmoud 3 (Cosmah) x 4 (Natalma), Banish Fear 4 (Cosmic Bomb) x 5 (Not Afraid)
SW	Nearco 3x4x5, Hyperion 4x5x5	Mumtaz Begum 3 (Nasrullah) x 5 (Dodoma II)
SW	Nearco 4x4x5	Mumtaz Begum 4 (Nasrullah) x 5 (Dodoma II)
G3SW	Native Dancer 4x4	
SW	Mahmoud 4x5, Nearco 5x4x5	
SW		Natalma 4 (Raise the Standard) x 3 (Northern Dancer), Almahmoud 5 (Cosmah) x 5 (Natalma) x 4 (Natalma)
G1SW	Nearco 4x4, Princequillo 4x5	
G2SW	Nearco 4x4, Hyperion 5x5	
SW	Turn-to 3x4, Nearco 5x4	
SW	Hype-rion 5x5, Princequillo 5x5	
SW	Nearco 5x4	
G2SW	Native Dancer 3x4, Nasrullah 4x5, Nearco 5x4, Bull Dog 5x5	
SW	Native Dancer 4x4, Nasrullah 5x5	
SW	Nasrullah 3x5, Nearco 4x4, Hyperion 5x5	
SW	Hype-rion 5x5, Nasrullah 5x5	
SW	Nearco 5x4x5, Native Dancer 5x4	
G2SW	Native Dancer 4x4	
SW	Mahmoud 4x5	
SW	Bold Ruler 4x4, Native Dancer 4x4, Nasrullah 5x5x5, Princequillo 5x5	
SW	Bold Ruler 4x4, Native Dancer 4x4, Nasrullah 5x5x5, Princequillo 5x5	
SW	Tudor Minstrel 4x4	
SW	Native Dancer 4x4	
SW	Nearco 5x5x4	
G3SW	Hype-rion 3x5, Papyrus 5x5	
SW	Hyperion 5x5, Pharos 5x5	
G3SW	Native Dancer 3x4, Nearco 5x4x5	
G1SW	Nearco 5x4x5, Native Dancer 5x4	
G3SW	Northern Dancer 5x2	
SW	Man o' War 5x5x5	
G2SW	Nearco 5x4	
G1SW		
G3SW	Nearco 5x4	
G2SW	Native Dancer 4x4, Ribot 4x4	
G2SW	Hail to Reason 5x4	
SW	Native Dancer 4x4, Nearco 5x4	
SW	Nearco 5x4x5	
SW	Nearco 5x4x5	
SW		

Appendix: Nijinsky II's Stakes Winners

HORSE	C/S/YOB	DAM	BROODMARE SIRE	STATUS
Caucasus	b.c. 1972	Quill	Princequillo	G1SW
Dancing Champ	b.c. 1972	Mrs. Peterkin	Tom Fool	G2SW
Green Dancer	b.c. 1972	Green Valley II	Val de Loir	G1SW
Lighted Glory	b.f. 1972	Lighted Lamp	Sir Gaylord	G3SW
Quiet Fling	b.c. 1972	Peace II	Klairon	G1SW
Summertime Promise	b.f. 1972	Prides Promise	Crozier	G3SW
Tanzor	b.c. 1972	Lady Victoria	Victoria Park	SW
African Dancer (GB)	b.f. 1973	Miba	Ballymoss	G2SW
Bright Finish	b.c. 1973	Lacquer	Shantung (Fr)	G2SW
Half an Hour	b.g. 1973	Be Suspicious	Porterhouse	SW
Javamine	b.f. 1973	Dusky Evening	Tim Tam	G2SW
La Jalouse	ch.f. 1973	Quadruple	Fleet Nasrullah	SW
Nijana	ch.f. 1973	Prodana Neviesta	Reneged	G3SW
Nuclear Pulse	ch.c. 1973	Solometeor	Victoria Park	SW
Popular Hero	b.c. 1973	Brave Lady	Herbager	SW
Baldski	dk.b.c. 1974	Too Bald	Bald Eagle	SW
Galletto	b.f. 1974	Gaia	Charlottesville (GB)	SW
Lucky Sovereign	b.c. 1974	Sovereign II	Pardao	G2SW
Maruzensky (Jpn)	b.c. 1974	Shill	Buckpasser	SW
Pas de Deux	ch.c. 1974	So Chic	Nasrullah	G3SW
Upper Nile	b.c. 1974	Rosetta Stone	Round Table	G1SW
Valinsky (GB)	b.c. 1974	Valoris II	Tiziano II	G2SW
Cherry Hinton	b.f. 1975	Popkins	Romulus (GB)	G3SW
Excitable	ch.c. 1975	Lady Graustark	Graustark	SW
His Honor	b.c. 1975	Bold Honor	Bold Ruler	SW
Ile de Bourbon	b.c. 1975	Roseliere	Misti	G1SW
Nizon	ch.c. 1975	Exit Smiling	Stage Door Johnny	G1SW
Piaffer	b.c. 1975	Strong Drink	Sound Track (GB)	SW
Stradavinsky (Ire)	b.c. 1975	Seximee	Hasty Road	G3SW
Summer Fling	b.f. 1975	Fast Approach	First Landing	G3SW
Terpsichorist	ch.f. 1975	Glad Rags II	High Hat (GB)	G2SW
Czaravich	ch.c. 1976	Black Satin II	Linacre (GB)	G1SW
Gleason	b.c. 1976	Gleam II	Spy Well	SW
Niniski	b.c. 1976	Virginia Hills	Tom Rolfe	G1SW
Sis C.	b.f. 1976	Fond Hope II	Sir Ivor	SW
Yeats	b.c. 1976	Lisadell	Forli	SW
Ballare	b.f. 1977	Morgaise	Round Table	SW
Muscovite	b.c. 1977	Alyne Que	Raise a Native	G3SW
Nice Havrais	ch.c. 1977	Shoubra	Bon Mot (Fr)	G3SW
Night Alert	b.c. 1977	Moment of Truth II	Matador (GB)	G2SW
Princesse Lida	b.f. 1977	Princesse Lee II	Habitat	G1SW
Shining Finish (GB)	b.c. 1977	Lacquer	Shantung (Fr)	G3SW
Street Ballet	b.f. 1977	Street Dancer	Native Dancer	SW
Water Dance	ch.f. 1977	Luiana	My Babu	SW
Balletomane	b.f. 1978	Nanticious	Nantallah	G3SW
De La Rose	b.f. 1978	Rosetta Stone	Round Table	G1SW
Kings Lake	b.c. 1978	Fish-Bar	Baldric	G1SW
Leap Lively	ch.f. 1978	Quilloquick	Graustark	G3SW
Netherby	b.c. 1978	Sweet Satina	Crimson Satan	SW
Nijinsky's Secret	ch.c. 1978	Secret Beauty	Raise a Native	G1SW
Shimmy	b.c. 1978	Amalesian	Ambiorix	SW
Sportin' Life	b.c. 1978	Homespun	Round Table	SW
Dearly Too	b.f. 1979	Dearly Precious	Dr. Fager	SW
Golden Fleece	b.c. 1979	Exotic Treat	Vaguely Noble	G1SW
Hostage	b.c. 1979	Entente	Val de Loir	G1SW

Appendix

HORSE	C/S/YOB	DAM	BROODMARE SIRE	STATUS
Khatango	b.c. 1979	Penny Flight	Damascus	G2SW
Number	b.f. 1979	Special	Forli	G2SW
Peacetime	b.c. 1979	Peace II	Klairon	G3SW
Rose Crescent	b.f. 1979	Roseliere	Misti	G3SW
Waving	ch.f. 1979	Top Round	Round Table	SW
Beaudelaire	ch.c. 1980	Bitty Girl	Habitat	G2SW
Bemissed	ch.f. 1980	Bemis Heights	Herbager	G1SW
Brogan	b.c. 1980	Drumtop	Round Table	G3SW
Caerleon	b.c. 1980	Foreseer	Round Table	G1SW
Down Stage	b.f. 1980	Flying Above	Hoist the Flag	SW
Fabuleux Dancer	ch.c. 1980	Fabuleux Jane	Le Fabuleux	SW
Gorytus	b.c. 1980	Glad Rags II	High Hat (GB)	G2SW
Rosy Spectre	ch.f. 1980	Like a Charm	Pied d'Or	SW
Russian Roubles	b.c. 1980	Squander	Buckpasser	SW
Solford	b.c. 1980	Fairness	Cavan	G1SW
Ultramate	ch.c. 1980	Gala Party	Hoist the Flag	SW
Val Danseur	b.c. 1980	Green Valley II	Val de Loir	G2SW
Dancing Slippers	ch.c. 1981	Chain	Herbager	SW
Empire Glory	dk.b.c. 1981	Spearfish	Fleet Nasrullah	G3SW
Esperanto	b.c. 1981	Bendara	Never Bend	SW
Greek Sky	b.c. 1981	Greek Victress	Victoria Park	SW
Key Dancer	dk.b.f. 1981	Key Partner	Key to the Mint	G2SW
Nagurski	b.c. 1981	Deceit	Prince John	G3SW
Tights	b.c. 1981	Dancealot	Round Table	G2SW
Trendy Gent	ch.c. 1981	Pucheca	Tom Rolfe	G2SW
Vidalia	b.f. 1981	Waya (Fr)	Faraway Son	G3SW
Vision	b.c. 1981	Foreseer	Round Table	G1SW
Western Symphony	b.c. 1981	Millicent	Cornish Prince	G3SW
Duty Dance	b.f. 1982	Discipline	Princequillo	G2SW
Fire of Life	b.c. 1982	Spark of Life	Key to the Mint	G1SW
Folk Art	b.f. 1982	Homespun	Round Table	G1SW
Gallant Archer	b.c. 1982	Belle of Dodge Me	Crème dela Crème	G3SW
Lightning Leap	ch.c. 1982	First Feather	First Landing	SW
Moscow Ballet	b.c. 1982	Millicent	Cornish Prince	G3SW
Perfect Point	b.f. 1982	Charm School	Dr. Fager	SW
Shadeed	b.c. 1982	Continual	Damascus	G1SW
Dance of Life	b.c. 1983	Spring Is Here	In Reality	G1SW
Dancing On a Cloud	b.f. 1983	Square Angel	Quadrangle	SW
Ferdinand	ch.c. 1983	Banja Luka	Double Jay	G1SW
Fred Astaire	b.c. 1983	Late Bloomer	Stage Door Johnny	G2SW
Manzotti	b.c. 1983	Shufleur	Tom Rolfe	G3SW
Shahrastani	ch.c. 1983	Shademah (Ire)	Thatch	G1SW
Ancient Times	b.c. 1984	Nellie Forbes	Secretariat	SW
Bound	b.f. 1984	Special	Forli	SW
Dancing All Night	ch.f. 1984	Blitey	Riva Ridge	G2SW
Helenska	b.f. 1984	In the Offing	Hoist the Flag	G3SW
Merce Cunningham	b.c. 1984	Foreseer	Round Table	G2SW
Seattle Dancer	b.c. 1984	My Charmer	Poker	G2SW
Sword Dance (Ire)	b.c. 1984	Rosa Mundi	Secretariat	G2SW
Banker's Lady	ch.f. 1985	Impetuous Gal	Briartic	G1SW
Dancing Goddess	b.f. 1985	Producer	Nashua	SW
Dancing Spree	ch.c. 1985	Blitey	Riva Ridge	G1SW
Jeanne Jones	b.f. 1985	Beautiful Glass	Pass the Glass	G1SW
Lake Como	b.c. 1985	La Dame Du Lac	Round Table	G3SW

Appendix: Nijinsky II's Stakes Winners

HORSE	C/S/YOB	DAM	BROODMARE SIRE	STATUS
Love You by Heart	b.f. 1985	Queen's Paradise	Summer Tan	G2SW
Maksud	ch.c. 1985	Jellatina (Ire)	Fortino II	SW
Maplejinsky	b.f. 1985	Gold Beauty	Mr. Prospector	G1SW
Mister Modesty	b.c. 1985	Dearly Precious	Dr. Fager	G3SW
Mystery Rays	ch.c. 1985	Rare Mint	Key to the Mint	G3SW
Nikishka	b.f. 1985	Bendara	Never Bend	G2SW
Classic Fame	b.c. 1986	Family Fame	Droll Role	G1SW
Classic Sport	b.c. 1986	Pump	Forli	SW
Connie's Gift	b.f. 1986	Connie Knows	Buckpasser	G2SW
Destiny Dance	b.f. 1986	Althea	Alydar	G3SW
Key Flyer	b.f. 1986	Key Partner	Key to the Mint	SW
Ryan's Gift	b.c. 1986	On the Bench	Good Behaving	G1SW
Committed Dancer	b.c. 1987	Committed	Hagley	SW
Crockadore	ch.f. 1987	Flo Russell	Round Table	G2SW
Glorify	ch.c. 1987	Autumn Glory	Graustark	G3SW
Land Rush	b.c. 1987	Faneuil Girl	Bolinas Boy	SW
Music Time J.	ro.c. 1987	Heather Road	The Axe II	G2SW
Nijinsky's Lover	ch.f. 1987	Luv Luvin'	Raise a Native	SW
Royal Academy	b.c. 1987	Crimson Saint	Crimson Satan	G1SW
Savina	ch.f. 1987	Wedding Reception	Round Table	G3SW
Single Combat	b.c. 1987	La Dame Du Lac	Round Table	G3SW
Sky Classic	ch.c. 1987	No Class	Nodouble	G1SW
Victory Piper	ch.c. 1987	Arisen	Mr. Prospector	G2SW
Friedland	b.c. 1988	Fenella (Ire)	Thatch	SW
Green Pola	b.f. 1988	Irish Valley	Irish River (Fr)	G3SW
Jaded Dancer	b.c. 1988	Lien	Never Bend	G3SW
Jendali	b.c. 1988	Jellatina (Ire)	Fortino II	G3SW
Mashaallah	b.c. 1988	Homespun	Round Table	G1SW
Nazoo (Ire)	b.f. 1988	La Dame Du Lac	Round Table	SW
Peplum	b.f. 1988	Chain Store	Nodouble	SW
Top Trestle	b.f. 1988	Trestle	Tom Rolfe	SW
Walim	ch.c. 1988	Splendid Girl	Golden Eagle II	SW
Chinese Empress	b.f. 1989	Execution	The Axe II	SW
Niodini	b.f. 1989	Home Thoughts	Tom Rolfe	G3SW
Thyer	b.c. 1989	Qui Royalty	Native Royalty	SW
Dardjini	b.g. 1990	Darara (Ire)	Top Ville	SW
Humam (Ire)	ch.c. 1990	Passamaquoddy	Drone	SW
Likeable Style	b.f. 1990	Personable Lady	No Robbery	G1SW
Matchless Dancer	gr.c. 1990	Matching	What Luck	SW
Russian Tango	dk.b.f. 1990	Brave Raj	Rajab	SW
Winged Victory	b.c. 1990	Wedding Picture	Blushing Groom (Fr)	G3SW
Munnaya	ch.f. 1991	Hiaam	Alydar	SW
African Dancer	b.c. 1992	Mandera	Vaguely Noble	G3SW
Ibuki New Star	b.f. 1992	Regal Endeavour	Roberto	G3SW
Lammtarra	ch.c. 1992	Snow Bride	Blushing Groom (Fr)	G1SW
Ninotchka	b.f. 1993	Purge Sound (GB)	High Top	SW

Vice Regent's Stakes Winners

HORSE	C/S/YOB	DAM	BROODMARE SIRE	STATUS
Christy's Mount	b.f. 1973	Snowmount	Sallymount	SW
Kirkfield Park	ch.f. 1973	Sweet Romance	Gun Bow	SW
Military Bearing	b.c. 1973	Midinette II	Tantieme (Fr)	SW
Canadian Regent	ch.c. 1974	Canadia	Canebora	SW
Captain Pat	b.c. 1974	Top Cabin	Admiral's Voyage	SW
Pro Consul	ch.c. 1974	Bingo Queen	Bing II	SW

HORSE	C/S/YOB	DAM	BROODMARE SIRE	STATUS
Regent Bird	b.c. 1974	Setting Sun	Sunny	SW
Regal Embrace	b.c. 1975	Close Embrace	Nentego	SW
Viceera	b.g. 1975	Little Bit O' Era	Victorian Era	SW
Porpourie	ch.f. 1976	Silly Sonata	Silly Season	SW
Girls'l Be Girls	ch.f. 1977	Ladys Holme	Noholme II	SW
New Regent	ch.c. 1977	Dobbinton	New Providence	SW
No Vices	dk.b.c. 1977	Come In Please	Narrator (GB)	SW
Northern Regent	b.c. 1977	Margay II	Tiger	SW
Sea Regent	b.f. 1977	Miss Tidal Wave	Captain's Gig	SW
Holiday Regent	b.f. 1978	Holiday Miss	Jubilate	SW
Kushog	ch.f. 1978	Nantopic	Ahoy	SW
Lady Sheppard	dk.b.f. 1978	Sir Ribots Lady	Sir Ribot	SW
No. One Bundles	ch.f. 1978	Hasty Gal	Maribeau	SW
Play the Hornpipe	b.g. 1978	Miss Tidal Wave	Captain's Gig	SW
Regal Stafford	b.c. 1978	Come Near	Nearctic	SW
Regent Cat	b.c. 1978	Cougar Cat	Cougar II	SW
Regent Miss	ch.f. 1978	Later Miss	Mister Jive	SW
Regimen	ch.c. 1978	Princess Game	Hasty Prince	SW
Brave Regent	dk.b.c. 1979	Buh Buh Buh Bold	Bold Monarch	SW
Deputy Minister	dk.b.c. 1979	Mint Copy	Bunty's Flight	G1SW
Fraud Squad	b.c. 1979	Three's a Crowd	Warfare	SW
Haliburton Huskie	b.c. 1980	Rolling Stoner	Traffic Mark	SW
Lady Ice	b.f. 1980	Dancing Castanet	Tambourine	SW
Mrs. Specklewing	ro.f. 1980	Maggie Muggins	Swerve	SW
Regal Taheka	ch.f. 1980	Taheka	Irmak	SW
Regents Rhythm	ch.f. 1980	Victory Songster	Stratus	SW
Royalesse	ch.f. 1980	Fun On Stage	Stage Door Johnny	SW
Sir Khaled	b.c. 1980	Khaled's Kaper	Prince Khaled	SW
Victorious Emperor	ch.c. 1980	Springlet	Young Emperor	SW
Archregent	b.c. 1981	Respond	Canadian Champ	SW
Bounding Away	ch.f. 1981	Bambee T. T.	Better Bee	SW
Centenarian	ch.c. 1981	Hildesheim	Carteret	SW
Deputy General	b.c. 1981	Summer Dreams	Victoria Park	SW
Lantana Lady	b.f. 1981	Friendly Ways	Green Ticket	SW
Park Regent	ch.f. 1981	Miss Attractive	Victoria Park	SW
Tip o' My Finger	ro.f. 1981	Ms. Dolly A.	New Providence	SW
Bessarabian	b.f. 1982	Tete de Linotte	Turn-to	G2SW
Deceit Dancer	ch.f. 1982	Deceit	Prince John	SW
In My Cap	ch.f. 1982	Passing Look	Buckpasser	SW
Noble Regent	dk.b.g. 1982	Spirited Away	Vaguely Noble	SW
Queen of Egypt	b.f. 1982	Forleana	Forum	SW
Quitman	ch.f. 1982	Close Embrace	Nentego	SW
Regal Remark	ch.f. 1982	Male Strike	Speak John	G3SW
Body Check	ch.c. 1983	Bude	Cornish Prince	SW
Dice Cup	ch.f. 1983	Rattling Fool	Rattle Dancer	SW
Grey Salute	ro.c. 1983	Night Out	Bustino (GB)	SW
Her Regency	ch.f. 1983	In Review	Reviewer	SW
Regency Silk	ch.f. 1983	Shanghai Melody	Shantung (Fr)	SW
Royal Treasurer	b.c. 1983	Waltz to the Mint	Key to the Mint	SW
Arcroyal	ch.f. 1984	Arch Miss	Mississippian	SW
Hangin On a Star	ch.f. 1984	Hangin Round	Stage Door Johnny	SW
Interrex	ch.c. 1984	Betty's Secret	Secretariat	SW
Love of Our Life	ch.f. 1984	Dreamy Bolina	Bolinas Boy	SW
Ruling Angel	ch.f. 1984	Loudrangle	Quadrangle	G3SW
Regal Classic	ch.c. 1985	No Class	Nodouble	G3SW
Regal Intention	dk.b.c. 1985	Tiffany Tam	Tentam	G3SW
Society Island	b.c. 1985	Gliding In	First Landing	SW
Sound the Fanfare	b.f. 1985	Nalee's Rhythm	Nalees Man	SW
Thaidah	b.f. 1985	Ballade	Herbager	SW
Presidential	ch.c. 1986	Sister Sal	Delta Judge	SW
Tarage	b.f. 1986	Timotara	Secretariat	SW

Appendix: Vice Regent's Stakes Winners

HORSE	C/S/YOB	DAM	BROODMARE SIRE	STATUS
Special Vice	b.f. 1987	Special Mah	Talc	SW
Trumpet's Blare	b.f. 1987	Passing Look	Buckpasser	G1SW
Excellent Tipper	b.g. 1988	Fast Tipper	Exceller	G3SW
Lady Regency	b.f. 1988	Funny Peculiar	Funny Fellow	SW
Platinum Paws	ro.f. 1988	Catcando	Al Hattab	SW
Victorian Angel	b.f. 1988	Twice an Angel	Halo	SW
Always Nettie	ch.f. 1989	Hail to Boldness	Bold Reason	SW
Classic Reign	ch.f. 1989	No Class	Nodouble	SW
Eishin Tennessee	b.f. 1989	Castle Royale	Slady Castle	G3SW
Great Regent	ch.c. 1989	Show Lady	Sir Ivor	SW
Harbor Springs	ch.f. 1989	Tinnitus	Restless Wind	SW
King's College	b.g. 1989	Choral Group	Lord Durham	SW
Victorious Lil	b.f. 1989	Glass House	Halo	SW
Bright Penny	ch.f. 1990	B's Overdraft	Damascus	SW
Carry The Crown	b.c. 1990	Tiffany Tam	Tentam	SW
Glenbarra	b.g. 1990	Supreme Excellence	Providential (Ire)	SW
Passing Vice	b.f. 1990	Passing Look	Buckpasser	G3SW
Swamp King	ch.c. 1990	Gladiolus	Watch Your Step	SW
Investalot	ch.f. 1991	Myun	Exclusive Native	G2SW
Seismic Report	ch.g. 1991	Prima Mara	First Landing	SW
Teewinot	ch.f. 1991	Double the Charm	Nodouble	SW
Twice the Vice	ch.f. 1991	Double Set	Resurgent	G1SW
Vice On Ice	ch.f. 1991	Wewarrenju	Damascus	SW
Virtuous Regent	ch.g. 1991	B's Overdraft	Damascus	SW
Lake George	ch.c. 1992	Esdiev	Secretariat	SW
Native Regent	b.c. 1992	Barkerville Belle	Ruthie's Native	G3SW
Once a Sailor	b.c. 1992	Cosmic Tiger	Tim the Tiger	SW
Londrina	ch.f. 1993	Play Around Honey	Exclusive Native	G3SW
Northern Hilite	b.f. 1993	Night Stand	Fluorescent Light	SW
Storm Regent	ch.g. 1993	Flee the Storm	Forceten	SW
Muskrat Sammy	b.g. 1994	Muskrat Love	Muscovite	SW
One O Seven	dk.b.f. 1994	Excruciation	Bold Hour	SW
Randy Regent	b.c. 1994	Carson City Gal	Silver Series	SW
Alce Canadense	ch.g. 1995	Enticed	Stage Door Johnny	SW
Cherie Yvonne	ch.f. 1995	Igmaar (Fr)	Don Roberto	SW
El Caleche	ch.g. 1995	La Caleche	Gregorian	SW
Vice n' Friendly	b.g. 1995	Very Best Friend	Best Turn	G2SW
Last Vice	ch.f. 1996	Donut's Pride	Nodouble	SW

Appendix: Lyphard's Stakes Winners

HORSE	C/S/YOB	DAM	BROODMARE SIRE	STATUS
Beaune (Fr)	ch.f. 1974	Barbra	Le Fabuleux	SW
Concertino	br.c. 1974	Isoline	Klairon	SW
Durtal (Ire)	b.f. 1974	Derna	Sunny Boy (Fr)	G1SW
Pharly	ch.c. 1974	Comely (Fr)	Boran (GB)	G1SW
President (Fr)	dk.b.c. 1974	Peisqueira	Free Man	G3SW
Bel Sorel (GB)	b.c. 1975	Belle Sorella	Ribot	SW
Calderina (Ity)	b.f. 1975	Cendres Bleues (Ity)	Charlottesville (GB)	G2SW
Dancing Maid (Fr)	b.f. 1975	Morana	Val de Loir	G1SW
Iron Ruler (Ire)	gr.c. 1975	Lindera	Linacre (GB)	G3SW
Lypheor (GB)	dk.b.c. 1975	Klaizia (Fr)	Sing Sing (GB)	G3SW
Lys River (Fr)	ch.f. 1975	Riverina	Snob (Fr)	SW
North Sea (Fr)	ch.f. 1975	Rough Sea (GB)	Herbager	G3SW
Reine de Saba (Fr)	b.f. 1975	Sirya	Sicambre (Fr)	G1SW
Bellypha (Ire)	gr.c. 1976	Belga (Fr)	Le Fabuleux	G3SW
Lyphard's Wish (Fr)	b.c. 1976	Sally's Wish	Sensitivo	G1SW
Lyric Dance	b.f. 1976	Ormentello	Elopement (GB)	SW

HORSE	C/S/YOB	DAM	BROODMARE SIRE	STATUS
Mogami	b.c. 1976	No Luck	Lucky Debonair	SW
Nain Bleu (Fr)	b.c. 1976	Emeraldine	Tanerko (Fr)	SW
San Feliou (Fr)	b.c. 1976	Streaming	Saint Crespin III (GB)	SW
Singapore Girl	b.f. 1976	Cheftaine	Tanerko (Fr)	G2SW
Three Troikas (Fr)	b.f. 1976	Three Roses (GB)	Dual	G1SW
Benicia (Ire)	b.f. 1977	Bashi (Fr)	Stupendous	G3SW
Chain Bracelet	b.f. 1977	Chain	Herbager	G1SW
Laquiola (Fr)	b.f. 1977	Kalila	Beau Prince II (GB)	SW
Leaf Fall (Fr)	dk.b.f. 1977	Sweet and Lovely	Tanerko (Fr)	SW
Monteverdi (Ire)	ch.c. 1977	Janina (Ire)	Match II	G1SW
Al Nasr (Fr)	dk.b.c. 1978	Caretta (Ire)	Caro (Ire)	G1SW
Euclid	dk.b.c. 1978	Lucky for Me	Appiani II	G2SW
Ghadeer (Fr)	b.c. 1978	Swanilda	Habitat	G3SW
Lydian (Fr)	ch.c. 1978	Miss Manon (Fr)	Bon Mot (Fr)	G1SW
Lyfessa (Fr)	b.f. 1978	Floressa	Sassafras (Fr)	SW
Lyllos (Fr)	b.c. 1978	Lybos (Fr)	Silly Season (GB)	SW
Phydilla (Fr)	b.f. 1978	Godzilla	Gyr	G3SW
Sangue (Ire)	b.f. 1978	Prodice (Fr)	Prominer	G1SW
Lichine	b.c. 1979	Stylish Genie	Bagdad	SW
Alzao	b.c. 1980	Lady Rebecca	Sir Ivor	G3SW
Au Point	b.c. 1980	Quillo Queen	Princequillo	G1SW
Esprit Du Nord	b.c. 1980	Rajput Princess	Prince Taj	G1SW
Idle Gossip	b.f. 1980	Toll Booth	Buckpasser	SW
Legend of France	b.c. 1980	Lupe II	Primera (GB)	G3SW
Lyphard's Princess	b.f. 1980	Avum	Umbrella Fella	SW
Lyphard's Special	b.c. 1980	My Bupers	Bupers	G3SW
Red Showers	b.f. 1980	Scarlet Rain	Rainy Lake	SW
Sabin	ch.f. 1980	Beaconaire	Vaguely Noble	G1SW
So Cozy	ch.f. 1980	Special Warmth	Lucky Mike	SW
Dahar	b.c. 1981	Dahlia	Vaguely Noble	G1SW
Ends Well	ch.c. 1981	Late Bloomer	Stage Door Johnny	G1SW
Premium Win	b.f. 1981	Classic Perfection	Never Bend	SW
Sicyos	ch.c. 1981	Sigy (Fr)	Habitat	G3SW
Vacarme	ch.c. 1981	Virunga (Fr)	Sodium	G2SW
Dreams to Reality	b.c. 1982	D'Arqueangel	Raise a Native	SW
Heraldiste	b.c. 1982	Heiress (Fr)	Habitat	G3SW
La Romance	b.f. 1982	L'Engadine	Secretariat	SW
Letkiss	dk.b.f. 1982	Limoya	Riva Ridge	SW
Proud Debonair	dk.b.c. 1982	Proud Delta	Delta Judge	G3SW
Amani	b.f. 1983	China Trade	Swaps	SW
Dancing Brave	b.c. 1983	Navajo Princess	Drone	G1SW
Kraemer	b.f. 1983	Rich and Riotous	Empery	SW
Lesotho	b.c. 1983	Sealy (Ire)	Filiberto	G3SW
Manila	b.c. 1983	Dona Ysidra	Le Fabuleux	G1SW
Storm On the Loose	dk.b.c. 1983	That's a Kennedy	Kennedy Road	G3SW
Thunderdome	dk.b.c. 1983	Mr. P's Girl	Mr. Prospector	SW
Imperial Frontier	ch.c. 1984	Hartebeest	Vaguely Noble	SW
La Grande Epoque	ro.f. 1984	Ancient Regime	Olden Times	SW
Mazilier	b.c. 1984	Marie Curie (Ire)	Exbury (Fr)	G3SW
Sure Locked	b.f. 1984	Double Lock (GB)	Home Guard	SW
Tenue de Soiree	b.f. 1984	River Rose (Fr)	Riverman	G3SW
Andaleeb	b.f. 1985	Bag of Tunes	Herbager	G3SW
Lyphka	ch.f. 1985	Veruschka	Venture (Fr)	SW
Reve Dore	ch.c. 1985	Riviere Doree	Secretariat	SW
Riviere D'or	b.f. 1985	Gold River (Fr)	Riverman	G1SW

Appendix: Lyphard's Stakes Winners

HORSE	C/S/YOB	DAM	BROODMARE SIRE	STATUS
Trick Question	b.c. 1985	Trick Chick	Prince John	SW
Ensconse	b.f. 1986	Carefully Hidden	Caro (Ire)	G1SW
Garm	ch.c. 1986	Peruvienne (Ire)	Luthier (Fr)	SW
Lyphard's Melody	b.f. 1986	Luth Music (Fr)	Mon Fils	SW
Pearl Bracelet	ch.f. 1986	Perlee (Fr)	Margouillat	G1SW
Funambule	ch.c. 1987	Sonoma (Fr)	Habitat	G3SW
Goofalik	dk.b.c. 1987	Alik (Fr)	Targowice	G2SW
Mais Oui	b.f. 1987	Affirmatively	Affirmed	SW
Ozal	ch.c. 1987	L'Attrayante (Fr)	Tyrant	SW
Witness Box	b.c. 1987	Excellent Alibi	Exceller	G3SW
Fairy Garden	b.f. 1988	Possible Mate	King's Bishop	G2SW
Rainbows for Life	ch.c. 1988	Rainbow Connection	Halo	G3SW
Darling Dame	b.f. 1989	Darling Lady	Alleged	SW
Jolypha	dk.b.f. 1989	Navajo Princess	Drone	G1SW
Polyxena	b.f. 1989	Minstrel Girl (Fr)	Luthier (Fr)	SW
Queens Court Queen	b.f. 1989	Turk O Witz	Stop the Music	G1SW
Skimble	ch.f. 1989	Nimble Folly	Cyane	G2SW
Finest City	b.f. 1990	True Lady	Le Fabuleux	SW
Llandaff	ch.c. 1990	Dahlia	Vaguely Noble	G2SW
Lost Prairie	b.f. 1990	Lady Lianga	Secretariat	SW
Lynton	b.c. 1990	Nashmeel	Blushing Groom (Fr)	SW
Lyphard's Delta	dk.b.f. 1990	Proud Delta	Delta Judge	G2SW
Pracer	gr.f. 1990	Shindy	Roberto	G2SW
Ski Paradise	gr.f. 1990	Ski Goggle	Royal Ski	G1SW
Tara Roma	b.f. 1990	Chic Shirine	Mr. Prospector	G2SW
Um Algowain	ch.c. 1990	Moonlight Serenade (Fr)	Dictus	SW
Ypha	b.f. 1990	Louisville (Fr)	Val de l'Orne (Fr)	SW
Beccari	b.c. 1991	Belle Pensee	Ribot	SW
Linney Head	b.c. 1991	Royalivor	Sir Ivor	G3SW
Quick Snooze	b.g. 1991	So She Sleeps	Seattle Slew	SW
Sarmatie (Ire)	b.f. 1991	Sonoma (Fr)	Habitat	SW
Tatami	dk.b.c. 1991	Tash	Never Bend	G3SW
Waldoboro	dk.b.c. 1991	Chic Shirine	Mr. Prospector	G2SW
Goldmark	b.c. 1992	Gold Rose (Fr)	Noblequest	G1SW
Labibeh	gr.f. 1992	Asl	Caro (Ire)	G3SW
Spicilege	b.g. 1992	Grabelst	Graustark	SW
Cap Beino	b.f. 1993	Capades	Overskate	SW
Hard News	b.g. 1993	Social Column	Vaguely Noble	G3SW
Lady Tabitha	b.f. 1993	Abidjan	Sir Ivor	SW
Lypink	b.f. 1993	Pink Valley	Never Bend	SW
Matchless	b.c. 1994	Unreality	In Reality	SW
Memorise	b.c. 1994	Shirley Valentine (GB)	Shirley Heights (GB)	G3SW
Tresoriere	dk.b.f. 1994	Time Deposit	Halo	G3SW
Azouz Pasha	b.c. 1996	Empress Club (Arg)	Farnesio (Arg)	SW

Appendix: Danzig's Stakes Winners

HORSE	C/S/YOB	DAM	BROODMARE SIRE	STATUS
Chief's Crown	b.c. 1982	Six Crowns	Secretariat	G1SW
Contredance	b.f. 1982	Nimble Folly	Cyane	G1SW
Danzig Darling	b.f. 1982	Middlemarch	Buckpasser	SW
Government Corner	b.c. 1982	Popachee	Apalachee	G3SW
Nordance	b.c. 1982	Sister Shu	Nashua	SW
Stephan's Odyssey	dk.b.c. 1982	Kennelot	Gallant Man	G1SW

HORSE	C/S/YOB	DAM	BROODMARE SIRE	STATUS
Trunk	b.f. 1982	Saratoga Fleet	Sir Gaylord	SW
Valiant Sweetheart	b.f. 1982	My Compliments	Delta Judge	SW
Ziggy's Boy	dk.b.c. 1982	Joe's Lil Girl	Sunrise Flight	G2SW
Brent's Danzig	b.c. 1983	Brent's Queen	Crozier	SW
Danzig Connection	b.c. 1983	Gdynia	Sir Ivor	G1SW
Free Water	b.c. 1983	Talk Out	Tobin Bronze	SW
Green Desert	b.c. 1983	Foreign Courier	Sir Ivor	G1SW
La Polonaise	dk.b.f. 1983	Princess Buddir	Bagdad	SW
Lotka	b.f. 1983	Kennelot	Gallant Man	G1SW
Mister C.	dk.b.c. 1983	Honey Deb	Herbager	SW
Soar to the Stars	b.c. 1983	Flitalong	Herbager	G2SW
Sweet Velocity	b.f. 1983	Madam Guillotine	Blakeney (GB)	SW
Wisla	b.f. 1983	Gauri	Sir Ivor	SW
Zigbelle	dk.b.f. 1983	Cornish Belle	Cornish Prince	SW
Ascot Knight	b.c. 1984	Bambee T. T.	Better Bee	SW
Danzidea	b.c. 1984	Merry Thought	Haveago	SW
I'm So Bad	b.c. 1984	Betcha	Riva Ridge	G3SW
Polish Navy	b.c. 1984	Navsup	Tatan	G1SW
Polonia	b.f. 1984	Moss	Round Table	G1SW
Qualify	b.c. 1984	So Endearng	Raise a Native	G1SW
Always Fair	b.c. 1985	Carduel	Buckpasser	G3SW
Foreign Survivor	dk.b.c. 1985	Lady Darrington	Drone	SW
Lustra	b.c. 1985	Glisk	Buckpasser	SW
Posen	b.c. 1985	Michelle Mon Amour	Best Turn	G2SW
Spark O'Dan	b.g. 1985	Sparklet	Sir Ivor	SW
Allied Flag	b.c. 1986	Up the Flagpole	Hoist the Flag	SW
Bravely Bold	b.g. 1986	Claerwen (GB)	Habat	G3SW
Broto	b.c. 1986	Bosk	Damascus	G3SW
Danehill	b.c. 1986	Razyana	His Majesty	G1SW
Diver	b.c. 1986	Coiffure	Sir Gaylord	G3SW
Grin	dk.b.g. 1986	Gleaming Smile	Gleaming	SW
Honoria	b.f. 1986	Royal Honoree	Round Table	G3SW
Magic Gleam	b.f. 1986	All Agleam	Gleaming	G2SW
Magical Strike	b.c. 1986	Egyptian Rose	Sir Ivor	SW
Nicholas	b.c. 1986	Lulu Mon Amour	Tom Rolfe	G2SW
One of a Klein	b.f. 1986	Barely Even	Crème dela Crème	G1SW
Polish Precedent	b.c. 1986	Past Example	Buckpasser	G1SW
Roi Danzig	b.c. 1986	Gdynia	Sir Ivor	G2SW
Royal Danzig	b.c. 1986	Royal Strait Flush	Seattle Slew	SW
Russian Bond	b.c. 1986	Somfas	What a Pleasure	G2SW
Shaadi	b.c. 1986	Unfurled	Hoist the Flag	G1SW
Silk Braid	b.f. 1986	Ribbon	His Majesty	SW
Adjudicating	dk.b.c. 1987	Resolver	Reviewer	G1SW
Asia	dk.b.g. 1987	Syria	Damascus	SW
Baltic Chill	b.f. 1987	Cold Hearted	The Axe II	SW
Danzig Queen	b.f. 1987	Queen of Bronze	Roberto	SW
Danzig's Beauty	b.f. 1987	Sweetest Chant	Mr. Leader	G2SW
Dayjur	dk.b.c. 1987	Gold Beauty	Mr. Prospector	G1SW
Harbour Club	b.f. 1987	Over Your Shoulder	Graustark	SW
Mukddaam	b.c. 1987	Height of Fashion (Fr)	Bustino (GB)	SW
Old Alliance	b.g. 1987	Nimble Folly	Cyane	SW
Slavic	b.c. 1987	Bamesian	Buckpasser	G2SW
Snaadee	dk.b.c. 1987	Somfas	What a Pleasure	G2SW
Aurora	b.f. 1988	Althea	Alydar	SW
Balwa	b.f. 1988	Princess Oola	Al Hattab	SW

Appendix: Danzig's Stakes Winners

HORSE	C/S/YOB	DAM	BROODMARE SIRE	STATUS
Dance Smartly	b.f. 1988	Classy 'n Smart	Smarten	G1SW
Dancing With Wings	b.f. 1988	Loudrangle	Quadrangle	SW
Danzante	b.f. 1988	Bold Captive	Boldnesian	SW
Lech	b.c. 1988	Wedding Reception	Round Table	G3SW
Majlood	dk.b.c. 1988	Qui Royalty	Native Royalty	SW
Monongahela	b.c. 1988	Sea Sister	Sea-Bird	SW
Polish Holiday	b.f. 1988	Kapalua Butterfly	Stage Door Johnny	G3SW
Polish Patriot	b.c. 1988	Maria Waleska (Ire)	Filiberto	G1SW
Run and Deliver	ro.c. 1988	Belga (Fr)	Le Fabuleux	G1SW
Versailles Treaty	b.f. 1988	Ten Cents a Dance	Buckpasser	G1SW
Arbusha	b.f. 1989	Lulu Mon Amour	Tom Rolfe	SW
Asaasy	b.c. 1989	Carduel	Buckpasser	SW
Belong to Me	dk.b.c. 1989	Belonging	Exclusive Native	G3SW
Dauberval	dk.b.c. 1989	Dancealot	Round Table	SW
Easy Now	dk.b.f. 1989	Relaxing	Buckpasser	G1SW
Furiously	dk.b.c. 1989	Whirl Series	Roberto	G1SW
Gdansk's Honour	dk.b.f. 1989	Royal Honoree	Round Table	SW
Hamas (Ire)	dk.b.c. 1989	Fall Aspen	Pretense	G1SW
Lure	b.c. 1989	Endear	Alydar	G1SW
Muhayaa	b.c. 1989	La Basque	Jean-Pierre	SW
Petit Loup	b.c. 1989	Bambee T. T.	Better Bee	G1SW
Pine Bluff	b.c. 1989	Rowdy Angel	Halo	G1SW
Polish Style	b.f. 1989	Family Style	State Dinner	SW
Tertian	b.c. 1989	Tertiary	Vaguely Noble	SW
Yousefia	b.f. 1989	Foreign Courier	Sir Ivor	SW
Ziggy's Act	dk.b.f. 1989	Comedy Act	Shecky Greene	G3SW
Boundary	b.c. 1990	Edge	Damascus	G3SW
Burooj (GB)	br.c. 1990	Princess Sucree	Roberto	G3SW
Dispute	b.f. 1990	Resolver	Reviewer	G1SW
Emperor Jones	dk.b.c. 1990	Qui Royalty	Native Royalty	G2SW
Kashani	b.c. 1990	Kashan	Damascus	SW
Lost Soldier	b.c. 1990	Lady Winborne	Secretariat	G3SW
Maroof	b.c. 1990	Dish Dash (GB)	Bustino (GB)	G1SW
Princess Polonia	b.f. 1990	My Celebrity	Sir Ivor	G3SW
Strolling Along	dk.b.c. 1990	Cadillacing	Alydar	G1SW
Tribulation	b.f. 1990	Graceful Touch	His Majesty	G1SW
Zieten	b.c. 1990	Blue Note (Fr)	Habitat	G1SW
Zignew	b.c. 1990	Newfoundland	Prince John	G2SW
Biko Pegasus	dk.b.c. 1991	Condessa (Ire)	Condorcet	G3SW
Dove Hunt	b.c. 1991	Hunt's Lark	Knightly Dawn	G3SW
Dumaani	gr.c. 1991	Desirable (Ire)	Lord Gayle	G2SW
Eagle Eyed	b.c. 1991	Razyana	His Majesty	G2SW
Foxhound	b.c. 1991	Lassie Dear	Buckpasser	SW
Grab	b.f. 1991	Snitch	Seattle Slew	SW
Kerfoot Corner	dk.b.g. 1991	Rokeby Rose	Tom Rolfe	SW
Polish Treaty	b.f. 1991	Infinite	Majestic Light	SW
Ago	dk.b.c. 1992	Far	Forli	SW
Anabaa	b.c. 1992	Balbonella (Fr)	Gay Mecene	G1SW
Appointed One	b.f. 1992	Qui Royalty	Native Royalty	SW
Crimson Guard	b.c. 1992	Wedding Reception	Round Table	SW
Langfuhr	b.c. 1992	Sweet Briar Too	Briartic	G1SW
Sesaro	dk.b.c. 1992	Royal Honoree	Round Table	SW
Smolensk	b.f. 1992	Blush With Pride	Blushing Groom (Fr)	G2SW
Truckee	b.c. 1992	Embellished	Seattle Slew	SW
Yamanin Paradise	b.f. 1992	Althea	Alydar	G1SW

HORSE	C/S/YOB	DAM	BROODMARE SIRE	STATUS
Blue Duster	b.f. 1993	Blue Note (Fr)	Habitat	G1SW
Chirico	b.c. 1993	Colour Chart	Mr. Prospector	SW
Dream Scheme	b.f. 1993	Dream Deal	Sharpen Up (GB)	G2SW
Everhope	b.f. 1993	Battle Creek Girl	His Majesty	SW
Mariuka	b.f. 1993	Tash	Never Bend	SW
Polish Love	b.c. 1993	Some Romance	Fappiano	SW
Skillington	b.g. 1993	Annie Edge (Ire)	Nebbiolo	SW
Elnadim	dk.b.c. 1994	Elle Seule	Exclusive Native	G1SW
Harpia	b.f. 1994	Razyana	His Majesty	G3SW
Hikari Cermet	b.c. 1994	Petalia	Sir Ivor	G3SW
Lil's Boy	b.c. 1994	Kentucky Lill	Raise a Native	SW
Military	dk.b.c. 1994	Wavering Girl	Wavering Monarch	G1SW
Partner's Hero	dk.b.c. 1994	Safely Home	Winning Hit	G2SW
Pas de Reponse	b.f. 1994	Soundings	Mr. Prospector	G1SW
Seebe	b.f. 1994	Annie Edge (Ire)	Nebbiolo	G3SW
Sheer Reason	b.f. 1994	Hiaam	Alydar	SW
Woven Silk	b.f. 1994	Ribbon	His Majesty	SW
Yashmak	b.f. 1994	Slightly Dangerous	Roberto	G1SW
Agnes World	dk.b.c. 1995	Mysteries	Seattle Slew	G1SW
Ashraakat	b.f. 1995	Elle Seule	Exclusive Native	SW
Baltic State	b.c. 1995	Kingscote (Ire)	Kings Lake	SW
Bianconi	dk.b.c. 1995	Fall Aspen	Pretense	G2SW
Duraid	b.c. 1995	Bialy	Alydar	SW
Grand Royale	b.c. 1995	Good Mood	Devil's Bag	SW
Jibe	dk.b.f. 1995	Slightly Dangerous	Roberto	SW
Moments of Magic	b.f. 1995	Cabiria	Raise a Native	SW
Recording	b.f. 1995	Ratings	Caveat	G3SW
Sophie My Love	b.f. 1995	Ramirena	Key to the Mint	SW
Time Changes	b.f. 1995	Make Change	Roberto	SW
Bertolini	b.c. 1996	Aquilegia	Alydar	G3SW
Black Rock Desert	b.c. 1996	City Dance	Seattle Slew	G3SW
Choice Spirit	b.f. 1996	Zaizafon	The Minstrel	SW
Golden Snake	b.c. 1996	Dubian (GB)	High Line (GB)	G1SW
Magnaten	b.c. 1996	Magic Night (Fr)	Le Nain Jaune (Fr)	G2SW
Mujahid	b.c. 1996	Elrafa Ah	Storm Cat	G1SW
Alyzig	b.c. 1997	Touch of Love	Alydar	SW
Brahms	dk.b.c. 1997	Queena	Mr. Prospector	G1SW
Chimes At Midnight	b.c. 1997	Surely Georgie's	Alleged	G3SW
Exchange Rate	gr/ro.c. 1997	Sterling Pound	Seeking the Gold	G2SW
Fath	b.c. 1997	Desirable (Ire)	Lord Gayle	G3SW
Monashee Mountain	b.c. 1997	Prospectors Delite	Mr. Prospector	G3SW
Mull of Kintyre	b.c. 1997	Retrospective	Easy Goer	G2SW
Shibboleth	b.c. 1997	Razyana	His Majesty	G3SW
Speak in Passing	b.c. 1997	Diese	Diesis (GB)	G3SW
Syncline	b.c. 1997	Annie Edge (Ire)	Nebbiolo	SW
War Chant	dk.b.c. 1997	Hollywood Wildcat	Kris S.	G1SW
Alshadiyah	gr/ro.f. 1998	Shadayid	Shadeed	SW
Iron Mask	b.c. 1998	Raise a Beauty	Alydar	G1SW
Ishiguru	b.c. 1998	Strategic Movement	Cryptoclearance	G3SW
Masterful	b.c. 1998	Moonlight Serenade (Fr)	Dictus	G2SW
Modigliani	b.c. 1998	Hot Princess (GB)	Hot Spark	G3SW
Shore Breeze	dk.b.c. 1998	Sea Breezer	Gulch	SW
Aramram	b.c. 1999	Felawnah	Mr. Prospector	SW
Bezrin	b.c. 1999	Darling Flame	Capote	SW
Burning Sun	b.c. 1999	Media Nox (GB)	Lycius	G2SW

225

Appendix: Danzig's Stakes Winners

HORSE	C/S/YOB	DAM	BROODMARE SIRE	STATUS
Century City (Ire)	b.c. 1999	Alywow	Alysheba	G2SW
Della Francesca	b.c. 1999	La Affirmed	Affirmed	G2SW
Line Rider	b.c. 1999	Freewheel	Arctic Tern	SW
War Zone	b.c. 1999	Proflare	Mr. Prospector	G3SW
Coherent	b.f. 2000	Unify	Farma Way	SW
Country Reel	b.c. 2000	Country Belle	Seattle Slew	G2SW
Etesaal	dk.b.c. 2000	Electric Society (Ire)	Law Society	SW
Miguel Cervantes	b.c. 2000	Warm Mood	Alydar	SW
Rimrod	b.c. 2000	Annie Edge (Ire)	Nebbiolo	SW
Walayef	b.f. 2000	Sayedat Alhadh	Mr. Prospector	G3SW
Antonius Pius	b.c. 2001	Catchascatchcan (GB)	Pursuit of Love	G2SW
Greek Sun	dk.b.c. 2001	Sunlit Silence	Trempolino	G2SW
Ulfah	b.f. 2001	Sayedat Alhadh	Mr. Prospector	SW
Ad Valorem	b.c. 2002	Classy Women	Relaunch	G1SW
Defer	b.c. 2002	Hidden Reserve	Mr. Prospector	G3SW
Survivalist	dk.b.c. 2002	Miner's Game	Mr. Prospector	G3SW
Librettist	b.c. 2002	Mysterial	Alleged	G1SW
Olympic	b.c. 2002	Queena	Mr. Prospector	SW
War Front	b.c. 2002	Starry Dreamer	Rubiano	G2SW
Phantom Rose	b.f. 2003	Honest Lady	Seattle Slew	SW
Soapy Danger (GB)	dk.b.c. 2003	On a Soapbox	Mi Cielo	G2SW
Suteki Shinsukekun	b.c. 2003	Autumn Moon	Mr. Prospector	SW
Wasseema	b.f. 2003	Vantive	Mr. Prospector	SW
Astronomer Royal	b.c. 2004	Sheepscot	Easy Goer	G1SW
Dijeerr	b.c. 2004	Sharp Minister	Deputy Minister	G3SW
Haatef	b.c. 2004	Sayedat Alhadh	Mr. Prospector	G2SW
Hard Spun	b.c. 2004	Turkish Tryst	Turkoman	G1SW
Pitamakan	b.f. 2004	Vantive	Mr. Prospector	SW
U S Ranger	b.c. 2004	My Annette	Red Ransom	SW
All Together	b.g. 2005	Unify	Farma Way	SW
Mawatheeq	b.c. 2005	Sarayir	Mr. Prospector	G3SW
Prussian	b.c. 2005	Crystal Downs	Alleged	G3SW

Appendix: Dixieland Band's Stakes Winners

HORSE	C/S/YOB	DAM	BROODMARE SIRE	STATUS
Box Office Gold	ch.f. 1986	Fearless Queen	Iron Ruler	G2SW
Dixie Dancer	dk.b.c. 1986	Debro	Gummo	SW
Dixieland Brass	ch.c. 1986	Windmill Gal	Gallant Romeo	G2SW
Dixieland Dream	dk.b.f. 1986	Par Three	Alleged	SW
Drum Taps	b.c. 1986	Lavendula Rose (GB)	Le Levanstell (GB)	G1SW
Rampart Road	b.c. 1986	Regal Road	Graustark	SW
Treat Tobeatyafeet	ch.g. 1986	Tort Lass	Grey Eagle	SW
Bedeviled	dk.b.c. 1987	Demetria	Raja Baba	G2SW
Dixie Accent	ro.f. 1987	Averell	Restless Native	SW
Dixie Card	b.f. 1987	Little Ferrous	Iron Ruler	SW
Blues Band	b.g. 1988	Bethenny's Star	Fappiano	SW
Donttellthefluff	b.f. 1988	Flag of Leyte Gulf	Hoist the Flag	SW
Golden Wave Band	b.f. 1988	Wind Talk	Drone	SW
He Is Risen	dk.b.c. 1988	Silver Design	Silver Series	G3SW
Lupescu (GB)	ch.f. 1988	Keep Me Posted	Stage Door Johnny	SW
Rally Run	b.c. 1988	Caronatta	Raise a Native	SW
Stark South	ch.c. 1988	Miss Stark	His Majesty	G3SW
Capitalimprovement	dk.b.c. 1989	Homewrecker	Buckaroo	SW
Dixie Brass	dk.b.c. 1989	Petite Diable	Sham	G1SW

Appendix: Dixieland Band's Stakes Winners

HORSE	C/S/YOB	DAM	BROODMARE SIRE	STATUS
For Dixie	b.f. 1989	Forain	Forli	SW
Primitive Hall	b.g. 1989	Dame Avie	Lord Gaylord	G3SW
Sing and Swing	ro.f. 1989	Sun and Snow	Hawaii	SW
Spinning Round	b.f. 1989	Take Heart	Secretariat	G1SW
Starlight Cove	dk.b.f. 1989	Sonia's Scamp	Warm Front	SW
Beal Street Blues	b.f. 1990	Windmill Gal	Gallant Romeo	G2SW
Daybreak Express	dk.b.g. 1990	Ms. Eloise	Nasty and Bold	SW
Del Mar Dennis	ch.g. 1990	Party Bonnet	The Axe II	G2SW
Devoted Brass	b.g. 1990	Royal Devotion	His Majesty	G2SW
Didyme	b.c. 1990	Soundings	Mr. Prospector	G2SW
Dixie Band	dk.b.f 1990	Halley's Comeback	Key to the Kingdom	SW
Dixie Hero	b.g. 1990	Queen's Statute	King's Bishop	SW
Dixieland Heat	dk.b.c. 1990	Evening Silk	Damascus	G3SW
Exclusivengagement	dk.b.c. 1990	Tiwa	Exclusive Native	SW
Piano Pleasure	b.c. 1990	Headin' West	Mr. Prospector	SW
Sheshallhavemusic	ch.f. 1990	Thought Provoker	Exceller	SW
Snake Eyes	b.g. 1990	Royalivor	Sir Ivor	G3SW
Ava Singstheblues	b.f. 1991	Ava Romance	Avatar	SW
Chimes Band	dk.b.c. 1991	Chimes	Mr. Prospector	G2SW
Dixie Luck	dk.b.f. 1991	Lucky Ole Queen	King's Bishop	G2SW
Dixie Power	dk.b.c. 1991	Clever Power	Lines of Power	SW
Rhapsodic	b.f. 1991	Tamanaco Day	Naskra	G2SW
Shoe Band	b.f. 1991	Other Shoe	Advocator	SW
Southern Rhythm	ch.f. 1991	Prospector's Queen	Mr. Prospector	G2SW
Dixie Pearl	dk.b.f. 1991	Pleasantly Free	Pleasant Colony	SW
Dixieland Gold	b.f. 1992	Easy 'n Gold	Slew o' Gold	G2SW
Fluffkins	b.f. 1992	Brass Needles	Twice Worthy	SW
Igotrhythm	b.f. 1992	Slew Princess	Seattle Slew	G2SW
Jambalaya Jazz	ch.c. 1992	Glorious Morning	Graustark	G3SW
Knockadoon	b.c. 1992	Double Smooth	Overskate	G3SW
Matula	ch.g. 1992	Manduria	Aloma's Ruler	SW
Placid Fund	ch.c. 1992	Sunset Strait	Naskra	SW
Tajannub	ch.f. 1992	Empress Jackie	Mount Hagen (Fr)	G3SW
Tajawall	b.g. 1992	Cojinx	Crafty Prospector	SW
Canyon Run	b.c. 1993	Miss Creeker	Red Ryder	SW
Dixie Bayou	ch.g. 1993	Marie de Chantilly	Alleged	G2SW
Freddie Frisson	b.f. 1993	Frisson	Fappiano	SW
Check the Band	gr/ro.c. 1994	Check Bid	Grey Dawn II	SW
Cotton Carnival	ch.f. 1994	Syrianette	Damascus	G3SW
Deal Breaker	dk.b.c. 1994	Tivli	Mt. Livermore	SW
Dixie Daylight	ch.f. 1994	Exclusive Love	Exclusive Native	SW
Dixie Flag	b.f. 1994	Thirty Flags	Hoist the Flag	G2SW
Land Boom	b.c. 1994	Boom and Bust	Mr. Prospector	SW
Love That Jazz	b.f. 1994	Love From Mom	Mr. Prospector	G3SW
A Lady From Dixie	ch.f. 1995	Wicked Witchcraft	Good Behaving	G2SW
Cool Dixie	b.f. 1995	Be Cool	Tank's Prospect	SW
Delta Music	dk.b.f. 1995	Prospectors Delite	Mr. Prospector	SW
Dixieland Sham	gr/ro.c. 1995	Sham Say	Oh Say	SW
Jazz Club	b.c. 1995	Hidden Garden	Mr. Prospector	G3SW
Lady Dixie	b.f. 1995	Chimes	Mr. Prospector	SW
Mission Park	b.f. 1995	Fretina	Star de Naskra	SW
Sazarac Jazz	b.f. 1995	Low Tolerance	Proud Truth	SW
Swear by Dixie	dk.b.c. 1995	Under Oath	Deputed Testamony	SW
Wised Up	b.c. 1995	Wising Up	Smarten	G3SW
Bought in Dixie	b.c. 1996	Shopping	Private Account	SW

Appendix: Dixieland Band's Stakes Winners

HORSE	C/S/YOB	DAM	BROODMARE SIRE	STATUS
Dootsie	b.f. 1996	Skybox	Spend a Buck	SW
Jena Jena	b.f. 1996	With a Wink	Clever Trick	SW
Mutaahab	b.c. 1996	Serene Nobility	His Majesty	G2SW
Rebel Account	b.f. 1996	New Account	Private Account	SW
Roaring Twenties	b.f. 1996	Questelavie	Conquistador Cielo	G1SW
Shag	ch.f. 1996	Ismelda	Wavering Monarch	SW
Away	ch.f. 1997	Be a Prospector	Mr. Prospector	SW
Dixie Union	dk.b.c. 1997	She's Tops	Capote	G1SW
Dixieland Diamond	dk.b.c. 1997	Sometimesadiamond	Mr. Prospector	SW
Egyptband	b.f. 1997	Egyptown (Fr)	Top Ville	G1SW
Hook and Ladder	dk.b.c. 1997	Taianna	Cox's Ridge	G2SW
Amelia	ch.f. 1998	Aquilegia	Alydar	SW
Bayou the Moon	ch.f. 1998	Lyin to the Moon	Kris S.	SW
Bowman's Band	ch.c. 1998	Hometown Queen	Pleasant Colony	G2SW
Shiny Band	gr/ro.f. 1998	Shiner	Two Punch	G2SW
Tap Your Feet	ch.f. 1998	Exotic Moves	Miswaki	SW
Music Club	b.f. 1999	Long View	Damascus	SW
Covering Ground	b.c. 2000	Serene Nobility	His Majesty	SW
Hippogator	b.f. 2000	Gastronomical	Sunshine Forever	SW
Makhlab	b.c. 2000	Avasand	Avatar	G3SW
My Ro	ch.f. 2000	Romy	Slew Machine	SW
Colony Band	b.f. 2001	Hostessante	Pleasant Colony	SW
Courtly Jazz	b.g. 2001	Serene Nobility	His Majesty	SW
Diputado	dk.b.c. 2001	Colonial Waters	Pleasant Colony	SW
Excellent Band	b.c. 2001	Excellentadventure	Slew City Slew	SW
Grand Bank	b.c. 2001	Starry Lake	Meadowlake	SW
Lutyens	ch.g. 2001	Hidden Garden	Mr. Prospector	SW
Menhoubah	dk.b.f. 2001	Private Seductress	Private Account	G1SW
Tigi	ch.f. 2001	Summit Park	A.P. Indy	SW
Welcome Home	b.f. 2001	Safe Return	Mr. Prospector	SW
Dixie Talking	b.f. 2002	Gin Talking	Allen's Prospect	G3SW
Marchonin	b.f. 2002	Pepita Ramoje	Capote	SW
Mogaamer	b.c. 2002	Dolly Talbo	Capote	SW
Ragtime Hope	b.f. 2002	Good 'n Smart	Smarten	SW
Sharp Lisa	ch.f. 2002	Winter's Gone	Dynaformer	G1SW
Kona Blend	b.g. 2003	Life in Seattle	Unbridled	SW
Southern Success	ch.c. 2003	My Success	A.P. Indy	SW
Barkley Sound	b.c. 2004	Class on Class	Jolie's Halo	SW
Sandwaki	b.c. 2004	Wakigoer	Miswaki	G3SW
Win With a Wink	b.f. 2004	With a Wink	Clever Trick	SW
Alwajeeha	b.f. 2005	Ridaa	Seattle Slew	G1SW
Simmard	ch.c. 2005	Dibs	Spectacular Bid	G2SW

Appendix: Nureyev's Stakes Winners

HORSE	C/S/YOB	DAM	BROODMARE SIRE	STATUS
Al Sylah (GB)	gr.f. 1982	Noiritza	Young Emperor	G3SW
Breath Taking (Fr)	ch.f. 1982	Cap d'Antibes (Aus)	Better Boy (Ire)	G3SW
Devalois (Fr)	ch.f. 1982	Dourdan	Prudent	G2SW
Eagling (GB)	dk.b.c. 1982	Magic Flute	Tudor Melody	SW
Gallanta (Fr)	ch.f. 1982	Gay Missile	Sir Gaylord	SW
Lidhame	br.c. 1982	Red Berry	Great Nephew	G3SW
Magic Mirror	gr.c. 1982	Turkish Treasure	Sir Ivor	G3SW
Nugget Point (Ire)	dk.b.c. 1982	Artists Proof	Ribot	SW

HORSE	C/S/YOB	DAM	BROODMARE SIRE	STATUS
Theatrical (Ire)	dk.b.c. 1982	Tree of Knowledge (Ire)	Sassafras (Fr)	G1SW
Vilikaia	ch.f. 1982	Baracala	Swaps	G3SW
Alex Nureyev	b.c. 1983	Solariat	Secretariat	SW
Lead On Time	dk.b.c. 1983	Alathea (GB)	Lorenzaccio	G2SW
Made of Pearl	dk.b.f. 1983	Mother of Pearl (Fr)	Sir Gaylord	SW
Only Star	ch.f. 1983	Rivermaid (Fr)	Riverman	G3SW
Sonic Lady	b.f. 1983	Stumped (GB)	Owen Anthony	G1SW
Truely Nureyev	ch.c. 1983	True Lady	Le Fabuleux	SW
Annoconnor	b.f. 1984	My Nord	Vent du Nord	G1SW
Fotitieng	dk.b.c. 1984	Dry Fly (Fr)	Mill Reef	G3SW
Gayane (GB)	b.f. 1984	Roussalka (GB)	Habitat	SW
Miesque	b.f. 1984	Pasadoble	Prove Out	G1SW
Mona Stella	b.f. 1984	Morana	Val de Loir	G2SW
Nuryana	b.f. 1984	Loralane (GB)	Habitat	SW
Professional Girl	b.f. 1984	Don't Sulk	Graustark	SW
Soviet Star	b.c. 1984	Veruschka	Venture (Fr)	G1SW
Stately Don	dk.b.c. 1984	Dona Ysidra	Le Fabuleux	G1SW
Timely Reserve	dk.b.f. 1984	Lady Trespass	Inverness Drive	SW
Action Francaise	dk.b.f. 1985	Allez France	*Sea-Bird	G3SW
Alwuhush	b.c. 1985	Beaming Bride (Ire)	King Emperor	G1SW
Angelina Ballerina	ch.f. 1985	Solariat	Secretariat	SW
Beaute Dangereuse	b.f. 1985	Allicance	Alleged	SW
Danseuse de Lune	ch.f. 1985	Blow Your Horn	Proud Clarion	SW
Exclusive Nureyev	dk.b.c. 1985	Balcony Dancer	Gallant Romeo	SW
Literati	ch.c. 1985	Lovelight II	Bleep-Bleep	SW
Most Precious	dk.b.f. 1985	Miss Summer (Ire)	Luthier (Fr)	SW
Movieland	b.f. 1985	Rivermaid (Fr)	Riverman	G3SW
Nureyev's Best	b.f. 1985	Meadow Blue	Raise a Native	SW
Pasakos	b.c. 1985	Cendres Bleues (Ity)	Charlottesville (GB)	G3SW
Pattern Step	br.f. 1985	Tipping Time	Commanding II	G1SW
Soviet Lad	b.c. 1985	Green Valley II	Val de Loir	SW
Vive	ch.f. 1985	Viva Regina	His Majesty	SW
Arsaan	dk.b.f. 1986	Anne Campbell	Never Bend	SW
Dancing Dissident	b.c. 1986	Absentia	Raise a Cup	G2SW
Eternity's Breath	dk.b.c. 1986	Sham's Princess	Sham	SW
Goldneyev	dk.b.c. 1986	Gold River (Fr)	Riverman	SW
Great Commotion	b.c. 1986	Alathea (GB)	Lorenzaccio	G3SW
Louveterie	ch.f. 1986	Lupe II	Primera (GB)	G3SW
Monsagem	b.c. 1986	Meringue Pie	Silent Screen	SW
Navratilovna	dk.b.f. 1986	Baracala	Swaps	G2SW
Taffeta and Tulle	ch.f. 1986	Miss Nymph (Arg)	Perugin	G3SW
Vanities	ch.f. 1986	Play It Safe (Ire)	Red Alert	SW
Zilzal	ch.c. 1986	French Charmer	Le Fabuleux	G1SW
Matador	ch.c. 1987	Allicance	Alleged	SW
Polar Falcon	dk.b.c 1987	Marie d'Argonne (Fr)	Jefferson	G1SW
Robin des Bois	b.c. 1987	Rare Mint	Key to the Mint	SW
Rudy's Fantasy	b.c. 1987	Rainbow's Edge	Crème dela Crème	G3SW
Silk Slippers	b.f. 1987	Nalee's Fantasy	Graustark	G2SW
Wajna	b.f. 1987	Wind Spirit	Round Table	SW
Anjiz	b.c. 1987	Prayers'n Promises	Foolish Pleasure	SW
Massaraat	b.f. 1988	Pasadoble	Prove Out	SW
Nucleus	b.g. 1988	Nellie Forbes	Secretariat	SW

Appendix: Nureyev's Stakes Winners

HORSE	C/S/YOB	DAM	BROODMARE SIRE	STATUS
Rinka Das	b.c. 1988	Tremulous	Gregorian	SW
Robin des Pins	b.c. 1988	Rare Mint	Key to the Mint	G2SW
Rudimentary	b.c. 1988	Doubly Sure (GB)	Reliance II	G2SW
Hydro Calido	dk.b.f. 1989	Coup de Folie	Halo	G2SW
King's Signet	ch.c. 1989	Sigy (Fr)	Habitat	SW
Kitwood	b.c. 1989	Kittiwake	Sea-Bird	G1SW
Manureva	b.f. 1989	Maximova (Fr)	Green Dancer	SW
Oumaldaaya	b.f. 1989	Histoire (Fr)	Riverman	G2SW
Red Slippers	ch.f. 1989	Morning Devotion	Affirmed	G2SW
Trishyde	ch.f. 1989	Rose Du Boele (Fr)	Rheffic	G2SW
What Katy Did	dk.b.f. 1989	Katies (Ire)	Nonoalco	SW
Wolfhound	ch.c. 1989	Lassie Dear	Buckpasser	G1SW
Baya	ch.f 1990	Barger	Riverman	G3SW
Caesour	dk.b.c. 1990	Don't Sulk	Graustark	G2SW
Jeune Homme	b.c. 1990	Alydariel	Alydar	G2SW
Neverneyev	b.c. 1990	River Rose (Fr)	Riverman	SW
Unusual Heat	dk.b.c. 1990	Rossard (Den)	Glacial	SW
Viviana	b.f. 1990	Nijinsky Star	Nijinsky II	SW
Fadeyev	b.c. 1991	Skating (Ire)	Mill Reef	G3SW
Flagbird	dk.b.f. 1991	Up the Flagpole	Hoist the Flag	G1SW
Heart Lake (GB)	ch.c. 1991	My Darling One	Exclusive Native	G1SW
La Confederation (GB)	b.f. 1991	Unite (Ire)	Kris (GB)	G2SW
Majestic Style	b.c. 1991	Fantastic Girl	Riva Ridge	SW
Mehthaaf	b.f. 1991	Elle Seule	Exclusive Native	G1SW
Opera Score	dk.b.c. 1991	Ballinderry (GB)	Irish River (Fr)	SW
Varsavia	dk.b.f. 1991	Header Card	Quack	SW
Wild Planet	b.f. 1991	Ivory Wings	Sir Ivor	SW
Atticus	ch.c. 1992	Athyka	Secretariat	G1SW
Dance Treat	ch.f. 1992	Office Wife	Secretariat	G3SW
Diffident	b.c. 1992	Shy Princess	Irish River (Fr)	G2SW
Isla Del Rey	ch.f. 1992	Priceless Pearl	Alydar	SW
Loyalize	b.f. 1992	Reloy	Liloy (Fr)	SW
Alamo Bay	b.c. 1993	Albertine (Fr)	Irish River (Fr)	SW
Joyeux Danseur	b.c. 1993	Fabuleux Jane	Le Fabuleux	G1SW
Russian Revival	ch.c. 1993	Memories	Hail the Pirates	G3SW
Spinning World	ch.c. 1993	Imperfect Circle	Riverman	G1SW
Black Hawk (GB)	b.c. 1994	Silver Lane	Silver Hawk	G1SW
Ice Ballet (Ire)	ch.f. 1994	Skating (Ire)	Mill Reef	SW
Peintre Celebre	ch.c. 1994	Peinture Bleue	Alydar	G1SW
Reams of Verse	ch.f. 1994	Modena	Roberto	G1SW
Romanov (Ire)	b.c. 1994	Morning Devotion	Affirmed	G2SW
Special Discount	b.g. 1994	Looks Sensational	Majestic Light	SW
Tekken (Ire)	b.c. 1994	Shannkara (Ire)	Akarad	SW
Diableneyev	dk.b.c. 1995	La Pitie	Devil's Bag	SW
Isle de France	b.f. 1995	Stella Madrid	Alydar	G3SW
Light Step	b.f. 1995	Nimble Feet	Danzig	SW
Social Charter	b.c. 1995	Aunt Pearl	Seattle Slew	G3SW
Eltawaasul	ch.c. 1996	Grand Falls	Ogygian	SW
European Rose	b.f. 1996	Lakab	Manila	SW
Good Journey	ch.c. 1996	Chimes of Freedom	Private Account	G1SW
Gracioso	ch.c. 1996	Don't Sulk	Graustark	G1SW
Istintaj	dk.b.c. 1996	Mathkurh	Riverman	G3SW
Senure	dk.b.c. 1996	Diese	Diesis (GB)	G1SW

Appendix: Nureyev's Stakes Winners

HORSE	C/S/YOB	DAM	BROODMARE SIRE	STATUS
Skimming	b.c. 1996	Skimble	Lyphard	G1SW
Stravinsky	b.c. 1996	Fire the Groom	Blushing Groom (Fr)	G1SW
England's Rose	dk.b.f. 1997	Infringe	Irish River (Fr)	G3SW
Fasliyev	b.c. 1997	Mr. P's Princess	Mr. Prospector	G1SW
No Matter What	ch.f. 1997	Words of War	Lord At War (Arg)	G1SW
Special Ring	b.g. 1997	Ring Beaune	Bering (GB)	G1SW
St. Petersburg (Aus)	br.c. 1997	Miss Bold Appeal	Valid Appeal	G3SW
Thady Quill	ch.c. 1997	Alleged Devotion	Alleged	SW
Valentino (GB)	ch.c. 1997	Divine Danse (Fr)	Kris (GB)	G2SW
Zentsov Street	b.c. 1997	Storm Fear	Coastal	SW
Binary File	b.c. 1998	Binary (GB)	Rainbow Quest	SW
Crystal Music	b.f. 1998	Crystal Spray (GB)	Beldale Flutter	G1SW
Dance Dreamer	dk.b.c. 1998	Revasser	Riverman	SW
King Charlemagne	b.c. 1998	Race the Wild Wind	Sunny's Halo	G1SW
Momentum	b.c. 1998	Imprudent Love	Foolish Pleasure	G3SW
Pure Theatre (Aus)	b.c. 1998	A Goodlookin Broad	Broad Brush	G3SW
Rock	b.c. 1998	Miswaki's Princess	Miswaki	SW
Stunning	b.f. 1998	Gorgeous	Slew o' Gold	SW
Toroca	ch.f. 1998	Grand Falls	Ogygian	G3SW
Dance Dress	dk.b.f. 1999	Private Line	Private Account	G3SW
Meshaheer	b.c. 1999	Race the Wild Wind	Sunny's Halo	G3SW
Stonemason	b.g. 1999	Sweet Times (GB)	Riverman	G3SW
Arakan	dk.b.c. 2000	Far Across (Gb)	Common Grounds	G3SW
Snipewalk	dk.b.c. 2000	Ramirena	Key to the Mint	SW

Appendix: Sadler's Wells' Stakes Winners

HORSE	C/S/YOB	DAM	BROODMARE SIRE	STATUS
Batshoof (Ire)	b.c. 1986	Steel Habit (Ire)	Habitat	G2SW
Braashee	b.c. 1986	Krakow	Malinowski	G1SW
Dolpour	b.c. 1986	Dumka	Kashmir II	G3SW
French Glory (Ire)	dk.b.c. 1986	Dunette	Hard to Beat	G1SW
In the Wings (GB)	b.c. 1986	High Hawk (Ire)	Shirley Heights (GB)	G1SW
Myth to Reality (Fr)	b.f. 1986	Millieme	Mill Reef	SW
Night of Stars	b.f. 1986	Glinting	Crepello (GB)	SW
Old Vic	b.c. 1986	Cockade	Derring-Do	G1SW
Pirouette (Ire)	b.f. 1986	True Rocket	Roan Rocket	SW
Prince of Dance	b.c. 1986	Sun Princess (GB)	English Prince	G1SW
Scenic (Ire)	dk.b.c. 1986	Idyllic	Foolish Pleasure	G1SW
Baylis (Ire)	b.c. 1987	Noblanna	Vaguely Noble	G3SW
Blue Stag (Ire)	dk.b.c. 1987	Snow Day (Fr)	Reliance II	SW
Northern Hal (Ire)	b.c. 1987	Northern Script	Arts and Letters	SW
Sagal Wells	b.c. 1987	Plume Au Vent (GB)	Posse	SW
Salsabil (Ire)	b.f. 1987	Flame of Tara (Ire)	Artaius	G1SW
Stagecraft (GB)	b.c. 1987	Bella Colora	Bellypha (Ire)	G2SW
Theatre Critic (Ire)	dk.b.c. 1987	Querida (Ire)	Habitat	SW
Theatrical Charmer (GB)	b.c. 1987	Very Charming	Vaguely Noble	SW
Adam Smith (GB)	b.c. 1988	Krakow	Malinowski	G3SW
Nimrouz (Ire)	b.g. 1988	Nilmeen	Right Royal (Fr)	SW
Opera House (GB)	b.c. 1988	Colorspin (Ire)	High Top	G1SW
Peking Opera (Ire)	b.c. 1988	Braneakins	Sallust	SW
Runyon (Ire)	b.c. 1988	Deadly Serious	Queen's Hussar (GB)	G1SW
Saddlers' Hall (Ire)	b.c. 1988	Sunny Valley	Val de Loir	G1SW

Appendix: Sadler's Wells' Stakes Winners

HORSE	C/S/YOB	DAM	BROODMARE SIRE	STATUS
Alnasr Alwasheek (GB)	b.c. 1989	Someone Special	Habitat	G2SW
El Prado (Ire)	gr.f. 1989	Lady Capulet	Sir Ivor	G1SW
Johann Quatz (Fr)	b.c. 1989	Whakilyric	Miswaki	G1SW
Masad	b.c. 1989	Marmolada	Sassafras (Fr)	G1SW
Miznah (Ire)	b.f. 1989	La Dame Du Lac	Round Table	SW
Modhish (Ire)	b.c. 1989	Arctique Royale (Ire)	Royal and Regal	G2SW
Soiree (Ire)	b.f. 1989	Seminar II	Don	SW
Sonus	b.c. 1989	Sound of Success	Successor	G3SW
Spring	b.f. 1989	Gull Nook (GB)	Mill Reef	G3SW
Admiral's Well (Ire)	b.c. 1990	Exotic Bride	Blushing Groom (Fr)	SW
Ballet Prince	b.c. 1990	Sun Princess (GB)	English Prince	SW
Barathea (Ire)	b.c. 1990	Brocade (GB)	Habitat	G1SW
Dancing Bloom	b.f. 1990	Dancing Shadow (Ire)	Dancer's Image	G3SW
Desert Secret (Ire)	b.c. 1990	Clandestina	Secretariat	G2SW
Fatherland (Ire)	b.c. 1990	Lisadell	Forli	G1SW
Fort Wood	b.c. 1990	Fall Aspen	Pretense	G1SW
Hunting Hawk (Ire)	b.c. 1990	High Hawk (Ire)	Shirley Heights (GB)	G2SW
Intrepidity (GB)	dk.b.f. 1990	Intrepid Lady	Bold Ruler	G1SW
Kirov Premiere (GB)	b.f. 1990	Querida (Ire)	Habitat	G3SW
Licorne (GB)	b.f. 1990	Catawba	Mill Reef	SW
Lille Hammer	b.f. 1990	Smeralda	Dschingis Khan	SW
Nassma	b.f. 1990	Pretoria	Habitat	SW
Pridwell (GB)	b.c. 1990	Glowing With Pride (GB)	Ile de Bourbon	SW
Royal Ballerina (Ire)	b.f. 1990	Fremanche	Jim French	G2SW
Scribe	b.c. 1990	Northern Script	Arts and Letters	G3SW
Taos (Ire)	b.c. 1990	Tenea (GB)	Reform (GB)	SW
Thawakib (Ire)	b.f. 1990	Tobira Celeste	Ribot	G2SW
Wakria (Ire)	b.f. 1990	Spirits Dancing	Melyno (Ire)	SW
Carnegie (Ire)	b.c. 1991	Detroit (Fr)	Riverman	G1SW
Correggio (Ire)	b.g. 1991	Rosa Mundi	Secretariat	G1SW
Foyer (GB)	b.c. 1991	Ela Romara	Ela-Mana-Mou (Ire)	G2SW
Hawker's News (Ire)	b.c. 1991	High Hawk (Ire)	Shirley Heights (GB)	G3SW
Interim (GB)	b.f. 1991	Intermission (GB)	Stage Door Johnny	G2SW
King's Theatre (Ire)	b.c. 1991	Regal Beauty	Princely Native	G1SW
Lady Reiko (Ire)	b.f. 1991	Willamae	Tentam	SW
Ming Dynasty (Ire)	b.g. 1991	Marie Noelle (Fr)	Brigadier Gerard (GB)	SW
Mohaajir	b.c. 1991	Very Charming	Vaguely Noble	SW
Northern Spur (Ire)	b.c. 1991	Fruition	Rheingold	G1SW
Sadler's Image (Ire)	b.c. 1991	Exclusive Order	Exclusive Native	SW
Sage Wells (Ire)	b.c. 1991	Forlene (Ire)	Forli	G3SW
Saxon Maid (GB)	b.f. 1991	Britannia's Rule	Blakeney (GB)	SW
Walter Willy (Ire)	b.c. 1991	Whakilyric	Miswaki	SW
Archive Footage (GB)	b.c. 1992	Trusted Partner	Affirmed	SW
Dance a Dream (GB)	b.f. 1992	Exclusive Order	Exclusive Native	SW
Election Day (Ire)	b.c. 1992	Hellenic	Darshaan (GB)	SW
Flowerdrum (Ire)	b.f. 1992	Mill Princess	Mill Reef	SW
Helen of Spain (GB)	b.f. 1992	Port Helene	Troy (GB)	G2SW
Honfleur (Ire)	b.f. 1992	Detroit (Fr)	Riverman	SW
Istabraq (Ire)	b.g. 1992	Betty's Secret	Secretariat	SW
Larrocha (Ire)	b.f. 1992	Le Melody (Ire)	Levmoss	SW
Moonshell (Ire)	b.f. 1992	Moon Cactus	Kris (GB)	G1SW
Muncie (Ire)	b.f. 1992	Martingale	Luthier (Fr)	G1SW
Poliglote (GB)	b.c. 1992	Alexandrie	Val de l'Orne (Fr)	G1SW

HORSE	C/S/YOB	DAM	BROODMARE SIRE	STATUS
Royal Solo (Ire)	b.c. 1992	Sharp Castan (GB)	Sharpen Up (GB)	G2SW
Russian Snows (Ire)	b.f. 1992	Arctique Royale (Ire)	Royal and Regal	G2SW
Song of Tara (Ire)	b.c. 1992	Flame of Tara (Ire)	Artaius	SW
Synergetic (Fr)	b.c. 1992	Gwydion	Raise a Cup	SW
Tamure (Ire)	b.c. 1992	Three Tails (Fr)	Blakeney (GB)	G3SW
Theatreworld (Ire)	b.g. 1992	Chamonis	Affirmed	SW
Balalaika (GB)	b.f. 1993	Bella Colora	Bellypha (Ire)	SW
Camporese (Ire)	b.f. 1993	Campestral	Alleged	G3SW
Chief Contender (Ire)	b.c. 1993	Minnie Hauk	Sir Ivor	G1SW
Dance Design (Ire)	b.f. 1993	Elegance in Design (Ire)	Habitat	G1SW
Darazari (Ire)	b.c. 1993	Darara (Ire)	Top Ville	G1SW
Double Leaf (GB)	b.g. 1993	Green Leaf	Alydar	G2SW
Dr Massini (Ire)	b.c. 1993	Argon Laser (GB)	Kris (GB)	SW
Dushyantor	dk.b.c. 1993	Slightly Dangerous	Roberto	G2SW
French Ballerina (Ire)	b.f. 1993	Filia Ardross (GB)	Ardross	SW
Lafitte the Pirate (GB)	b.g. 1993	Reprocolor	Jimmy Reppin	SW
Luna Wells (Ire)	dk.b.f. 1993	Lunadix (Fr)	Breton (GB)	G1SW
On Fair Stage (Ire)	b.f. 1993	Fair Salinia (Ire)	Petingo (GB)	SW
Otaiti (Ire)	b.f. 1993	Ode	Lord Avie	SW
Reine Wells (Ire)	b.f. 1993	Rivoltade	Sir Ivor	SW
Royal Court (Ire)	b.c. 1993	Rose of Jericho	Alleged	G3SW
Time Allowed (GB)	b.f. 1993	Time Charter	Saritamer	G2SW
Water Poet (Ire)	dk.b.c. 1993	Love Smitten	Key to the Mint	SW
Allurement (Ire)	b.f. 1994	Alydaress	Alydar	G3SW
Ashley Park (Ire)	b.c. 1994	Maiden Concert (Ire)	Condorcet	G3SW
Ballarat (Ire)	b.c. 1994	Bex	Explodent	SW
Casey Tibbs (Ire)	b.c. 1994	Fleur Royale (Ire)	Mill Reef	SW
Cloudings (Ire)	gr.c. 1994	Ispahan (Ire)	Rusticaro	G1SW
Crimson Tide	b.c. 1994	Sharata (Ire)	Darshaan (GB)	G2SW
Ebadiyla (Ire)	b.f. 1994	Ebaziya (Ire)	Darshaan (GB)	G1SW
Entrepreneur (GB)	b.c. 1994	Exclusive Order	Exclusive Native	G1SW
Family Tradition (Ire)	b.f. 1994	Sequel (Ire)	Law Society	SW
Ghataas (GB)	b.c. 1994	Harmless Albatross	Pas de Seul	SW
Go Boldly (Ire)	b.c. 1994	Diavolina	Lear Fan	SW
In Command (Ire)	b.c. 1994	Flying Melody (Ire)	Auction Ring	G1SW
Kayf Tara (GB)	b.c. 1994	Colorspin (Ire)	High Top	G1SW
Legend Maker (Ire)	b.f. 1994	High Spirited (Ire)	Shirley Heights (GB)	G3SW
Loco	b.c. 1994	La Colorada (Ire)	Surumu (Ger)	SW
New Frontier (Ire)	b.c. 1994	Diamond Field	Mr. Prospector	G3SW
Palme d'Or (Ire)	b.f. 1994	Pampa Bella (Fr)	Armos (Ire)	G3SW
Saafeya (Ire)	b.f. 1994	Safa (GB)	Shirley Heights (GB)	SW
Sabadilla	b.c. 1994	Jasmina	Forli	SW
Solo Mio (Ire)	b.c. 1994	Marie de Flandre (Fr)	Crystal Palace	G3SW
Strawberry Roan (Ire)	b.f. 1994	Doff the Derby (Ire)	Master Derby	SW
Swalina (Ire)	b.f. 1994	Dinalina (Fr)	Top Ville	SW
Tanaasa (Ire)	dk.b.c. 1994	Mesmerize (Ire)	Mill Reef	SW
Yalaietanee (GB)	b.c. 1994	Vaigly Star (GB)	Star Appeal	G3SW
Amusing Time (Ire)	b.f. 1995	Ozone Friendly	Green Forest	SW
Desert Fox (GB)	b.c. 1995	Radiant	Foolish Pleasure	SW
Dream Well (Fr)	b.c. 1995	Soul Dream	Alleged	G1SW
Eminence Grise (Ire)	b.g. 1995	Impatiente	Vaguely Noble	SW
Greek Dance (Ire)	b.c. 1995	Hellenic	Darshaan (GB)	G1SW
Insight (Fr)	b.f. 1995	Or Vision	Irish River (Fr)	G1SW

Appendix: Sadler's Wells' Stakes Winners

HORSE	C/S/YOB	DAM	BROODMARE SIRE	STATUS
Kadaka (Ire)	b.f. 1995	Kadissya	Blushing Groom (Fr)	SW
King of Kings (Ire)	b.c. 1995	Zummerudd (Ire)	Habitat	G1SW
Leggera (Ire)	b.f. 1995	Lady Ambassador (GB)	General Assembly	G1SW
Sea Wave (Ire)	b.c. 1995	Three Tails (GB)	Blakeney (GB)	G2SW
Commander Collins (Ire)	b.c. 1996	Kanmary (Fr)	Kenmare (Fr)	G1SW
Daliapour (Ire)	b.c. 1996	Dalara	Doyoun (Ire)	G1SW
Daring Miss (GB)	b.f. 1996	Bourbon Girl	Ile de Bourbon	G2SW
Doowaley (Ire)	b.c. 1996	Dwell	Habitat	SW
Festival Hall (Ire)	b.c. 1996	Handsewn	Sir Ivor	G3SW
Hijaz (Ire)	b.f. 1996	Bex	Explodent	SW
Historic (Ire)	b.g. 1996	Urjwan	Seattle Slew	SW
Montjeu (Ire)	b.c. 1996	Floripedes	Top Ville	G1SW
Moon Dragon (Ire)	b.c. 1996	Moonsilk (Ire)	Solinus (Ire)	SW
Mother of Pearl (Ire)	b.f. 1996	Sisania	High Top	SW
Peach Out of Reach (Ire)	b.f. 1996	Cocotte (GB)	Troy (GB)	SW
Saffron Walden (Fr)	b.f. 1996	Or Vision	Irish River (Fr)	G1SW
Sagittarius (GB)	b.c. 1996	Ste Nitouche (Fr)	Riverman	SW
String Quartet (Ire)	b.f. 1996	Fleur Royale (Ire)	Mill Reef	SW
Trebizond (Ire)	b.g. 1996	Karri Valley	Storm Bird	G1SW
Yeoman's Point (Ire)	b.g. 1996	Truly Bound	In Reality	SW
Amethyst (Ire)	b.f. 1997	Zummerudd (Ire)	Habitat	SW
Among Equals (GB)	b.g. 1997	Epicure's Garden	Affirmed	SW
Aristotle (Ire)	b.c. 1997	Flamenco Wave	Desert Wine	G1SW
Beat Hollow (GB)	b.c. 1997	Wemyss Bight (GB)	Dancing Brave	G1SW
Chiang Mai (Ire)	b.f. 1997	Eljazzi	Artaius	G3SW
Glyndebourne (Ire)	b.c. 1997	Heaven Only Knows	High Top	G3SW
Grand Finale (Ire)	b.c. 1997	Final Figure	Super Concorde	SW
Hatha Anna (Ire)	b.c. 1997	Moon Cactus	Kris (GB)	G2SW
Interlude (GB)	b.f. 1997	Starlet	Teenoso	G2SW
Pittsburgh Phil (Ire)	b.g. 1997	Broadway Joan	Bold Arian	SW
Roscius (Ire)	b.c. 1997	Rosefinch	Blushing Groom (Fr)	SW
Rostropovich (Ire)	gr.g. 1997	Infamy (Ire)	Shirley Heights (GB)	SW
Sadler's Flag (Ire)	b.f. 1997	Animatrice	Alleged	G3SW
Samsaam (Ire)	b.g. 1997	Azyaa	Kris (GB)	G3SW
Snob Wells (Ire)	b.c. 1997	Galitizine	Riverman	SW
St Expedit (GB)	b.c. 1997	Miss Rinjani (GB)	Shirley Heights (GB)	G3SW
Subtle Power (Ire)	b.c. 1997	Mosaique Bleue	Shirley Heights (GB)	G1SW
Wellbeing (GB)	b.g. 1997	Charming Life (NZ)	Sir Tristram	G3SW
Adonesque (Ire)	b.f. 1998	Mira Adonde	Sharpen Up (GB)	SW
Carnival Dancer (GB)	b.c. 1998	Red Carnival	Mr. Prospector	G3SW
Covent Garden (GB)	b.g. 1998	Temple Row (GB)	Ardross	SW
Crimphill (Ire)	b.f. 1998	Vernon Hills	Hard Fought	SW
Galileo (Ire)	b.c. 1998	Urban Sea	Miswaki	G1SW
Ice Dancer (Ire)	b.c. 1998	Tappiano	Fappiano	SW
Imagine (Ire)	b.f. 1998	Doff the Derby (Ire)	Master Derby	G1SW
Inchiri (GB)	b.f. 1998	Inchyre (GB)	Shirley Heights (GB)	SW
Lime Gardens (GB)	b.f. 1998	Hatton Gardens (Ire)	Auction Ring	G3SW
Luna Sacra (Fr)	b.f. 1998	Luna Blue (Fr)	Cure the Blues	SW
Milan (GB)	b.c. 1998	Kithanga	Darshaan (GB)	G1SW
Moon Queen (Ire)	gr/ro.f. 1998	Infamy (Ire)	Shirley Heights (GB)	G2SW
Musha Merr (Ire)	b.c. 1998	Valdara (GB)	Darshaan (GB)	SW
Nalani (Ire)	b.f. 1998	Narwala (Ire)	Darshaan (GB)	SW
Narrative (Ire)	b.c. 1998	Barger	Riverman	G2SW

HORSE	C/S/YOB	DAM	BROODMARE SIRE	STATUS
Perfect Soul (Ire)	b.c. 1998	Ball Chairman	Secretariat	G1SW
Relish The Thought (Ire)	b.f. 1998	Viz	Kris S.	SW
Roman Saddle (Ire)	b.c. 1998	Galitizine	Riverman	G3SW
Sensible (Fr)	b.c. 1998	Raisonnable (GB)	Common Grounds	SW
Sequoyah (Ire)	b.f. 1998	Brigid	Irish River (Fr)	G1SW
Side of Paradise (Ire)	b.f. 1998	Mill Princess	Mill Reef	SW
Sligo Bay (Ire)	b.c. 1998	Angelic Song	Halo	G1SW
Wareed (Ire)	b.c. 1998	Truly Special	Caerleon	G2SW
Xtra (GB)	b.g. 1998	Oriental Mystique (Ire)	Kris (GB)	SW
Ballingarry (Ire)	b.c. 1999	Flamenco Wave	Desert Wine	G1SW
Black Sam Bellamy (Ire)	b.c. 1999	Urban Sea	Miswaki	G1SW
Cane Brake (Ire)	b.g. 1999	Be My Hope (Ire)	Be My Native	SW
Carib Lady (Ire)	b.f. 1999	Belle Passe (Ire)	Be My Guest	G3SW
Dance Routine (GB)	b.f. 1999	Apogee (GB)	Shirley Heights (GB)	G2SW
Diaghilev (Ire)	b.g. 1999	Darara (Ire)	Top Ville	G1SW
Gossamer (GB)	b.f. 1999	Brocade (GB)	Habitat	G1SW
High Chaparral (Ire)	b.c. 1999	Kasora	Darshaan (GB)	G1SW
Islington (Ire)	b.f. 1999	Hellenic	Darshaan (GB)	G1SW
Kiltubber (Ire)	b.f. 1999	Priory Belle (Ire)	Priolo	SW
Kournakova (Ire)	b.f. 1999	Bemuda Classic	Double Form	SW
Mer de Corail (Ire)	b.f. 1999	Miss Tahiti (Ire)	Tirol	SW
Morozov	b.c. 1999	High Hawk (Ire)	Shirley Heights (GB)	G2SW
Mutinyonthebounty (GB)	dk.b.c. 1999	Threatening (GB)	Warning (GB)	G2SW
Nysaean (Ire)	b.c. 1999	Irish Arms (Fr)	Irish River (Fr)	G3SW
On The Nile (Ire)	b.f. 1999	Minnie Habit	Habitat	SW
Phoenix Park (GB)	b.c. 1999	Park Appeal (Ire)	Ahonoora (GB)	SW
Quarter Moon (Ire)	b.f. 1999	Jude (GB)	Darshaan (GB)	G1SW
Sholokhov (Ire)	b.c. 1999	La Meilleure	Lord Gayle	G1SW
Short Pause (GB)	b.c. 1999	Interval	Habitat	G3SW
Stage Call (Ire)	b.c. 1999	Humble Eight	Seattle Battle	SW
Starbourne (Ire)	b.f. 1999	Upper Circle	Shirley Heights (GB)	SW
Adopted Hero (Ire)	b.g. 2000	Lady Liberty (NZ)	Noble Bijou	SW
Alberto Giacometti (Ire)	b.c. 2000	Sweeten Up (GB)	Shirley Heights (GB)	G1SW
Bouthan (Fr)	b.c. 2000	Baiser Vole	Foolish Pleasure	SW
Brian Boru (GB)	b.c. 2000	Eva Luna	Alleged	G1SW
Doyen (Ire)	b.c. 2000	Moon Cactus	Kris (GB)	G1SW
Dubai Success (GB)	b.c. 2000	Crystal Spray (GB)	Beldale Flutter	G3SW
Essex (Ire)	b.g. 2000	Knight's Baroness	Rainbow Quest	SW
Fontanesi (Ire)	b.c. 2000	Northern Script	Arts and Letters	SW
Humilis (Ire)	b.c. 2000	Humble Eight	Seattle Battle	SW
Icklingham (Ire)	b.g. 2000	Braiswick (GB)	King of Spain	SW
In The Limelight (Ire)	b.f. 2000	Minnie Habit	Habitat	SW
Juliette (Ire)	b.f. 2000	Arutura	Riverman	SW
Julius Caesar (GB)	b.g. 2000	Stiletta	Dancing Brave	SW
Look Honey (Ire)	b.c. 2000	Middle Prospect	Mr. Prospector	G2SW
Policy Maker (Ire)	b.c. 2000	Palmeraie	Lear Fan	G2SW
Powerscourt (GB)	b.c. 2000	Rainbow Lake	Rainbow Quest	G1SW
Refuse To Bend (Ire)	b.c. 2000	Market Slide	Gulch	G1SW
Royal Devotion (Ire)	b.f. 2000	Alleged Devotion	Alleged	SW
Visions of Clarity (Ire)	b.f. 2000	Imperfect Circle	Riverman	SW
Yesterday (Ire)	b.f. 2000	Jude (GB)	Darshaan (GB)	G1SW
Acropolis (Ire)	b.c. 2001	Dedicated Lady (Ire)	Pennine Walk (Ire)	SW

Appendix: Sadler's Wells' Stakes Winners

HORSE	C/S/YOB	DAM	BROODMARE SIRE	STATUS
All Too Beautiful (Ire)	b.f. 2001	Urban Sea	Miswaki	G3SW
Asti (Ire)	dk.b.f. 2001	Astorg	Lear Fan	SW
Australie (Ire)	b.f. 2001	Asnieres	Spend a Buck	G3SW
Day Flight (GB)	b.c. 2001	Bonash (GB)	Rainbow Quest	G3SW
Fire Dragon (Ire)	b.g. 2001	Cattermole	Roberto	SW
Lucky (Ire)	b.f. 2001	Zummerudd (Ire)	Habitat	G3SW
Meath (Ire)	b.c. 2001	Twyla	Habitat	G3SW
Mikado (Ire)	b.g. 2001	Free At Last (GB)	Shirley Heights (GB)	SW
Modesta (Ire)	b.f. 2001	Modena	Roberto	SW
Moscow Ballet (Ire)	b.c. 2001	Fire the Groom	Blushing Groom (Fr)	SW
New Morning (Ire)	b.f. 2001	Hellenic	Darshaan (GB)	G3SW
Percussionist (Ire)	b.g. 2001	Magnificent Style	Silver Hawk	G3SW
Prospect Park (GB)	b.c. 2001	Brooklyn's Dance (Fr)	Shirley Heights (GB)	G3SW
Quiff (GB)	b.f. 2001	Wince (GB)	Selkirk	G1SW
Rave Reviews (Ire)	b.f. 2001	Pieds de Plume	Seattle Slew	SW
Two Miles West (Ire)	b.g. 2001	User Friendly (GB)	Slip Anchor (GB)	SW
Wolfe Tone (Ire)	b.c. 2001	Angelic Song	Halo	SW
Yeats (Ire)	b.c. 2001	Lyndonville (Ire)	Top Ville	G1SW
Zaiyad	b.g. 2001	Zaila (Ire)	Darshaan (GB)	SW
Argentina (Ire)	b.f. 2002	Airline	Woodman	SW
Briolette (Ire)	b.f. 2002	Cocotte (GB)	Troy (GB)	SW
Gypsy King (Ire)	b.c. 2002	Love for Ever (Ire)	Darshaan (GB)	G3SW
Kitty O'Shea (GB)	b.f. 2002	Eva Luna	Alleged	SW
Kong (Ire)	b.c. 2002	Hill of Snow (Ire)	Reference Point	G3SW
Playful Act (Ire)	b.f. 2002	Magnificent Style	Silver Hawk	G1SW
Queen Titi (Ire)	b.f. 2002	Litani River	Irish River (Fr)	SW
Silk And Scarlet (GB)	b.f. 2002	Danilova	Lyphard	G2SW
Yehudi (Ire)	b.c. 2002	Bella Vitessa (Ire)	Thatching (Ire)	SW
Alexandrova (Ire)	b.f. 2003	Shouk (GB)	Shirley Heights (GB)	G1SW
Alma Mater (GB)	b.f. 2003	Alouette (GB)	Darshaan (GB)	SW
Arosa (Ire)	b.f. 2003	Sharata (Ire)	Darshaan (GB)	SW
Ask (Ire)	b.c. 2003	Request (GB)	Steinhatchee	G1SW
Atlantic Waves (Ire)	b.c. 2003	Highest Accolade (GB)	Shirley Heights (GB)	SW
Dragon Dancer (GB)	b.c. 2003	Alakananda (GB)	Hernando (Fr)	SW
Fermion (Ire)	b.f. 2003	Pieds de Plume (Fr)	Seattle Slew	SW
Judge Roy Bean (Ire)	b.g. 2003	Be My Hope (Ire)	Be My Native	SW
Linda's Lad (GB)	b.c. 2003	Colza	Alleged	G1SW
Millennium Wing (Ire)	b.c. 2003	Angelic Song	Halo	SW
Mount Kilimanjaro (Ire)	b.c. 2003	Hill of Snow (GB)	Reference Point (GB)	SW
Nakheel (GB)	b.c. 2003	Matiya (Ire)	Alzao	SW
Novellara (Ire)	b.f. 2003	Modena	Roberto	SW
Poseidon Adventure (Ire)	b.c. 2003	Fanny Cerito	Gulch	SW
Puerto Rico (Ire)	b.c. 2003	Commanche Belle (GB)	Shirley Heights (GB)	G3SW
Saddex (GB)	b.c. 2003	Remote Romance	Irish River (Fr)	G1SW
Septimus (Ire)	b.c. 2003	Caladira	Darshaan (GB)	G2SW
Synchronised (Ire)	b.g. 2003	Mayasta (Ire)	Bob Back	SW
Time On (GB)	b.f. 2003	Time Away (Ire)	Darshaan (GB)	G2SW
Tusculum (Ire)	b.g. 2003	Turbaine	Trempolino	SW
Ashkazar (Fr)	b.g. 2004	Ashama (Ire)	Darshaan (GB)	SW
Ballet Boy (Ire)	b.g. 2004	Happy Landing (Fr)	Homing (GB)	SW
Concentric (Ire)	b.f. 2004	Apogee (GB)	Shirley Heights (GB)	SW

HORSE	C/S/YOB	DAM	BROODMARE SIRE	STATUS
Ezima (Ire)	b.f. 2004	Ezilla (Ire)	Darshaan (GB)	SW
Liscanna (Ire)	b.f. 2004	Lahinch (Ire)	Danehill Dancer (Ire)	G3SW
Measured Tempo (GB)	b.f. 2004	Allez Les Trois	Riverman	SW
More's Wells (GB)	b.f. 2004	Endorsement (GB)	Warning (GB)	G3SW
Royal and Regal (Ire)	b.g. 2004	Smart 'n Noble	Smarten	G3SW
Changing Skies (Ire)	b.f. 2005	Magnificient Style	Silver Hawk	G3SW
Curtain Call (Fr)	b.c. 2005	Apsara (Fr)	Darshaan (GB)	G2SW
Doctor Fremantle (GB)	b.c. 2005	Summer Breeze (GB)	Rainbow Quest	G2SW
Front House (Ire)	b.f. 2005	Adjalisa (Ire)	Darshaan (GB)	G2SW
Gagnoa (Ire)	dk.b.f. 2005	Gwynn (Ire)	Darshaan (GB)	G3SW
Hindu Kush (Ire)	b.g. 2005	Tambora (Ire)	Darshaan (GB)	SW
Honoria (Ire)	b.f. 2005	Tedarshana (GB)	Darshaan (GB)	SW
Listen (Ire)	b.f. 2005	Brigid	Irish River (Fr)	G1SW
Pouvoir Absolu (GB)	b.c. 2005	Pine Chip	Nureyev	SW
Prospect Wells (Fr)	b.c. 2005	Brooklyn's Dance (Fr)	Shirley Heights (GB)	G2SW
Sail (Ire)	b.f. 2005	Pieds de Plume (Fr)	Seattle Slew	SW
The Fist of God (Ire)	b.g. 2005	Hula Angel	Woodman	SW
Black Bear Island (Ire)	b.c. 2006	Kasora (Ire)	Darshaan (GB)	G2SW
Claremont (Ire)	b.c. 2006	Mezzo Soprano	Darshaan (GB)	G3SW
Fantasia (GB)	b.f. 2006	Blue Symphony (GB)	Darshaan (GB)	G3SW
Golden Stream (Ire)	b.f. 2006	Phantom Gold (GB)	Machiavellian	SW
Peinture Rare (Ire)	b.f. 2006	Peinture Bleue	Alydar	G2SW
Precious Gem (Ire)	b.f. 2006	Ruby (Ire)	Danehill	G3SW
Roses for the Lady (Ire)	b.f. 2006	Head in the Clouds (Ire)	Rainbow Quest	SW
Tactic (Ire)	b.g. 2006	Tanaghum (GB)	Darshaan (GB)	G3SW
Tamarind (Ire)	b.f. 2006	Sharata (Ire)	Darshaan (GB)	G3SW
Veiled (GB)	b.f. 2006	Evasive Quality (Fr)	Highest Honor (Fr)	SW
Big Occasion (Ire)	b.g. 2007	Asnieres	Spend a Buck	SW
Bullet Train (GB)	b.c. 2007	Kind (Ire)	Danehill	G3SW
Magnificence (GB)	b.f. 2007	Doctor's Glory	Elmaamul	SW
Mellon Martini	b.c. 2007	Sand Springs	Dynaformer	SW
Saddler's Rock (Ire)	b.c. 2008	Grecian Bride (Ire)	Groom Dancer	G2SW
Sadler's Risk (Ire)	b.g. 2008	Riskaverse	Dynaformer	SW

Appendix: Northern Dancer as a Sire of Sires

This section lists Northern Dancer's most prominent sire sons and a sampling of their most significant sons and other male descendants on the racetrack or in the stud.

******

Nijinsky II (1967–1992) bay colt, Northern Dancer—Flaming Page, by Bull Page: Won England's Triple Crown (1970); champion two-year-old colt England 1969; champion three-year-old colt, Horse of the Year England 1970; leading sire in England 1986; 155 stakes winners (18% from foals); leading broodmare sire in the United States 1993, 1994. Sire of:

> **Caerleon** (1980–1998): champion three-year-old colt France 1983; Classic winner; leading sire in England 1988, 1991; leading sire in Ireland 1991. Sire of:
>> *Generous [Ire]* (1988): Horse of the Year Ireland 1991; champion three-year-old colt Ireland 1991; Classic winner of $1,848,544.

> **Green Dancer** (1972–2000): leading sire in France 1991. Sire of:
>> *Green Tune* (1991): highweight older miler France 1995; Classic winner.
>> *Oak Dancer* (1979), 1990 Argentine champion sire

> **Ile de Bourbon** (1975): champion three-year-old colt England 1978; champion older horse England 1979. Sire of:
>> *Kahyasi [Ire]* (1985): champion three-year-old colt Ireland 1988; Classic winner.

> **Lammtarra [Ire]** (1992): champion three-year-old colt Europe 1995; Classic winner.

> **Niniski** (1976–1998): multiple group I stakes winner. Sire of:
>> *Hernando [Fr]* (1990): highweight older horse 11-14 furlongs France 1994; Classic winner. Sire of:
>>> *Sulamani [Ire]* (1999): highweight three-year-old male 11-14 furlongs France 2002; highweight older horse 11-14 fur-

longs United Arab Emirates 2003; highweight older horse 9.5-11 furlongs England 2004; Classic winner.

Lomitas [GB] (1988): champion three-year-old colt and Horse of the Year Germany 1991; highweight older horse 11-14 furlongs Germany 1992; leading sire in Germany 2001. Sire of:

> *Silvano [Ger]* (1996): highweight older horse 9.5-11 furlongs Germany 2001.

Royal Academy (1987): champion three-year-old colt England, Ireland; sire of 167 stakes winners (6% of foals). Sire of:

Ali-Royal [Ire] (1993–2001): highweight older horse 7-9.5 furlongs England 1997.

Oscar Schindler [Ire] (1992): highweight three-year-old stayer Ireland 1995; highweight older horse 11-14 furlongs Ireland 1996, 1997; highweight older stayer Ireland 1996, 1997.

Val Royal [Fr] (1996): Breeders' Cup Mile winner of $1,186,687.

Sky Classic (1987): champion two-year-old colt Canada 1989; champion older male Canada 1991; champion grass horse Canada 1991; champion grass horse United States 1992; earned $3,320,398.

******

Vice Regent (1967–1995) chestnut colt, Northern Dancer—Victoria Regina, by Menetrier: A leading sire in Canada and the United States; 105 stakes winners (15% from foals); a leading broodmare sire in Canada and the United States. Sire of:

Deputy Minister (1979–2004): champion two-year-old colt and Horse of the Year Canada 1981; champion two-year-old colt United States 1981; leading sire in the United States 1997, 1998. Sire of:

> *Awesome Again* (1994): Breeders' Cup Classic 1998; graded stakes winner of $4,374,590. Sire of:
>
> > *Ghostzapper* (2000): Horse of the Year and champion older horse United States 2004.
>
> *Dehere* (1991): champion two-year-old colt United States 1993.
>
> *Silver Deputy* (1985): sire of 88 stakes winners (8% from foals).
>
> *Touch Gold* (1994): Classic winner.

Regal Classic (1985): champion two-year-old colt Canada 1987; leading sire in Canada.

******

Lyphard (1969–2005) bay colt, Northern Dancer—Goofed, by *Court Martial: Leading sire in France 1978, 1979; leading sire in the United States 1986; 115 stakes winners (14% from foals); leading broodmare sire in France 1985. Sire of:

Alzao (1980): sire of 100 stakes winners. Sire of:
> *Waky Nao [GB]* (1993): highweight older horse 9.5-11 furlongs Italy 1998.

Bellypha [Ire] (1976): group stakes winner. Sire of:
> *Mendez [Fr]* (1981): group stakes winner. Sire of:
>> *Linamix [Fr]* (1987): Classic winner; leading sire in France 1998, 2004. Sire of:
>>> *Fragrant Mix [Ire]* (1994): highweight older horse 11-14 furlongs France 1998.
>>> *Sagamix [Fr]* (1995): highweight three-year-old male 11-14 furlongs France 1998.
>>> *Slickly [Fr]* (1996): highweight older miler England 2001; highweight older miler Italy 2001, 2002.

Dancing Brave (1983): champion three-year-old colt England and France 1986; champion miler England 1986. Sire of:
> *Commander in Chief [GB]* (1990): champion three-year-old colt Europe 1993; a leading sire in Japan 1999.
> *White Muzzle [GB]* (1990): highweight three-year-old male 11-14 furlongs England, France, Italy 1993; highweight older horse 11-14 furlongs England 1994.

Ghadeer [Fr] (1978): leading sire in Brazil 1990/91 through 1997/98; leading broodmare sire in Brazil 1997/98 through 2003/04 and 2006/07 through 2012/13.

Lypheor [GB] (1975): a leading sire in Japan 1986, 1987.

Manila (1983): champion grass horse United States 1986; leading broodmare sire in Turkey 2003.

******

Danzig (1977–2006) bay colt, Northern Dancer—Pas de Nom, by Admiral's Voyage: Leading sire in the United States 1991, 1992, 1993; 188 stakes winners (17% from foals). Sire of:

Anabaa (1992): champion sprinter in Europe 1966; internationally prominent sire (Europe and Australia). Sire of:

Anabaa Blue [GB] (1998): Classic winner.

Ascot Knight (1984): a leading sire in Canada.

Bertolini (1986): group stakes winner; leading British-based first-year sire 2005.

Boundary (1990): Sire of:

Minardi (1998): highweight juvenile colt England, Ireland 2000.

Chief's Crown (1982–1997): champion juvenile colt United States 1984; among the leading sires in the United States. Sire of:

Chief Bearhart (1993): champion grass horse Canada 1996, 1997, 1998; Horse of the Year Canada 1997, 1998; champion older horse Canada 1997; champion grass horse United States 1997.

Concerto (1994): graded stakes winner of $1,308,118.

Grand Lodge (1991–2003): champion juvenile colt Europe 1993. Sire of:

Indian Lodge (1996): co-highweight older miler England 2000.

Sinndar (1997): champion three-year-old colt Europe 2001.

Grandera (1998): champion older horse Europe 2002.

Danehill (1986–2003): champion in Europe 1989; international leading sire (Australia and Europe). All-time leading sire of stakes winners (311 [12% from foals]). Sire of:

Danehill Dancer [Ire] (1993): champion male Ireland 1995.

Danetime [Ire] (1994): leading first-crop sire in Europe 2002.

Danewin (1992): champion three-year-old Australia 1995.

Dansili [GB] (1996): champion older male England, France 2000.

Redoute's Choice [Aus] (1996): champion Australia 1999; leading sire in Australia 2009/10 and 2013/14; leading broodmare sire in Australia 2018/19, 2019/20, and 2021/22.

Rock of Gibraltar [Ire] (1999): Classic-winning Horse of the Year Europe 2002.

Tiger Hill [Ire] (1995): highweight three-year-old male 11-14 furlongs Germany 1998; highweight older horse 11-14 furlongs Germany 1999; a leading sire in Europe.

Dayjur (1987): champion three-year-old colt England, France 1990; Horse of the Year England 1990.

Green Desert (1983): a leading sire in Europe. Sire of:

Cape Cross [Ire] (1994): highweight older miler England 1999; leading sire in England, France 2009.

> *Sea the Stars [Ire]* (2006): Horse of the Year and champion three-year-old male Europe 2009; a leading sire in England, France, Germany, Ireland, Italy

Desert Prince [Ire] (1995): Classic-winning champion 1998; a leading sire in Germany, Italy.

Desert Style [Ire] (1992): highweight three-year-old sprinter Ireland 1995.

Volksraad [GB] (1988): leading sire in New Zealand 2001/02 through 2006/07, 2008/09, and 2009/10.

Oasis Dream [GB] (2000): champion sprinter Europe 2003; a leading sire in England, France, and Ireland.

Langfuhr (1992): champion sprinter Canada 1996. Sire of:

Wando (2000): champion three-year-old colt and Horse of the Year Canada 2003.

Mobil (2000): champion older male Canada 2004.

National Assembly (1984): nine-time leading sire in South Africa.

War Chant (1997): Breeders' Cup Mile winner of $1,130,600; among the leading juvenile sires in the United States 2004.

******

Dixieland Band (1980) bay colt, Northern Dancer—Mississippi Mud, by Delta Judge: Graded stakes winner of $441,320; 107 stakes winners (9% from foals); leading broodmare sire in the United States 2004. Sire of:
Chimes Band (1991–2005): graded stakes winner of $416,961.

Dixie Union (1997): grade I stakes winner of $1,233,190. Sire of:
Union Rags (1990): 1993 Belmont Stakes

******

Nureyev (1977–2001) bay colt, Northern Dancer—Special, by *Forli: Champion miler France 1980; leading sire in France 1987, 1997; 137 stakes winners (17% from foals). Sire of:
Fasliyev (1997): champion two-year-old colt Europe 1999.

Peintre Celebre (1994): champion three-year-old colt Europe 1999; horse of the year Europe 1997; Classic winner.

Polar Falcon (1987–2001): champion older horse Europe 1991; champion older horse France 1991. Sire of:
Pivotal [GB] (1993): grade I stakes winner; a leading sire in England, France, Germany, Ireland. Sire of:
Kyllachy [GB] (1998): champion older horse England 2002.
Siyouni [Fr] (2007): group I stakes winner; leading sire France 2020, 2021.

Soviet Star (1984): champion sprinter England 1988; Classic winner. Sire of:
Ashkalani [Ire] (1993): highweight three-year-old colt France 1996; Classic winner.

Spinning World (1993): highweight three-year-old miler Ireland 1996; highweight older miler France 1994; Classic winner of $1,734,477.

Stravinsky (1996): champion sprinter Europe 1999.

Theatrical [Ire] (1982): champion grass horse United States 1987; Breeders' Cup Turf winner of $2,940,036. Sire of :
> *Zagreb* (1993): highweight three-year-old male 11-14 furlongs Ireland 1996; Classic winner.

Zilzal (1986): Horse of the Year England 1989; champion three-year-old colt England 1989; champion miler England 1989.

******

Sadler's Wells (1981) bay colt, Northern Dancer—Fairy Bridge, by Bold Reason: Champion miler France 1984; Classic winner; leading sire in England fourteen years; 265 stakes winners (13% from foals); leading broodmare sire in England, France, Ireland, and the United States. Sire of:
> **Barathea [Ire]** (1990): highweight three-year-old miler England and Ireland 1993; European Horse of the Year and champion older horse 1994; Classic winner. Sire of:
>> *Tobougg [Ire]* (1998): champion two-year-old colt Europe 2000.

> **Beat Hollow [GB]** (1997): highweight three-year-old male 9.5-11 furlongs France 2000.

> **Carnegie [Ire]** (1991): highweight three-year-old male 11-14 furlongs France 1994.

> **Doyen [Ire]** (2000): highweight older horse 11-14 furlongs England 2004.

> **El Prado [Ire]** (1989): champion two-year-old colt Ireland 1991; leading sire in the United States 2002. Sire of:

Kitten's Joy (2001): champion grass horse United States 2004; leading sire United States 2013, 2018.

Megdalia d'Oro (1999): grade I stakes winner; a leading sire United States.

Entrepreneur [GB] (1994): highweight three-year-old miler England 1997; Classic winner.

Fort Wood (1990): leading sire in South Africa 1999. Sire of:

Horse Chestnut [SAf] (1995): Triple Crown winner South Africa; Horse of the Year South Africa 1999; champion three-year-old colt South Africa 1999.

Galileo [Ire] (1998): champion three-year-old colt Europe 2001; Classic winner; leading sire England ten times; leading sire France 2016, 2019; leading sire Ireland 13 times. Sire of:

Frankel [GB] (2008): Horse of the Year and champion three-year-old male Europe 2011; Horse of the Year and champion older horse Europe 2012; leading sire England 2021, 2023; leading sire France 2022.

In the Wings [GB] (1986): champion older horse France 1990; Breeders' Cup Turf winner; leading sire in the Slovak Republic 1998. Sire of:

Singspiel [Ire] (1992): champion grass horse United States 1996; champion older horse United Arab Emirates 1997; leading sire in the United Arab Emirates 1997. Sire of:

Moon Ballad [Ire] (1999): Horse of the Year and champion older horse United Arab Emirates 2003.

Montjeu [Ire] (1996): champion three-year-old colt Europe 1999; highweight older horse 11-14 furlongs England, France 2000; highweight older horse 9.5-11 furlongs Ireland 2000; Classic winner; leading sire France 2005. Sire of:

Hurricane Run [Ire] (2002): Horse of the Year and champion three-year-old colt Europe 2005; Classic winner.
Motivator [GB] (2002): Classic winner.
Scorpion [Ire] (2002): Classic winner.

Northern Spur [Ire] (1991): champion grass horse United States 1995.

Refuse To Bend [Ire] (2000): highweight three-year-old male 9.5-11 furlongs Ireland 2003; Classic winner.

******

Storm Bird (1978–2004) bay colt, Northern Dancer—South Ocean, by New Providence: Champion two-year-old colt England and Ireland 1980; 63 stakes winners (9% from foals). Sire of:
   Bluebird (1984): champion sprinter Ireland 1987; leading sire in Italy 1993, 1994. Sire of:
      Dolphin Street [Fr] (1990): highweight three-year-old miler Germany 1993; champion older horse Europe 1994.
      Fly to the Stars [GB] (1994): highweight older miler England 1999.

Storm Cat (1983): leading sire in the United States 1999, 2000; seven-time leading juvenile sire in the United States; sire of 177 stakes winners (12% from foals). Sire of:
      Cat Thief (1996): Breeders' Cup Classic winner of $3,951,012.
      Giant's Causeway (1997): Horse of the Year Europe 2000; champion three-year-old colt England and Ireland 2000; leading sire in the United States 2009, 2010, 2012. Sire of:
         Footstepsinthesand [GB] (2002): Classic winner.
         Shamardal (2002): champion two-year-old colt Europe 2004; Classic winner; a leading sire in England, France, Germany, Ireland, Italy.
      Hennessy (1993): leading juvenile sire in the United States 2001. Sire of:
         Johannesburg (1999): champion juvenile colt Europe and United States 2001; Breeders' Cup Juvenile winner.

Tabasco Cat (1991–2004): Classic winner of $2,347,671.
Tale of the Cat (1994): leading juvenile sire in the United States 2003.

Summer Squall (1987): Classic winner of $1,844.282. Sire of:
Charismatic (1996): Horse of the Year and champion three-year-old colt 1999; Classic winner.

*I*ndex

Index

Index

Index

Index

Index

Index

Acknowledgments

Few books are ever written as solo efforts, and this one would not have come into being without contributions from many others. In particular, I would like to thank Ron Turcotte, Manny Ycaza, Joe Hickey Jr., and Norman Bowles for generously providing their time and memories during interviews, and the Keeneland Library staff for their assistance with research. Without them this book would have lacked many of the details that helped bring Northern Dancer back to life as a personality. I would also like to thank the members of the Pedigree Query message board who helped me track down the contact information for my interviews; their work was very much behind the scenes but nonetheless much appreciated.

And, again, I want to thank my husband, whose patience and support have been incredible throughout the development of my writing career.

I am grateful to Eclipse Press for publishing the original version of *The Kingmaker* and for making this updated version possible. And no list of acknowledgments would be complete without remembering God and his many gifts — to Him be the glory.

Avalyn Hunter
September 12, 2023

$\mathcal{P}$hoto $\mathcal{C}$redits

About the Author

One of the first pedigree books **Avalyn Hunter** can recall reading as a fifteen-year-old is Sir Charles Leicester's classic work *Bloodstock Breeding*, which twenty-five years later served as a model and an inspiration for Hunter's first book, *American Classic Pedigrees 1914-2002*. Covering the race records, antecedents, and descendants of the winners of the American Triple Crown races plus the Kentucky Oaks and Coaching Club American Oaks for fillies, the massive work took some two years to write and was released in May 2003 by Eclipse Press. It was followed by the original version of *The Kingmaker* in 2006 and by *Gold Rush: How Mr. Prospector Became Racing's Billion-Dollar Sire* in 2007, both Eclipse Press releases. Her most recent books are *Dream Derby: The Myth and Legend of Black Gold*, which was released by the University Press of Kentucky in 2023, and *The Kentucky Oaks: 150 Years of Running for the Lilies*, a 2024 University Press of Kentucky release.

Hunter has also published the award-winning fiction stories "The Passing of the Torch" and "The Foundation," both prizewinners in the Thoroughbred Times' Biennial Fiction Contest. She has written articles on Thoroughbred pedigrees and history for *The Blood-Horse, MarketWatch, Owner-Breeder International, Thoroughbred Times*, and *Louisiana Horse*. A former Air Force officer, Hunter is a graduate of Vanderbilt University (BA, psychology) and Southern Illinois University at Edwardsville (MA, clinical psychology). She lives in Florida with her husband and spends much of her free time expanding her own website on Thoroughbred breeding and history, American Classic Pedigrees (www.americanclassicpedigrees.com).